Countermelodies

A Memoir in
Sonata Form

Ernestine Whitman

SHE WRITES PRESS

Published 2024
Printed in the United States of America
Print ISBN: 978-1-64742-732-0
E-ISBN: 978-1-64742-733-7
Library of Congress Control Number: 2024911666

For information, address:
She Writes Press
1569 Solano Ave #546
Berkeley, CA 94707

Interior Design by Tabitha Lahr

She Writes Press is a division of SparkPoint Studio, LLC.

Names and identifying characteristics have been changed to protect the privacy of certain individuals.

Trigger Warning: This book contains subjects that might be troubling to some readers, including rape and suicide. Please be mindful of these and other possible triggers.

For my two favorite feminists,
Howard and Elliott

*Pain reaches the heart with electrical speed,
but truth moves to the heart
as slowly as a glacier.*

—Barbara Kingsolver, *Animal Dreams*

Sonata Form

Sonata form is the structure often used for single movements of symphonies and other large-scale works of classical music. In this story, as in sonata form, two themes of contrasting character generate the entire work. The narrative divides into three parts. In sonata form, the divisions are called exposition, development, and recapitulation.

Contents

EXPOSITION

FIRST THEME: FATHER FIGURES

Chapter 1: Liberty 3

Chapter 2: My Sister's Shadow 10

Chapter 3: Music Teachers 21

Chapter 4: Family Myth 39

SECOND THEME: BECOMING A MUSICIAN

Chapter 5: The Flute 53

Chapter 6: Expanding Horizons 66

Chapter 7: Hope 84

Chapter 8: Resignation 92

Chapter 9: College 104

DEVELOPMENT: PART I

Chapter 10: Dream Job 115

Chapter 11: Work/Study 128

Chapter 12: Downward Spiral 143

Chapter 13: Recovery 164

Chapter 14: Better Days 175

Chapter 15: Big City 205

Chapter 16: Hard Decisions 215

DEVELOPMENT: PART II

Chapter 17: Conservatory 227

Chapter 18: Isthmus 239

Chapter 19: Therapist 252

Chapter 20: Darkness 266

Chapter 21: Endings and Beginnings 280

RECAPITULATION

Chapter 22: Resolution, Second Theme 303

Chapter 23: Resolution, First Theme 307

Afterword 321

Acknowledgments 323

About the Author 325

Exposition

The exposition of sonata form presents the two themes in succession. The first theme is usually the more dramatic of the two; in the past, music theorists labeled such themes masculine. In Beethoven's famous Symphony No. 5, for example, the first theme is a repeated four-note motif that is abrupt, choppy, and restless; the second theme (less than one minute into the work) is smooth and graceful.

First Theme:
Father Figures

Chapter 1: Liberty

Hey, girls, your mother says it's time to come down," Uncle Russell called from the foot of the curved staircase. "Dinner's almost ready." He sounded tense and irritable, out of character for our jovial uncle.

Even in Grandmother's well-built antebellum house, we'd overheard Mother ordering Russell to stop playing his silly tunes and call us to supper. Strains of "In the Mood" and other old songs often floated up from one of the two out-of-tune grand pianos in the parlor, usually the white one, which Russell preferred. With the heating vent open, the sound from the first floor went straight into the spacious upstairs bedroom we shared with Mother. In past years, Melinda and I had eavesdropped on adult conversations through the vent, but now that she was a cool teenager, I had to spy on my own, which wasn't as much fun.

"Can't we keep our shorts on just this one day?" I asked. At eleven, I still idolized my fifteen-year-old sister and thought she could solve any problem.

"No, you know we can't." Melinda sighed. "We'd better get dressed quickly."

The midsummer heat, building all day in our grandmother's house, peaked in the late afternoon. We'd been playing canasta, sitting close to the fan in the bedroom—even steamier than downstairs, but the only room where shorts were allowed. My grandmother's rigid ideas about attire for proper young ladies did not include shorts, even in hundred-degree heat. Accepting the inevitable, my sister and I stuffed our sweaty bodies back into hot dresses with wide skirts that were held aloft by starched, scratchy crinolines.

Each summer, Melinda, Mother, and I left our father in Atlanta and took a two-day train ride to Kansas City, Missouri, for a monthlong visit with Grandmother and weird Uncle Russell. They lived in the town of Liberty on Grandmother's sizable piece of property, known as Forest Hill. Built next to William Jewell College in 1857, exactly one hundred years old that summer, Forest Hill had been an impressive residence, with two large parlors that ran along the front of the house. After three house fires and years of neglect, the paint on the white columns outside was peeling, and many of the red bricks were tinged with black. Although the house looked more decrepit than stately, Grandmother lived in the past, and on the rare occasions when she spoke to us, she recounted stories of parties and of handsome young men from William Jewell who came to call in the afternoons.

I had no interest in the dark wood antiques crowding the rooms or the three sets of bone china in the dining room cabinets, though I liked the deeply colored blue and burgundy glasses we used for iced tea in the late afternoons. Inadequate lighting made the rooms dark, and Grandmother's refusal to open windows kept the air musty. With no bathroom upstairs and no pajamas allowed downstairs, at night we used a chamber pot. Despite Mother's constant cleaning, the bathroom was almost as disgusting as the pot. I never imagined how grand the place must have been. To me, the house was simply old and dreary—and in August, very, very hot.

Despite the heat, dresses, and gloomy house, I loved being in Liberty because it meant four whole weeks of my sister's company. With no other kids around, Melinda deigned to play with me. In the front yard on the edge of the property, a huge maple tree had fallen during one of the many theatrical summer storms. As with most things at Forest Hill, Russell did nothing about it. For years Melinda and I climbed all over it, using it as a horizontal tree house. (We could wear shorts outside, as long as we didn't leave the property.) That summer, Melinda refused to join me outside, so we played card games and Monopoly, which she always won. Knowing she was stuck with me, I didn't mind losing.

The only Grandmother-approved activity was performing little concerts for her friends. Arrayed in our best dresses, we sang and acted out songs from *Your Hit Parade*. For years we'd simply sung the top ten, but in 1957 Elvis topped the charts, so we had to be selective. "Honeycomb" and "That'll Be the Day" were fine, but not "Jailhouse Rock," my favorite.

Uncle Russell was the fun, if somewhat zany relative. Unlike our grandmother, who viewed us merely as projects for instilling manners and a rigid dress code, Russell paid attention to Melinda and me. He told lots of jokes and whimsical stories, even played cards with us, the only grown-up who would do that. Instead of saying goodnight, he'd say, "See you in the funny papers," wiggling his dark, bushy eyebrows with Groucho Marx dexterity. He kept hard candies and bubble gum in his pockets, cautioning us not to let Grandmother catch us sucking or chewing. When I was little, I adored Russell; that summer I found his jokes corny and his behavior a little strange. But unlike Mother, I liked hearing him play the piano.

Russell never went to work. I was surprised when Mother told us he had single-handedly built the small, eight-unit apartment house that sat at the back of the property. Having accomplished that, however, he didn't bother to keep track of who paid rent, resulting in lots of squatters. Most days, Russell spent hours inventing and constructing gadgets. That summer, Russell made a one-eighth-cup measure with six concentric circles etched inside, marking a tablespoon down to one-eighth teaspoon. He must've applied for over a hundred patents, without success. When he wasn't making gadgets, Russell attended VFW meetings (he'd served in World War II), read newspapers assiduously, and cooked all the meals. I loved Russell's cooking. He used lots of lard.

Mother cooked that night, a rare exception that may have been the catalyst for what happened. Melinda and I, suitably dressed, came downstairs and walked to the end of the dining room next to the kitchen.

"Russell, put the glasses around," Mother said. She seemed agitated—abrupt manner, flushed face. If we'd been older, we might've sensed the tension between our mother and her older brother.

"How many do we need?" Russell asked.

"Looks like you could figure that out for yourself, but maybe your head's too full of stupid songs." Then she muttered something we didn't hear, something that enraged Russell. He rushed into the kitchen and grabbed the large kitchen knife.

"I'm not putting up with this another week. I'm going to kill you," he snarled, stopping about ten feet from my mother. The savage look on his face bore no resemblance to the uncle I knew.

For a few seconds, we all froze, motionless except for the pendulum of the grandfather clock. Mother recovered first.

"Melinda, call the police." Mother's voice sounded urgent but controlled. "The number's in the front of the phone book."

Instead, Melinda stepped between Mother and Russell and shouted, "Don't hurt my mother!" Russell went around her and lunged at Mother, cutting a deep gash in her right arm.

Again, no one moved, as blood dripped onto the dark wooden floor. After several seconds Russell dropped the knife, dashed out of the room, and ran into his bedroom, slamming the door behind him.

"Go to our bedroom right now," Mother ordered. Melinda and I hurried up the stairs, terrified.

"Get a towel, I've cut myself," we heard Mother say to Grandmother, who'd entered the kitchen unaware of what happened. Ten minutes later Mother came upstairs, her arm wrapped in a threadbare blue towel. She didn't bother shutting the door and seemed unconcerned about her arm, though I could see blood beginning to seep through.

"Are we going to call the police?" Melinda asked.

"No," Mother said firmly. "We're not going to tell anyone about this."

"Can we leave early, maybe tomorrow?" I asked, unaware of the added expense.

"Of course not. Russell will settle down." Mother sounded more irritated than scared. Then she turned to face us, making sure she had our full attention. Raising her voice, she said sternly, "And you will *not* tell your father about any of this, either in a letter or when we get home." Mother seemed more concerned about Daddy finding out than about Russell attacking again.

"But what about your arm?" I asked.

"Yes," Melinda added, "shouldn't you see Doctor Goodson?" The physician and longtime family friend lived a few houses down the street.

"No!" Mother almost yelled. "We won't tell anyone what happened. I'll take care of my arm." We never ate supper that night; no one wanted to go back into the kitchen.

The remaining week of the visit, though strained, was uneventful, except that Russell's teasing, upbeat persona disappeared completely, leaving a distant, disinterested uncle, much like our grandmother.

When my father picked us up at the train station, Mother wore a long-sleeved blouse, despite the Atlanta heat. I heard her tell Daddy she'd cut herself while fixing dinner—hard to imagine, since she was right-handed. The incident was never mentioned. If not for the large scar on Mother's arm, I might've thought I'd imagined the whole thing. But the visit left me with lots of questions. Why couldn't we tell our father what happened? Why was Mother more afraid of Daddy than of Russell? Why had Daddy never come with us to Missouri? And more disturbingly, how could the fun-loving uncle turn into the monster who attacked Mother?

For weeks afterward I tried to listen in on conversations between my parents. When they talked about Grandmother and Russell, I could tell by the tension in my father's voice that he disliked Russell. At some point, I found out my father sent them a monthly check. Given Daddy's anxiety about money, that alone would have caused friction. Russell's refusal or inability to hold a steady job no doubt infuriated Daddy. In the past year or so, I'd seen more of the harsh, judgmental side of my father.

We didn't return to Liberty after that summer, and Mother never again spoke to us about her brother or mother, other than to inform us, many years later, that her mother had died. She made a quick trip to Liberty for the funeral. When Russell died shortly after that, she did not attend his funeral.

Uncle Russell's attack on Mother haunted me for a long time and forced me to rethink my simplistic views of Russell and, more importantly, my father. I also learned a lot about my mother: her composure in a crisis, her refusal to talk about anything upsetting, a penchant for secrecy, and—the trait I struggled with most—her cynical view of men. Each of these traits lay hidden beneath a sweet, calm demeanor.

Melinda and I sometimes talked about Russell, trying to figure out why he attacked Mother. The one positive thing Mother told us about him—said with more jealousy than admiration—was that, despite his refusal to take lessons, Russell was a facile pianist who could play anything by ear, from jazz pieces to popular songs to operatic arias. His musical talent, like his other abilities, remained undeveloped. After a few years in the military, which he never spoke about, Russell's life consisted of failed projects and taking care of his mother in her childhood home until she died at age ninety-six. Did Russell begrudge Mother for escaping Liberty? Or, did he resent having his sister and nieces in his mother's house for a whole month? Did Mother communicate with Russell or Grandmother after that summer, other than to send checks? These questions remained; Melinda and I knew if we'd asked, Mother would not have answered.

My memory of the attack got one major detail wrong. Recounting the story decades later, my sister corrected me: when Mother yelled at her to call the police, Melinda just stood there, as stunned and incapable of movement as I was. Mother despised her older sibling; I cast mine as the heroine.

Chapter 2: My Sister's Shadow

"*The Naughty Lady of Shady Lane*," I sang, swinging up to the treetops and rocking the old, green metal frame with each apex. Gripping the bumpy chains, I belted out songs from *Your Hit Parade*, accompanied by the rhythmic squeak of the swing.

When I was two and three years old, my mother claimed, I woke up from naps singing. I don't remember that, but I do remember many blissful hours singing and swinging in the secluded backyard of our house on Andrew Circle. We moved into the neighborhood of rental housing for Emory University faculty in 1948, when I was two, and stayed for fourteen years.

Andrew Circle was a great place for kids. The grassy field in the center of the circle, a hundred yards or so in diameter, served as a large playground. The end farthest from our house was the kickball/softball field, with worn places in the grass for bases. Younger girls occupied the other half of the field, making daisy chains, looking for four-leaf clovers, or simply talking. I remember my excitement when I was finally old enough to join the games, though my feeble kicks sent the ball wobbling straight to the pitcher, who easily tagged me for an out. Melinda wasn't as good as the boys, but her kicks earned her at least one base, often two; kickball was one of countless things Melinda did much better than I. By the time I was big enough to kick the ball successfully, Melinda had outgrown kickball.

With the field for pickup games, big magnolia trees to climb, and woods to explore behind the houses, kids in the neighborhood grew up with a sense of freedom and expansiveness. On summer days, we played into the evening, mixing kickball with dodgeball, tag, and improvised games. Each family had a unique whistle call to summon us for supper. Ours was short-short-long-short. With the K-12 school next to Andrew Circle, everything we needed was within walking distance. No carpools, no buses. Just a safe, boringly homogeneous neighborhood.

Though the rooms in our narrow house were small, we had a den as well as separate dining and living rooms. The back end of the house, away from the road, featured a wide, screened-in porch. Due to the steep pitch of the yard, the porch floor was higher than the top of the swings, like a second floor. Underneath it was a small, unfinished basement containing a filthy coal furnace. A flight of rickety wooden steps with one splintery railing led from the porch to the ground. We were warned to stay off the rotting steps. Of course, we ignored that.

The wooded area behind the house led downhill to a set of railroad tracks. When we heard a train coming, we'd run to the tracks for bubble gum and occasional baseball cards the caboose-man tossed us. My childhood memories are punctuated by the haunting sound of train whistles. When I couldn't sleep, I heard the eleven o'clock night train. The train whistle evoked a feeling I later identified as melancholy, but it also comforted me. Still does.

My happiest childhood memories date from the early years in that house, and the scenes I treasure most are those with my father. When Daddy interacted with young kids, he was playful and imaginative, a side of him adults seldom saw. As a little girl, I relished the rare treat of my father's company. I loved the bedtime stories he made up about Rufus, a redheaded adventurous boy with ears even bigger than my father's. In my earliest memory of Daddy, he's sitting in his big, brown corduroy armchair, and I'm standing beside the chair as I attempt to put Mother's curlers in his silky, straight black hair. Daddy repeatedly pushes my hand away, somehow conveying affection even as he's telling me to stop. It's a striking memory, given how rarely my father and I had any physical contact. I don't remember ever sitting in his lap, much less any horsing around.

Melinda and I shared a bedroom until she turned thirteen. It was so small that if you opened the closet door very wide, it banged into the foot of my bed. The iron frames of our twin beds had thick, curved bars on both ends. When I was little, I'd put a pillow over the bar to make a saddle and loop the ends of my bathrobe sash to create stirrups. Then I'd wrap a belt around the closet doorknob for reins and gallop away on my gorgeous palomino horse. I hated the two pictures mounted on one wall of the bedroom, situated so you faced them when you were in bed. They were scenes of ships on stormy seas, all browns and grays. The gray radiator was also ugly, though more interesting after I left a box of crayons on it.

My untroubled worldview changed when I was six, beginning one summer evening shortly after we'd returned from Liberty. I'd taken a bath while Melinda played outside, and as I was drying off, I heard Mother shout.

"Then for our fifteenth wedding anniversary, we can just get a divorce," she said as she stomped out of the den. A moment later, the front door slammed. My stomach plummeted and my legs turned to jelly as I sank to the bathroom floor. I'd never heard Mother shout at Daddy or anyone else.

Wrapped in a towel, I started shivering even though it was a hot night. Sometime later—it could've been two minutes or twenty—my sister barged into the bathroom.

"What are you doing on the floor?" Melinda asked, then looked at me more closely. "Were you crying?"

"I guess so," I said, dazed.

"Well, put on your pajamas and get out of here so I can use the bathroom." Her gentle tone softened the harshness of the words.

After Mother said a terse goodnight, I waited impatiently for Melinda's bedtime. As soon as she appeared, I told her what I'd heard.

"What's going to happen?" I asked, imagining the two of us in an orphanage.

"Nothing. Don't worry about it," Melinda said. "I've heard them say things like that before. It doesn't mean anything."

"You mean you've heard them talking about divorce before?" I asked, afraid of the answer.

"Maybe not those exact words, but they've certainly argued."

"Isn't their anniversary soon?"

"Yes, today's August twelfth, so four days from now."

"Will Mother change her mind before then?"

"Sure, she will. Look, I told you, Mother didn't mean it. For Pete's sake, don't take everything so seriously. Now go to sleep."

I lay awake for a long time, trying to believe Melinda. She always knew what was going on, but it upset me that Mother had yelled at Daddy. How could Melinda be so dismissive when Mother had threatened divorce? In the dim light cast from the streetlamp outside the window, I stared at the gloomy pictures on the wall.

Melinda, as always, was right. On their anniversary, Daddy gave Mother what he always gave her, a box of Russell Stover candy wrapped in flowery paper by the store clerk. Despite the reassuring kiss my parents shared when Daddy presented the candy, I wondered how long it would be before they had another argument. But for the next few months, they seemed fine. My anxiety gradually subsided, and by late fall I'd forgotten all about it.

Every Thanksgiving we got together with the Bullocks, a family of four who lived in Tucker, about thirty miles from our house. We got to know them because my mother and Eleanor Bullock were best friends in college. I loved visiting the Bullocks. I had a crush on the older son, who was Melinda's age, but I didn't care for the boy my age. The father, Charles, had an administrative position with Southern Railroad. I was about eleven when I figured out why those visits were so much fun: Charles wasn't an Emory colleague. Instead of collegial one-upmanship, Daddy and Charles traded stories, and they were both hilarious storytellers.

That year it was our turn to host, and Daddy devised an elaborate joke to play on Charles. He made a gizmo consisting of a small inflatable disc with a long tube that was connected to a bulb. He placed the disc under the turkey platter, ran the tube under the tablecloth, and hid the bulb in his lap. During dinner Daddy occasionally squeezed the bulb to make the turkey platter jump—not much, but enough to be noticeable. Everyone except Charles was in on the joke.

"Did you see that?" Charles asked.

"What?" Daddy said.

"The turkey, I thought it moved," Charles said, bewildered.

"The turkey? What do you mean it moved?" my father asked.

"Well, it just sort of jumped up," Charles said.

"Did anyone else see it?" Daddy asked.

We shook our heads. I concentrated hard on keeping a straight face. Daddy waited a while before he squeezed the bulb again. Eventually, Charles noticed that every time the turkey jumped, my father had only one hand above the table, and he figured it out.

I love that memory because it epitomizes the fun times, which were rare, and most of them were with the Bullocks. Even Mother, who'd had the pressure of cooking the big meal, was happy. Other than those dinners, I remember very few times we laughed—or even relaxed completely—as a family.

As a kid, I thought of Daddy as the funny parent, Mother the grumpy one. Her grumpiness peaked early in the day or late in the afternoon. After breakfast I often saw her grimace when she looked at Daddy's plate, a cigarette butt squashed into the egg yolk residue.

—————

"Damn!" I heard Mother say a few days after Thanksgiving. I could tell she was trying to stifle her voice so I wouldn't hear. It shocked me. Though I'd heard Mother threaten divorce, I'd never heard her swear. Even my father rarely did that. Then there was a sound I couldn't identify, a sort of soft crunch.

She was preparing dinner, so I tiptoed toward the kitchen to see what she was doing. Her foot rested on a flattened egg carton, apparently an empty one, since no cracked eggs were seeping out.

"Damn, damn, damn!" she fumed, as she reached for another egg carton. More angry foot stomping, another flattened egg carton.

Did she keep empty egg cartons just so she could stomp on them? I wondered. She turned to the stove and resumed cooking, a deep scowl on her face. She hadn't raised her voice, but she looked really mad, and I wondered what I'd done wrong. It happened several times before I connected the episodes with dinnertime. I continued to think it was my fault: she was stuck at home with two kids, so she had to cook, which she hated.

Mother's threat of divorce and her egg carton stomping occurred at the end of what I came to think of as The Good Daddy Years. Gradually, Daddy the fun parent disappeared, replaced by a harsh, judgmental father whom I always disappointed. Much of the change in my father was prompted by the change in me: I was losing my cute-little-girl status. Melinda had outgrown that phase long ago, but she maintained Daddy's attention by being brilliant at everything she did.

As far back as I can remember, I thought everything about Melinda was perfect. When we were little and took baths together, I scrubbed my arms and legs incessantly to get them as clean and white as Melinda's. But she had fairer skin. Later, I slept in uncomfortable curlers, hoping to transform my straight brown hair into Melinda's lovely auburn curls. I couldn't do much about my brown eyes, other than wish they were hazel, like hers. The natural tendency to look up to an older sibling was compounded by my father's preference for her. Daddy often complimented her on schoolwork and listened carefully when she talked. He didn't seem to enjoy my company as much and often ignored my comments. I thought if I looked more like Melinda, and could be as good at things as she was, Daddy might find me interesting too.

My sister naturally preferred the company of kids her

age, but on rainy days she occasionally played with me, though games were one-sided, even those that depended on chance. Melinda managed to win every time by baiting me into doing something stupid. Playing rummy, she might hint that she had only low-score cards, leading me to slough off a face card, which she then picked up for a meld. She liked to push me past the breaking point, then run to Mother, complaining I had bitten her. (I had.)

In first grade, following in Melinda's footsteps, I began both piano and ballet lessons. Mother enjoyed chauffeuring us because she liked both dance and classical music, interests my father didn't share. I liked ballet better because Melinda had quit after one year, so I didn't have to compete with the perfect role model. Like most young dancers, getting my first pair of toe shoes was one of the highlights of my short ballet career. At age twelve, my pointe work was good enough to earn me a solo part in the end-of-year recital. The theme for the program was seasons and weather; our class depicted storm clouds and sunshine, and I was the first ray of sunshine to come on stage and chase the clouds away. But I got mixed up and bourréed onto the stage several measures early, where the music sounded almost the same as it did for my entrance. Realizing my mistake, I simply bourréed across the stage and waited backstage until the right moment, when I entered again, this time with a red face.

I was mortified, but Mother consoled me.

"You just made the first ray of sun peek out briefly from behind a cloud," she said, "and later it came all the way out, like it often does after storms."

The pep talk worked. I didn't give it another thought.

With piano, unlike ballet, sibling comparisons were inevitable. Our secondhand, upright piano sat against a wall in the den, the center of our small house. Melinda always got to practice first. After she'd worked through the intricacies of Bach and Schubert, I plunked out short pieces with stupid titles — "Wee Willy Will," "Sleep Baby Sleep," "My Little Wigwam."

The staid piano teacher, Mrs. Siefkin, wore straight skirts, silk blouses, and white-framed, cat-eye glasses that dangled from a gold chain around her neck. She taught in a strict, no-nonsense manner, sitting with perfect posture on a straight-backed chair to our right, never beside us on the piano bench. Lessons were joyless, practicing worse. After I'd studied for a couple of years and was playing pieces with sixteenth notes, the titles were better, but I couldn't get the runs as fast as Melinda played hers. And my father noticed.

"You've got a long way to go if you ever want to catch up to Melinda," my father said with a chuckle one day. He'd heard me struggling with a run. Whenever Daddy compared me to Melinda, piano comments bothered me the most, because he showed little interest in music other than to contrast our achievements. I tried to avoid practicing when Daddy was home, but even when he wasn't there, I often got so frustrated and angry — at both myself and the piano — that I thought of the Bible verse: "If thy right hand offend thee, cut it off."

The nadir came during my fifth-grade year, when I played Debussy's "Clair de Lune" in a Christmas recital. Mrs. Siefkin had transformed her living room into a small recital space; a large tree decorated with lovely homemade ornaments shared the stage with the grand piano. I felt calm while the first five students played their pieces. Then the person before me, an eighth grader, sat down to play. From her dress, hairstyle, and demeanor, she appeared even more poised and grown-up than Melinda, who was a year older. Miss Utmost Confidence performed one of Bach's Two-Part Inventions flawlessly, which delighted the audience.

By the time I sat down to play, my knees felt wobbly and my hands shook. Despite this, the first part of the piece went well. Then my mind went blank. I stopped abruptly. "Damn" tumbled out of my mouth. Shocking language from a well-bred southern girl—and in front of my parents' friends. After what seemed like hours of silence, Mrs. Siefkin spoke from the darkness of her living room.

"Just start over," she said stiffly.

The second time, the piece went well, but that didn't lessen the shame. I felt disgraced, as if I'd stripped in front of everyone. Melinda never forgot a piece, much less swore in front of an audience. At the post-recital reception, I stood by myself, my cheeks flaming, too upset to eat the fancy cookies. In the car ride home, no one said a word.

Mrs. Siefkin greeted me coolly at the first lesson after Christmas. My awful blunder at the recital had destroyed any shred of positive connection between us. Every few days I begged Mother to let me quit piano. She wanted me to finish out the year; I wanted to avoid the May recital. In mid-March, after five years of playing in the same recitals as my accomplished sister, I got permission to stop taking lessons on the condition I tell Mrs. Siefkin in person, an unpleasant but satisfying task.

I was second-best in everything, not just piano. Melinda set impossibly high standards, both socially and academically. When she was in the seventh grade, four boys each gave her a box of Valentine candy.

"Maybe it's your auburn curls those boys like so much," Mother said, making me wonder if any boy would ever like my straight, lank hair. At twelve, Melinda was already the pretty teenager she would become. In the third grade, my Buster Brown haircut accentuated a too-round face, and my new front teeth looked like they belonged to a giant beaver.

Melinda's academic record was equally intimidating—
not simply all As but perfect scores on most of her tests. In
both junior high and high school, my sister and I had many of
the same teachers. When they called me Melinda, I might've
taken it as a compliment—she was, after all, an extraordinary student. Instead, I felt erased—not merely in my sister's
shadow but obliterated by it.

As the burden of comparison increased, however, I
stumbled upon an escape route.

Chapter 3: Music Teachers

A defining period in my life began in the most ordinary way—a desire to please my classmate Anne, the most sophisticated eleven-year-old I knew. At an age when most girls barely thought about hair, Anne wore her black hair short and stylishly cut, with a natural, dramatic white streak in front. I envied her sharp wit, easy self-confidence, and, especially, her position in the clique of popular girls. When she suggested we join the junior high band and play the flute, I went along, hoping to get closer to Anne's inner circle.

Right away I felt a personal connection with the flute, a sharp contrast to my adversarial struggle with the piano. Instead of hitting keys, I made the sound with my breath. That felt magical, as if my breath transformed the flute into an extension of my body. And unlike a piano, it was portable. With the music stand squeezed into my bedroom, I had to angle the flute carefully to avoid hitting the walls, but it was worth it to practice away from my father's critical presence.

Although the secondhand flute was a bit tarnished, the blue velvet lining of the case worn in spots, it was mine, and playing the flute was *my* skill, a skill my sister never had. Following Anne's suggestion didn't raise my popularity status, but I spent less time comparing myself to Melinda.

The fact that Daddy didn't care about my interest in the flute didn't matter; I met surrogate father figures who did care.

A cute, olive-skinned man with an engaging grin, the junior high band director had a knack for striking just the right balance between disciplined learning and good humor. Mr. Barron seemed to relish both band music and interacting with sixth and seventh graders. I loved the sound of his soft, deep laugh, and like everyone else in the band, I thought he was the epitome of cool.

Meeting Mr. Barron was my first encounter with a warm-hearted, encouraging man. I don't know which I liked more—the flute, or the thrill of Mr. Barron's undivided attention when I played solo flute parts. In addition to directing the band, Mr. Barron owned a music store just off the square in Decatur. Anne and I invented reasons for stopping by to see him in the late afternoons. We worried he'd wonder why we kept losing our camphor and cork grease, but he was probably used to junior high girls inventing excuses to come into his store. Despite our frequent visits and unconvincing excuses, he always seemed pleased to see us.

The first year of band coincided with the opening of Fernbank, the new elementary school built when baby boomers overcrowded the K-12 school next to our house. Because Fernbank had no band room, we rehearsed every day on the stage of the auditorium, surrounded by gleaming, light-colored wood and dark red velvet curtains.

Other than developing a crush on Mr. Barron, all I remember from the first year of band is the Christmas concert. Mr. Barron asked me to play "White Christmas" as a solo, which was a little scary because I'd be standing in front of the band, performing from memory, in an auditorium packed with parents. The five years of piano recitals were for audiences of only about thirty. There were twice that many just in the band.

And it was exactly one year since the piano recital when I forgot my piece. My stomach churned every time I thought about that recital.

When the night of the band concert arrived and I walked to the front of the stage, I did indeed feel exposed, trapped between two large groups—the band seated behind me on the brightly-lit stage and the audience facing me in the big, dark hall. My heart raced as I wondered how many eyes were focused on me. Probably hundreds. But only briefly— one verse of "White Christmas" goes by quickly. Though nerve-racking, my first public flute solo went well—one short but satisfying minute.

A few months after joining the band, I began daydreaming about Mr. Barron. I remember my favorite fantasy with such clarity, it's as if I dreamed it last night: Mr. Barron finds me after I've fallen down the flight of concrete stairs outside the band room. He carries me back up the stairs, my head resting against his broad chest, and . . . that was as far as I got.

I'd been fascinated by a similar passage in *Gone with the Wind*, where Rhett Butler grabs Scarlett and carries her up a winding staircase. The summer before, I read that passage over and over, trying to figure out what happened when they reached the top of the stairs. I probably sensed it was about sex, but at that age I neither understood nor thought about sex. Like many daughters of distant fathers, what I yearned for was not sex but affection, and the part that fascinated me was Scarlett leaning her head against Rhett's chest. (That Rhett grabbed Scarlett against her will didn't occur to me.) Fantasies about a cute band director are pretty normal for preteen girls. My longing to have an older man care about me, however, persisted.

"Ernestine," Mother called from the kitchen one night while I was practicing, "what's the name of that piece you're playing? It sounds so familiar."

I was in my bedroom, about fifteen feet from the kitchen. Three weeks before, Mother had purchased *Everybody's Favorite Flute Solos*, a collection of tunes ranging in difficulty from simple to intermediate.

"It's 'Ah, So Pure' by Von Flotow," I said.

"Why don't you practice in here? I can listen while I wash dishes."

I brought the music stand into the dingy kitchen, turned one of the chairs to face the stand, and sat down. The room was dominated by a square, light green wooden table my father had made. It was a bit wobbly, due to the unevenness of the rust-colored linoleum floor. The only place with enough room was the side of the kitchen table by the front door. The flute stretched out about two feet to my right, a few inches from the door.

"Are you sure that melody isn't from an opera?" Mother asked.

I looked more closely at the title. "It says 'Martha' underneath the title."

"Oh yes, though it would be pronounced 'Marta' in German."

That she knew the name of the opera didn't surprise me. My parents used to listen to the Saturday afternoon broadcast of the Metropolitan Opera, following librettos they borrowed from the Emory University library that had the original language on one page, with an English translation on the facing page. My mother's knowledge of German pronunciation, however, puzzled me.

"I thought you studied French at Duke," I said. She sometimes helped Melinda with high school French assignments.

"My master's degree was in Romance languages," she explained, "and even though German isn't a Romance language, I learned some things about German from studying French, Spanish, and Italian. And from listening to German operas."

I knew it had been my mother's idea to listen to the opera broadcasts. It saddened me to remember they stopped listening to the Met because Daddy decided he'd rather watch college football on Saturday afternoons.

The next night, I brought the music stand into the kitchen before I started practicing. At the end of my practice, I flipped through the book looking for more melodies to play. When I got to page 139, I froze: an arrangement of Debussy's "Clair de Lune." After more than a year, seeing the title still triggered the memory of that awful night. I quickly flipped forward to my favorite piece, Schubert's "Ave Maria." Something about the lovely melody made me play with a slightly different tone. Mother noticed right away.

"You sound your best when you play that piece," she said.

We decided the arrangement worked well—she had something to listen to while she worked in the kitchen; I had an audience and a resonant, flattering place to play. Sometimes Mother would even stop working, sit down, and listen attentively. When she listened, I played more expressively. She never said much, but I loved sharing music with her, knowing she, too, experienced its beauty.

Daddy, on the other hand, had no interest in my flute studies or in classical music. The few times I went to concerts with my parents, my father fidgeted through most of the program, as he did when Mother persuaded him to go to church. Daddy did, however, love musicals.

Each summer Atlanta had a season of shows called "Theater Under the Stars," presented in the outdoor Chastain Amphitheater and performed by Broadway casts accompanied by musicians from the Atlanta Symphony. My father, always tight with money, splurged on season tickets for several years, beginning when I was ten. He bought LPs of all the musicals we attended, plus others, some quite obscure. I loved going to those shows; they were the only activity we did as a family other than dinners with the Bullocks and the annual Whitman reunions, which were fun for Daddy (verbal sparring with his sisters), boring for the rest of us.

My favorite show was *Kismet*. Based on music by Alexander Borodin, many of the melodies come from his orchestral piece, "Polovetsian Dances." When I fell in love in the eighth grade, if I was alone in the house, I walked around singing "And This Is My Beloved" and "Stranger in Paradise." Dozens of songs from those musicals remain etched into my brain, alongside those from *Your Hit Parade.*

My father also liked folk singers, especially if they sang funny songs, like Burl Ives singing about an old woman who swallowed a fly. To his credit, he never objected to the Elvis records I bought with my small allowance; he even liked "You Ain't Nothin' But a Hound Dog." A few years later, he liked "Wake Up Little Susie," which was interesting, given the strict curfews he set for his daughters.

Daddy must've had a pretty good ear, because when he whistled—which was often—his pitch was very good. So many memories of my father are scenes when he was angry, but that wasn't all the time. No one whistles when they're angry. The song he whistled ad nauseum was "Lara's Theme" from the movie *Doctor Zhivago*. I suspect he had a crush on Julie Christie.

makeup, and actually needed bras. I felt like Miss Skinny Little Nobody.

Anne and I mourned the loss of Mr. Barron. We'd traded our cute idol for a strange man named Mr. Little. Oddly, Mr. Little was big—tall and overweight, with a large, round face and straight black hair swept back from his high forehead. His rimless glasses and ill-fitting brown suit did nothing to enhance his awkward appearance. In striking contrast to Mr. Barron, Mr. Little seemed ill at ease with the band. His face registered two expressions: irritated and bored. Our junior high crushes certainly didn't transfer to this weird man.

As unappealing as the director, the band room in the old high school was dingy, the metal chairs uncomfortable, the gray linoleum floor permanently soiled. The acoustical tiles on the walls, originally white, now matched the gray of the floor. Like many band rooms, it had three tiers. The highest tier, at the back, was for the percussion and some of the brass players. As usual the flutes were in front on the main floor, closest to the front wall that was part corkboard, part blackboard with music staves. Closest to the dorky band director.

During the second week of band, we read through a piece with several flute solos. The first chair flutist was a pretty, curvy senior named Lenore. Right before one of her solos, Mr. Little winked at her, which seemed out of character for this large, awkward man. Listening carefully, I tried to figure out why Mr. Little was so pleased with her playing. Her solos sounded okay, but nothing special.

After the rehearsal, I caught up with Anne.

"Did you see Mr. Little wink at Lenore?" I asked.

"I sure did," Anne said, "and it was weird. She seems kind of stuck up. You never see her talking to anyone."

"She's well-endowed, I'll give her that." My entire bra might cover half of her.

"Don't you think she looks kind of cheap?" Anne asked. "I mean, all that makeup."

"Yeah, especially the blue eye shadow. And she didn't even sound that great on her solos."

"But Mr. Little looked impressed." Anne sounded puzzled.

"I don't know why he liked her playing so much. I sure miss Mr. Barron."

"No kidding, makes you almost wish we were back in seventh grade, just to see him," Anne said, before we hurried off to our next classes.

Druid Hills was a big high school, at that time supposedly the best of the five public schools in the Atlanta area. I had expected the first chair flutist in the band to be really good. It bothered me that Mr. Little liked her playing so much. I didn't covet Mr. Little's attention, but I did covet the solos. In junior high, I'd liked playing the solo parts, hearing my sound soar above the whole band. Now that I'd heard Lenore, I swore I'd earn that first chair spot, well before my senior year.

While Anne and I compared our uncool band director with Mr. Barron, Mother took steps to follow Mr. Barron's advice. He'd said my flute talent would develop more quickly if I had private flute lessons, and he'd recommended the principal flutist in the Atlanta Symphony, reputed to be the best flutist not only in Atlanta but in the entire South. Unfortunately, the one open time slot was 8:00 a.m. on Saturday.

The first lesson occurred in early fall, when most Atlantans feel a sense of renewed energy after summer's oppressive heat and humidity. But I was a teenager. I didn't want to be up at that hour on Saturday in any weather. I sulked all the way to the teacher's house, sighing noisily in protest. As I opened the car door, Mother turned to me.

"You should probably know this man's name; it's Mr. Little," she said.

"Mother, for Pete's sake," I said, almost yelling, "that's the weird band director. Why didn't you tell me? I don't want to take lessons with him. Why can't I study with Mr. Barron?"

"Well, for one thing, he's not a flutist. You know that," she said.

"But he could still teach me a lot."

"Mr. Barron recommended Mr. Little, said he's the best flutist in town. He even plays professionally with the symphony."

"But—"

"Just take one lesson and then we can talk about it. Go on, it's already eight."

As I climbed the steps to the front door of Mr. Little's house, I thought how embarrassing it would be if my friends found out I was studying with the uncool band director. Reluctantly, I rang the doorbell. When he appeared, framed in the doorway, Mr. Little seemed twice as tall and far more imposing than he'd seemed in the band room. I felt a little nervous..

"You must be Ernestine," he said, somewhat awkwardly.

"Yes," was all I could think of to say. Even though I didn't like him, I kind of resented the fact that I'd been in his band for two weeks, yet he had no idea which flutist I was. Another strike against him. As he stepped aside to let me in, I considered backing down the steps.

Mr. Little led me to the back of his small house where a den had been converted into a music room. Two chairs sat side by side, with a music stand in front of one of them. Somehow the room felt inviting, maybe because it was right off the kitchen. It was 8:00 a.m. and I was in an unfamiliar house with a strange man, but at least I recognized the smell of bacon. In the crowded room, a small, faded couch sat against one wall, perpendicular to the chairs. The wall opposite the couch contained bookshelves crammed with untidy stacks of music.

"Did you bring a piece to play?" he asked after we sat down.

"Yes," I said, putting my book of solos on the music stand. I turned to the fast movement of a Handel sonata, a solo I knew well.

"Okay, go ahead, take whatever tempo you like," Mr. Little said.

"Very good," he said, after I finished.

I turned to face him and was astonished to see a big smile on his face, a genuine smile that made his eyes crinkle up. The awkward band director had disappeared, replaced by someone who radiated warmth and reassurance. Despite my previous opinion of him, I wanted to crawl inside the warmth of his remarkable smile.

"So, how about some sight-reading?" Mr. Little asked, opening volume 2 of Voxman's *Selected Duets for Flute.*

"Sure."

I wanted to impress him with my sight-reading ability, but it was hard to focus on the music, because I'd never sat beside such a lovely flute sound. Having heard only fellow band members, I had no idea a flute tone could be beautiful. Mr. Little's sound had none of the fuzzy, white noise that plagued most band flutists, and it was fuller, even when he was playing softly—as if it was composed of lots of colors. When we stopped, I almost blurted out, "Wow!"

"You're a good sight-reader," he said. "There are a couple of books of music I'd like you to purchase, by next week if you can. Did you bring a notebook?"

"Oh, I'm sorry, I didn't," I said.

"Doesn't matter. I've got some paper here," he said, reaching for a notebook. His arms looked kind of short and stubby for such a tall man. He ripped a sheet out and started writing on it. "The closest place for you is probably Ritter's Music Store, in Buckhead."

"Okay," I said as he handed me the paper, which listed a scale book and two volumes of Mozart duets.

"Don't worry," Mr. Little said, sensing my disappointment that no book of solos was listed. "After another lesson or two, we'll decide which solos you'll be studying. For next week, I'd like you to prepare 'Flight of the Bumblebee' from the solo book you have. It's short but very challenging. Don't go too fast at first, just try to make it clear and even." He got up from his chair as I finished putting my flute in its case.

"I'm glad you've decided to take lessons, Ernestine. I'll see you next week," he said, walking me to the door. "Sorry it has to be so early," he added.

I almost skipped to the car. I wanted to shout, "Hey, I just played duets with the principal flutist of the Atlanta Symphony!"

"Well, how did it go?" Mother asked.

"Much better than I thought," I admitted.

I called Anne as soon as I got home.

"Anne, you have to take lessons too," I said.

"You mean with Mr. Little? Are you kidding?" she asked.

"No, really, you should. You'll be surprised how nice he is."

"I find that hard to believe," Anne said. "And besides, I thought you had to take the 8:00 a.m. slot."

"Well, maybe someone will cancel, or maybe he teaches another day. He's really different in lessons," I said.

"You were right," Anne said two weeks later, after her first lesson. "I guess he just doesn't like the band."

"I knew you'd like him. Now, can we switch so my lesson's on Sunday afternoon?"

"For Saturday morning? Ha, fat chance."

At the beginning of each lesson, Mr. Little greeted me warmly and seemed eager to hear me play. I continued to be captivated by his smile—one that enveloped you and conveyed not just friendliness but delight and encouragement. Before long Anne and I had transferred our crushes to Mr. Little. His eccentricities intrigued us. For some of my Saturday morning lessons, Mr. Little wore a rumpled tux, probably from the previous night's concert. He left his outside Christmas lights up all year, turning them on randomly in April and May. He was both the kindest and the most fascinating man we knew.

Eventually, we met Mrs. Little, a petite, glamorous brunette. Even at 8:00 a.m., she wore bright red lipstick and sheath dresses in solid, vivid colors, a sharp contrast to my mother's pastel, flowered shirtwaist dresses. Anne and I found Mrs. Little fascinating because she didn't seem like a housewife. We were right, as we later found out; Jane Little played string bass with the Atlanta Symphony.

"Just think what it would be like," Anne said one day, "to have Mr. Little as a father."

"Oh, that would be so great," I said. "Hey, then Mrs. Little would be our mother. Wouldn't that be cool? She seems a lot younger than my mother."

"Well, she probably is, you know. I mean, he looks way younger than our dads."

"It's really too bad he doesn't have any kids," I said, and Anne agreed.

Thus began our weekly flute lessons and the quick transformation of Mr. Little from strange band director to beloved teacher and father figure.

By the time I was in the eighth grade, my real father had begun to frighten me. This, too, was part of a transformation, but a gradual one that had begun years earlier, when Daddy compared my piano skills to Melinda's. After I quit piano, my father found other areas to compare: "Your handwriting isn't nearly as neat as Melinda's," and "Melinda is such a clever conversationalist; why don't you talk more?" In the past year or so, his disapproval had been mixed with anger. Although my father never resorted to physical violence, his verbal attacks were bad enough.

Melinda coped with Daddy's outbursts better than I did, standing up to him with anger of her own. Like Mother, I deflected his anger by shrinking into myself, saying nothing. Even when I thought he was wrong, fear made me hesitate to speak up. After he had lashed out at me, the shame lingered — sometimes hours, sometimes days — leaving a residue that never went away.

One Friday night, a couple of months after I'd begun lessons with Mr. Little, my father invited me to come with him to the new Lenox Square shopping mall while he looked for a Christmas present for my mother. We didn't talk much on the way there, which was fine with me. My father almost never asked me to accompany him; I didn't want to spoil things by making him angry. Silence was safer.

We saw the bright lights from Lenox Square as soon as we crested a hill two blocks from the mall. The stores were laid out in a large L-shaped pattern, around a huge Christmas tree in the center of the open space. It took me a moment to figure out why everything seemed so bright: the stores featured glass front walls. In addition to the walkway lampposts, much of the light from the stores spilled out into the mall. Although not a recent development, the widespread use of glass walls in stores was, like shopping malls, a new phenomenon in

1959. The number of stores in one space astonished me too. When Daddy let me wander around by myself, I felt quite sophisticated to be on my own in such a cosmopolitan place.

By the time we left, the mall's parking lot was almost empty, so Daddy drove across the rows of parking spaces, making a diagonal line for the exit. But we seemed to be heading straight for one of the light poles that dotted the parking lot. As we came closer and closer, thoughts raced through my head.

Why is Daddy driving straight toward that post? Can't he see it? Should I say something and get yelled at?

My heart started pounding. Time seemed to stretch as crucial seconds went by while I struggled to decide whether to risk my father's anger. The lamppost remained dead center to the windshield.

"STOP!" I yelled, right before the moment of impact.

The dashboard filled my mouth as my head shattered the windshield. A deafening sound of crunching metal was followed by stunned silence. Moments after the initial shock, I noticed blood on my shirt. My head felt bludgeoned, and my tongue found a gaping hole in my mouth; my front upper left tooth was gone.

Daddy appeared to be okay. He asked if I was all right; unable to speak, I just nodded.

"Why didn't you tell me the lamppost was there? Didn't you see it?" Even if my mouth hadn't been bleeding, I couldn't have answered him. Long after I'd managed to stand up to him in some ways, I still couldn't tell my father how much his anger terrified me.

A man who saw the accident drove us to Grady Hospital. I remember very little about the hospital visit other than holding gauze on my upper gum. When we got home, my mother called Mr. Little to cancel the next day's flute lesson.

"Mr. Little is very concerned about you," Mother said when she came to my room.

I nodded—slowly.

"He said to tell you that you shouldn't worry, you'll be able to keep playing the flute, even with a missing tooth."

Whether I could play the flute was something I hadn't even considered. But Mr. Little's words were comforting; knowing he'd thought about me meant a lot to me that night. Daddy, on the other hand, said nothing, either in the taxi ride home or after we arrived. I assumed he was angry because I hadn't spoken up. The exciting trip to Lenox Square led to a miserable weekend. My mouth hurt, I looked ridiculous, and my father remained angry at me.

Knowing how embarrassed I was to have a missing front tooth, Mother let me stay home from school for a few days. My father arranged a couple of meetings with a dentist at the Emory University School of Dentistry. By the time I returned to school, I had a retainer with a fake tooth. Not too bad as long as I didn't smile. And Mr. Little was right; I could still play the flute.

Once my mouth healed, I began a series of lengthy, painful dental appointments, preparing for and installing a bridge that had a permanent front tooth. To save on costs, the work was done by a student at the Emory dental school. Unfortunately, the inexperienced student chose a tooth that didn't match my other front tooth in shape or color. It was, in fact, a worse match than the temporary tooth. I looked like Ollie, the snaggletoothed dragon on the TV show *Kukla, Fran and Ollie.*

Although Mother explained that they chose the dental student to do the work because it was less expensive, I had other suspicions. Because my father had said nothing, I thought I didn't deserve better—the mismatched tooth was my scarlet letter, a reminder that the accident was my fault. It was many years before I understood my father's concern about dental costs; in the early 1960s, faculty salaries at Emory University were modest. I wish he could've talked to me about it, maybe expressed regret over the quality of the work. It's possible the tooth seemed fine to him because he never looked closely at me. As the years passed, I stopped blaming myself for not saying, "Stop," in time. It took longer to believe I deserved a good-looking front tooth.

Chapter 4: Family Myth

The sudden jump in the volume and difficulty of homework in high school jolted me and forced me to make a difficult choice. I'd studied ballet for seven years and loved everything about it—the fanciful costumes, the smooth pink satin of new toe shoes, and, especially, the sheer joy of moving to music. We danced to the accompaniment of an out-of-tune, upright piano played by a so-so pianist, but it was exhilarating to leap and turn to live music—always classical, lots of Chopin. At the end of the previous year, I'd been accepted into the Atlanta Ballet Apprentice Company. To keep up with the company, I would need to practice ballet at home, in addition to taking daily, after-school classes.

This year, band also took more time, with extra practices scheduled during football season that conflicted with ballet class. Even if I could get permission to miss part of a band practice and part of a ballet class, the burden of homework would still make it impossible to keep up with all three.

If I gave up band, I'd probably have to give up the flute. Now that I'd started lessons with Mr. Little, I wanted to practice every day. I was beginning to explore ways to improve the sound with subtle changes of my lip muscles. It amazed me that a minute change in the flute embouchure (lip formation) could alter tone quality. And there were other things that excited me about staying in the band. Compared to junior high, the high school band's sound was richer, the players more in tune, the music more challenging. The first week of band, I'd been disappointed to be eleventh chair in the flute section, but once I realized all sub-freshmen were placed at the bottom of sections, I welcomed the challenge of working my way up. There were also cute older boys. No boys, cute or otherwise, in ballet class.

Did I choose band because, at thirteen, I felt a passion for the flute? No. I picked it because, relative to others my age, I was the best flutist I knew, something I would never achieve as a dancer. After dropping ballet, I tried to ignore the gnawing sense of loss. But the love for dance remained part of me and greatly enriched my life. When I watch ballerinas, I can still feel the muscles that contract for a pirouette.

—

"Ernestine, come here," Mother called from the kitchen one night, "it's time to help with the dishes." Mother sounded tired and cross, as she usually did at suppertime.

Although a lengthy history assignment was due the next day, I thought I could grab a half hour of practicing before tackling schoolwork. I was about to shut my bedroom door when Mother called.

"I really want to practice flute. Can't Melinda do it?" I asked, wishing I'd shut the door before opening the flute case. If I hadn't been within earshot, Mother might've called Melinda. Though these days, that was unlikely.

"You know she has a lot more studying to do than you, and that's certainly more important than playing your flute."

"But I have a lot of homework tonight too."

"I thought you said you wanted to practice," Mother said. I could hear her stacking dinner plates.

"I was going to practice for just thirty minutes, and then do homework."

"Well, you'll just have to skip the flute tonight."

The den was opposite my bedroom, off the short hallway to the kitchen. As usual, my father was in the den, sitting in his big, brown corduroy armchair. He'd put his newspaper aside and was watching TV. With Melinda.

"Melinda's just watching TV," I said, as I entered the kitchen.

"What?" Mother asked, hunched over the sink.

"Well, she's just watching TV, so maybe she could put the food away and dry the dishes," I pointed out—reasonably, I thought.

"Just let her be. She needs some time to relax."

We'd had many similar exchanges, each one a reminder that Melinda's needs came first. I swallowed my resentment and grabbed a dish towel. The flute would have to wait another day. I thought wistfully of the evenings when Mother had enjoyed my practicing in the kitchen, only two years ago. Sometime during my seventh-grade year, for reasons unknown to me, Mother had decided she preferred my help with dishes to hearing me play the flute.

Mother must have heard me sigh.

"Sit down, Ernestine, we need to talk," she said, after I'd dried a couple of dishes.

With a sense of dread, I pulled out one of the kitchen chairs and sat down. Mother sat down as well, abandoning the dishes for the moment. This must be serious.

"Your sister is brilliant, and you're going to have to make peace with that," she said. "Melinda is like your father; you're more like me."

"What do you mean?" I asked, though I was pretty sure I didn't want to know.

"Your father and Melinda are brilliant and very ambitious, and they need our support." I frowned. "You're good at things too," she added hastily. "So far, you've done as well in school as Melinda, but that was just junior high. Now that you're in high school, and Melinda is getting ready to go to college next year, you have to accept that her needs come first."

I could think of nothing to say. It wasn't as if her words shocked me; they merely confirmed what I'd sensed in the past couple of years about the hierarchy in our little family.

"I'm not trying to discourage you," she went on. "It's just that you're growing up, and I don't want you to be disappointed because you're not like Melinda."

You mean not as good as, I thought. She had confirmed the thing I dreaded most—that I would remain in my sister's shadow forever. Mother and I were supposed to reflect the values of the TV show *Father Knows Best*, which we watched every week; our roles were the gracious wife and daughter of the wise father. But my volatile, judgmental father was nothing like the calm, supportive dad Robert Young portrayed, and what was Melinda's role? Was she the son? It wasn't the first time I'd wondered if Daddy's disappointment with me was because he'd hoped for a son. Melinda was the next best thing. In any case, I was expected to be sweet and compliant. How infuriating.

I wanted to scream that I was nothing like Mother, but I knew we shared many similarities that contrasted with the other half of the family. Melinda and Daddy took charge of situations and stated their opinions with assurance. Mother and I were quieter, more likely to listen than to jump into a conversation. Much to my annoyance, the pairings also fit our appearance: like Mother, I had dark eyes, straight hair, and skin that tanned easily; like Daddy, Melinda had hazel eyes, curly hair, and fair skin. Mother could see I was upset.

"Don't worry, honey, you know you've always been pretty. And people appreciate your sweet nature."

I did not feel sweet. When I resumed drying the dishes, I wanted to fling every one of them at my mother. But of course I didn't, which merely proved her point. Swallowing my anger was part of a skill I later perfected: the art of hiding emotions. Hiding meant dismissing them, which suited Mother because she hated emotional confrontation. But it felt dishonest, pretending everything was fine.

In the following months, Mother occasionally reminded me of our designated roles, especially when I objected to having more chores than Melinda. If Mother thought defining the family dichotomy would make things less frustrating for me, or perhaps seal a bond between the two of us, it didn't work. Sensing her need for an ally, and without being conscious of it, I began to pull away from her, even physically. Whenever she embraced me, I felt smothered, pressured to be like her. Which was worse, I wondered, being sweet and passive like Mother or a pale imitation of Melinda?

At thirteen I knew enough about my parents' early years to make me wonder why Mother had become subservient to my father. Daddy often told the story of seeing Mother's glamorous picture in the Duke University newspaper, part of an article about the smart graduate student who was president of the International Club and excelled in dancing the tango. The daughter of a diplomat, she'd traveled all over the world. Mother's unusual upbringing was the very thing that caught Daddy's attention.

In sharp contrast to Mother, Daddy grew up in the tiny town of Boaz, Alabama, with seven older sisters who all did chores to help their hardworking parents. I don't know if my father had any chores; I suspect being both male and the youngest child exempted him. Daddy was used to women taking care of things, whereas in Mother's family, servants had done all the cooking and housekeeping.

Perhaps pursuing Mother simply reflected my father's ambitious nature—of course he would go after someone exotic and smart. (She earned Phi Beta Kappa; he didn't.) How sad, then, that when Mother married him she gave up her academic ambitions; sadder still that she became so quiet and submissive. After a childhood spent in many of the world's great cities, at age twenty-five my mother set aside her master's degree to begin a new life. She was now the wife of a modestly paid college professor in the South. No wonder she found cooking and housework tedious.

Suddenly, a memory from seven years earlier came to me: I'd heard Mother yell at Daddy, "Then for our fifteenth anniversary, we can just get a divorce." That had upset me at the time; now I questioned my memory. Had she really stood up for herself like that? I wished I could go back and cheer her on, "Way to go, Mother!"

But trying to understand it did nothing to alter my situation. Whether I liked it or not, throughout my teenage years I grew to look more and more like my mother. Yes, Mother was pretty, but I wanted to be like Melinda and Daddy. I wanted to be one of the achievers.

A few weeks after band started, I noticed the tuba player staring at me. Surely, I was imagining it. He was a cute junior;

I, a lowly sub-freshman who wore glasses and barely needed a bra. The next day when I caught him looking at me, he smiled. I smiled back. In the Friday afternoon marching band practice, I noticed how broad his shoulders were, the tuba resting comfortably. He could probably carry four tubas on those shoulders. I found myself imagining how it would feel to rub my hand over his blond crew cut.

From exchanged glances we progressed to brief conversations before band practices; a month or so later, he asked me to go with him to a party on December 4. As soon as I said yes, I began to panic. What would my parents think? Would they disapprove of Ken? Maybe I wasn't ready for this. When I sought Melinda's advice, she said it would probably be okay to go, but that I might be a little too young. (She started dating in the ninth grade.) A week before the date, I began pawing through my closet, looking for the impossible: something that would give me a 36-22-36-inch figure. At least I had the 22 part. I settled for a baby-blue sheath dress that gave the illusion of a slightly hourglass figure.

On December 4, I met Ken at the back door (the only door accessible from the street in our crazy house) and led him through the house to the rarely used living room. My parents sat on the only sofa, looking as welcoming as a seated version of *American Gothic*. After stiff introductions, Ken and I each sat on a straight-backed chair, as far apart as we could be in that small room. To break the awkward silence, Mother got up and showed Ken her collection of angel figurines, housed in a glass bookcase at one end of the room.

"And this is your prettiest angel," Ken said, pointing at me.

I cringed, expecting my father to voice his disapproval. I assumed my parents would consider any comment about my appearance improper, if not downright lewd. I was sure they could see my cheeks burning. Daddy showed no reaction one way or the other, but to my surprise, Mother smiled as if Ken's remark had been merely a sweet compliment. I was too worried and self-conscious to realize she was right.

After what seemed like endless minutes of forced small talk, we left the house and walked to the curb. Ken opened the passenger door of a white 1954 Ford station wagon, with fake wood panels on the sides. The interior smelled like smoke, as most cars did in those days. It was his parents' car; no teenager I knew had a car of his own. Since Ken could drive, we avoided the awkwardness of having a parent take us to the party.

I don't remember much about the party, other than feeling out of place because I didn't know anyone. When Ken drove me home, right before we got out of the car, he reached across the back of the wide front seat, gently touched my right shoulder, and kissed me on the cheek. I pulled away from him, too surprised to register whether I liked it or not. On the second date, when the kiss was longer and on the lips, I discovered I liked it—a lot.

In early spring, Ken took me to the movie *Spartacus*. Finally, we were alone in a darkened room. When he held my hand, I felt warm and secure. After several minutes, he began gently stroking my palm and wrist in a circular, clockwise motion. Coziness gave way to strange sensations—my heartbeat sped up, the lower half of my body seemed to be melting, and I felt an unfamiliar but strong yearning. I remembered what my mother had warned me about.

"If you get carried away, you won't be able to think, and you'll be ruined."

Is this what ruination feels like? What if I like being ruined? Maybe it was bad for her but good for me?

Other than *Spartacus*, our dates were well-chaperoned school dances that offered no opportunities for being alone. Ken resorted to stealing a few kisses in stairwells between classes. When his hand first slipped under my blouse, the thrill and hunger were overwhelming. So was the guilt. That night I confessed in my diary that I'd done something "really awful." I couldn't bring myself to be specific, even in a diary, but I vowed never to do it again. Shortly after that I stopped writing in the diary.

At the end of the year, Ken invited me to the junior-senior prom, held in a ballroom of the new, downtown Marriott Hotel. One of only two sub-freshmen invited, I achieved my social pinnacle at age fourteen. Melinda was also there, but we never saw one another. Despite our extreme nearsightedness, we'd decided glasses were not part of prom wear—in my case a strapless, lavender, frilly concoction with a wide, stiff skirt puffed out by robust crinolines was. The dress and the wrist corsage of white carnations Ken gave me made me feel glamorous, especially next to Ken, handsome in his white coat and black bow tie. Behind his glasses his blue eyes sparkled; I mistook that sparkle for the look of love.

The DJ played a nice mix of fast and slow songs, though we looked pretty silly doing the twist in formal wear. I loved leaning into Ken and feeling his arm around my waist during the Shirelles' "Will You Still Love Me Tomorrow," one of my favorite songs. After an hour or so of mostly slow dancing, Ken led me to an emergency exit door (no alarm) that opened onto a steep, outside staircase leading to the ground. Looking down from the top of that long flight of concrete stairs, I wondered if I could make it down without tripping, given my limited sight, puffy dress, and high heels, but I was highly motivated. I'd decided a big event like the prom justified progressing a little further down the road to ruination.

We made it down the stairs and tried to progress, but the stiff dress, which had seemed so romantic, made subtle moves impossible. No slipping a hand beneath a blouse or under a short skirt. Unlike Ken, I wasn't frustrated when formal wear thwarted our desire; I thought Ken and I were destined to be together for a long time. I didn't understand that the more enthralled I became, the less interesting I was to him. Shortly after the prom, Ken broke up with me. I took it hard, as if I'd lost a part of me I'd only recently discovered. The loss caused me to doubt myself in a way I hadn't before I dated Ken.

For more than a year, I spent an excessive amount of time in my bedroom sobbing, playing Elvis's "Are You Lonesome Tonight?" over and over. One day, Mother came into my room to put some laundry away and caught me.

"What's wrong?" she asked, more impatient than concerned.

"Nothing really, I'm just sad."

"Well, if it's about Ken Skillern, don't waste your time. Here, make yourself useful." She handed me some blouses to hang up. I've never forgotten her next comment.

"You might as well learn this now rather than later. Where women are concerned, men want only two things: sex and a cook."

Years later, I found out Mother's father abandoned the family when Mother was seventeen. No wonder she mistrusted men. When we were growing up, Mother told Melinda and me that our grandfather had died before we were born; we learned the truth only when he actually did die, and Mother had to explain a sudden trip to Missouri. But she refused to talk about her father's desertion.

Mother's cynical remark made me question both Ken's feelings about me and my feelings toward him. Other than band, we had nothing in common. I was an A student, Ken a mediocre one. I was a rule follower; he'd been in juvenile prison for stealing a car. I came from an academic family; his father owned a garage. Given such differences, why did I fall so hard for him? Perhaps because Ken had chosen me. For a few months, being singled out made me feel cherished, exceptional. I hungered for male attention; when it was withdrawn, I felt diminished.

For the next three years, I spent boring evenings with guys I didn't particularly like. It never occurred to me I could say no, though my chilly demeanor sent them away after one or two dates. The experience with Ken soured me on romance; I turned once again to music teachers and conductors for the male attention I craved.

Second Theme:
Becoming a Musician

Second themes, formerly labeled feminine, are usually lighter, more lyrical than first themes. For example, when the first theme is in a minor key, the second theme is often in a major key, such as in Beethoven's Fifth Symphony, which makes it sound more positive, less intense.

Chapter 5: The Flute

The first year I studied with Mr. Little, lessons were fun, a pleasant diversion from homework. Although Anne and I talked about our crushes on Mr. Little, neither of us was serious about the flute; we simply enjoyed having the attention of a kind, encouraging man. Like me, Anne had a distant father, though hers was less volatile.

After a few months of lessons, Mr. Little suggested I upgrade my flute from the cheap Artley model. A friend of my father's, eager to sell his daughter's abandoned instrument, sold us a Haynes flute for only $250. At fourteen, I had no idea Haynes made the best flutes in the country, if not the world, but as soon as I tried the flute, I heard the difference in tone. Thrilled by the added richness of the sound, I wanted to practice more. Mr. Little never told me how much to practice, and my parents certainly didn't care. My motivation was simply that I wanted to sound better. And, of course, Mr. Little's praise.

In spring of that year, Mr. Little assigned Giulio Briccialdi's "Carnival of Venice," a set of variations on a simple theme, a far more virtuosic piece than anything I'd studied previously. I wondered if I could conquer all the thirty-second note runs in the hardest variation. To my surprise, the challenge turned out to be fun. I played it faster and faster, until it sounded like two flutes were playing—one voicing the melody in the top part, the other with crazy-fast, accompanying notes in the lower voice. Although I didn't think about it at the time, the fun and sense of accomplishment had nothing to do with playing for anyone else. Instead, I had discovered the fundamental joy of practicing: working toward a goal—just me, my flute, and the piece of music. Like finding the solution to a difficult math problem all on my own, except more personal. Math solutions were universal; a piece of music varied with each person who played it.

At the end of the school year, I told Mother I wanted to continue flute lessons, even over the summer, when most kids took a break. Although Anne stopped lessons after that year, I was hooked. Yearning for an attentive father intensified my attachment to Mr. Little, but I was also intrigued by the sound of the flute, now that I had a better instrument.

It would be years before I could appreciate Mr. Little's extraordinary teaching; at the time, I simply did what he asked because I enjoyed it. The first year of lessons, a typical weekly assignment would include an Andersen étude (a piece of music that focuses on developing technique, or finger dexterity), several scale exercises, and part of a solo piece. By the second year, I knew all the major and minor scales so well that I could play a two-octave run in E-flat melodic minor, the hardest key, as easily as in C major, the easiest.

When I had conquered the scales, Mr. Little added other technical exercises—patterns of thirds and sixths. Even when I had an imminent performance of a solo piece, études and technical patterns were part of the week's assignment. It was a strict regimen for a high school student, one that developed facile technique. (The more finger patterns a player knows by rote, the easier it is to play fast.)

Although other good flute teachers used the same materials—scales, études, and solos—two things made Mr. Little an exceptional teacher: his ability to connect with students, giving each one his thoughtful, undivided attention, and his sense of when and how much to push a student. If a student easily learned an étude a week, he assigned two. When a student successfully memorized one section of a solo, he doubled the length of the section assigned the following week.

One of the things I learned to do better than most flutists was play very softly without going flat in pitch—very difficult on the flute because it requires a lot of subtle lip control. Mr. Little assigned a simple but effective exercise to develop this ability: play a dynamics diamond (<>) on a single pitch; that is, crescendo from pianissimo (very soft) to fortissimo (very loud) and back down to *niente* (silence). As you use more air to get louder, you have to relax your lip muscles to keep the pitch from going sharp, sort of like widening the nozzle on the hose when you add water volume so you won't cut off the heads of the flowers. Mr. Little told me to do the exercise on every note in the flute range. I'm sure most students skipped a few notes, if they did the exercise at all. But I did the diamond exercise faithfully. Was this extreme? Probably, but it certainly developed my lip control, dynamic range, and sensitivity to intonation.

Although Mr. Little didn't say much about interpretation or musicality, he emphasized legato (connecting notes smoothly). "Use your air to fill the space between the notes," he would say. A good pianist can play legato without using the pedal, but I never could. I loved how easy it was to connect the notes on the flute. I also found the variety of articulation styles fascinating—staccato and legato were merely opposite ends of a spectrum that included countless variations.

Unlike my rigid, nonresponsive piano teacher, Mr. Little was generous with his praise whenever I learned something well. Often the lessons ran past the scheduled half hour, which drove my father, waiting in the car, crazy. After a good lesson, I felt elated, but if I was more than five minutes late, Daddy's anger quickly extinguished my enthusiasm. My father, I began to understand, disliked Mr. Little, and as my adoration of Mr. Little increased, so did my father's animosity toward him.

———

In March of my freshman year, Mr. Little assigned a solo I hated, Kent Kennan's *Night Soliloquy*. Its strange melody never seemed to settle into a key, and half the time I couldn't even tell if I was playing the right notes. The piece's quirky rhythmic groupings were unlike anything I had tackled up to that point. How the heck can a composer write more—a lot more—than eight thirty-second notes in a beat? After two weeks, I thought about refusing to learn it. A *Night Soliloquy* boycott.

One day at dusk, on a whim I took my music stand to our screened-in back porch. The porch's seclusion drew me. We rarely went out there, maybe because of the moldy furniture: a once-green love seat swing and a chaise lounge covered in tattered dark green terry cloth. Because the coal furnace in the basement was directly underneath, everything on the porch was coated with soot. But, surrounded by treetops, it offered the best view in the house. I decided to give the crazy piece one more shot, and, phrase by phrase, *Night Soliloquy* began to make sense. Its eerie melancholy seemed to reflect a quality in the twilight's fading light. Alone on the porch, looking out over the treetops, something happened: I forgot who I was, where I was. Kennan's piece became my own soliloquy.

That evening on the porch was my first experience of being wholly absorbed in a piece of music while practicing. Being fully immersed in the music, I felt free. Nowhere else could I be both in control and entirely unselfconscious. From that day on, playing the flute became a refuge, a way to work through the troubling emotions of adolescence.

The used Haynes flute I'd gotten in the eighth grade served me well; by the end of my sophomore year, however, I found the instrument's limitations frustrating. To continue improving my sound and intonation, I needed another upgrade. One of Mr. Little's former students was selling a Haynes open-hole (a high-end model) flute for $1,000. My father said it was too much. After my persistent begging, he agreed to lend me the money, but only after I signed a formal, notarized contract setting the interest rate and schedule of repayment. Daddy pointed out his generosity in giving me a low interest rate, and in postponing repayments until college graduation. If he expected me to feel grateful, it backfired. I resented the formal arrangement, a constant reminder of my father's anxiety about my being able to pay back the loan. The threat of having to sell the flute in order to repay him loomed over me for years.

"Now try it the other way," Mr. Little said at one of my lessons in the spring of my sophomore year. We'd been working on the presto section at the end of Chaminade's Concertino. Chaminade wrote two versions of the section's most difficult bar, one with fast articulation (like saying *tut-tut* many times per second), the other with an awkward high register run that repeats four times. I'd just played the first version.

"Go back to the beginning of the presto," Mr. Little added, "so I can hear it in context."

I played the presto, this time with the gnarly sixteenth-note runs.

"Hey," Mr. Little said, giving me one of his extraordinary smiles, "you can do either one, so you can choose. Which one would you rather play?"

"I think it sounds more exciting with the runs," I said, after replaying both versions in my head. "Unless the runs slow me down."

"Yes," Mr. Little chuckled. "I know you like to play flashy things fast. Just keep working those runs with the metronome—every notch."

"I will," I promised. I couldn't imagine *not* practicing something the way he asked. After two and a half years of weekly lessons, I could tell Mr. Little's teaching had made me a better flutist. And that wasn't all. His weekly support and encouragement had become a lifeline, filling the void left by my distant and judgmental father. I loved Mr. Little's enthusiasm and ability to be fully present every minute of each lesson. I wondered if he made every student feel as special as I felt.

"Have you heard of the Transylvania Music Camp in North Carolina?" Mr. Little asked at the end of the lesson.

"I think so, if that's the one in Brevard," I answered, turning toward him.

"Yes, that's right. It's a very good summer program, and two weeks from today the Georgia Power Company is holding auditions for a scholarship to go there. I thought you might try out for it."

Stunned and pleased, I didn't know what to say, so I just looked at him, probably with my mouth hanging open.

"You could play Concertino," he said. "You've had that piece memorized for a while now, and you showed me today that you've got the hardest part under control. Are you interested in auditioning?"

"S-sure. Are a lot of people trying out?"

"Quite a few. The applicants will be mostly juniors and

seniors, so you may be the youngest. It's open to all wind instrumentalists, though you have to be recommended by a teacher. I'll write the recommendation and send it in, but you need to send in this application," he said, handing me a two-page form.

"Okay, thanks," I said, as I stood up to leave, putting the form carefully into my music folder.

"Mother, guess what," I said as soon as I got to the car.

"What?" she asked, smiling. She could see my excitement.

I told her about the scholarship. Each year the Georgia Power Company held auditions in seven locations around the state, picking a winner from each district. The most competitive district was Atlanta.

Two weeks later, I took a seat on one of the gray metal folding chairs that lined a dingy hallway in the Georgia State University music building. Saturday morning, waiting for my name to be called, a routine that would become familiar. That first time, I experienced no racing heart, no queasy stomach. Minutes earlier I'd warmed up in a noisy room filled with woodwind and brass players. I didn't mind that my chances of winning were slim. Mr. Little had recommended me, and that was enough.

After a pleasant middle-aged lady called my name, I entered a classroom where the student desks had been moved against the walls. Two male judges sat behind a small table; a music stand stood in the center of the room. Since I was performing from memory, I stood to the side of the stand.

The auditions were unaccompanied, but as I closed my eyes to begin, I imagined the introductory bars of the piano part to Chaminade's Concertino. For the opening theme, I began with as sweet a tone as I could summon and tried to shape the melody so it expressed a quiet sense of serenity. Remembering to take a huge breath for the end of the first section, I focused on keeping the sound full and open for the louder, more assertive part of the theme that goes into the high register.

Concertino was the first solo piece I studied that featured constant changes in tempo, or rubato. Performing unaccompanied allowed me to take more liberties with the stringendos (speeding up) and ritards (slowing down) to highlight changes in mood. That day I exaggerated the stringendos in the first few sections, building momentum to bring out the restlessness and yearning in the music. After a dramatically paced cadenza, I finished the piece with the fastest tempo I'd ever tried for the final presto section. I wouldn't win, but I was happy with my performance.

When the forty performers had played, we crowded around the door to the audition room, waiting to hear the result. Some of the parents were there, but most, including my mother, waited around the corner in the hallway. Ten minutes later, the lady who had ushered us into the audition room emerged.

"Thank you all for your wonderful performances. The level this year was excellent. The judges have decided to award the scholarship to Ernestine Whitman."

Had I heard correctly? The other applicants walked away to join their parents, but for a few moments I was too dumbfounded to move.

Then I ran down the hall. "Mother, I won!"

As soon as we got home, I called Mr. Little.

"Hello, Mr. Little?" I asked, hoping I wasn't interrupting a lesson.

"Yes, who is this?" He sounded friendly.

"It's Ernestine. I'm sorry to call you on the weekend, but I have something to tell you." I rushed ahead. "I won the scholarship to Brevard," I said, a little out of breath, my heart beating fast.

"Well, well, Ernestine, congratulations! That's quite an achievement, especially at your age. I'm glad you called to tell me." Although I couldn't see it, I heard the warm smile in his voice.

Despite the brevity of the conversation, Mr. Little's warm response meant as much to me as winning the scholarship. He'd sounded pleased. And something else, something I didn't identify until much later because it was so unfamiliar. He sounded proud of me.

My state of shock continued over the next few hours as I tried to make sense of what had happened. I knew I was no child prodigy. Earning top ratings at the Solo and Ensemble Festival didn't mean much. Nor did being first chair in a high school band, even a good one. But this was different. Competing with the best high school musicians in Atlanta, I'd been singled out, chosen.

I couldn't wait to tell Daddy. On Saturdays he worked in his office at the Emory Business School until about 5:00 p.m. As soon as he walked through the door, I pounced on him.

"Daddy, guess what."

"What?" he asked, bewildered.

"I won the Georgia Power Company scholarship to attend Transylvania Music Camp!"

"Well . . . good. What does that mean?"

"I have a full scholarship to go to Brevard this summer to study music."

"When is it exactly?"

"I don't know the dates, but it's eight or nine weeks this summer." Maybe the length of the camp would impress him.

"Okay, but what are the actual costs here?" he asked.

"Um, well, I know the scholarship covers tuition to the camp." Think, *think*. "And it covers meals too," I added.

"What about where you stay?"

"Students stay in cabins, so that should be covered." I could feel his impatience building.

"Well, you'd better find out before we do much planning around this. I'd hate for you to be unable to go because of hidden costs Mr. Little didn't bother to tell you about."

Would you really hate that? I wondered. In the past few months, Daddy's disapproval of Mr. Little had become more pronounced. Thank goodness there were no hidden costs.

———

A month after winning the Brevard scholarship, Mr. Little suggested I try out for the Atlanta Symphony Orchestra's (ASO) youth soloist competition—high school musicians competing for a chance to be the featured soloist in one of the ASO's fall children's concerts. For the competition, Mr. Little chose Briccialdi's "Carnival of Venice" because it had lots of flashy runs to impress the audience of elementary school kids, and its minimal accompaniment made it easy to put together with the orchestra. This was important because the winner got only one rehearsal with the symphony—very challenging for a high school student. When Mr. Little first proposed it, I hadn't felt ready to compete at that level, but the more I practiced, the more confident I became. Then I found out the date.

"Daddy, do I have to go to Boaz in two weeks?" Every couple of months, we visited two elderly aunts living in northern Alabama, in the old house where they and my father grew up. "There's a competition I want to enter that Saturday," I said.

"No, you have to go with us," he said, not looking up from the newspaper.

"Couldn't we go another weekend?" I asked.

"You know we worked all this out with Melinda. She's

got a busy schedule at Emory, and that's the weekend she picked," he said.

"Well, she didn't go the last two times, so maybe I could stay home this time."

"No." He put the paper down and glared at me. "Whatever it is, visiting your aunts is more important. You probably wouldn't win anyway."

He'd forgotten that, barely a month ago, I'd won the scholarship to Brevard Music Camp. I thought of reminding him, but his rebuff had already sent me into the familiar cowed, defensive position.

"But Mr. Little really wants me to do it, and—"

"No!" he said, frowning. He rose to his feet and towered over me, standing way too close. "Can't you think about anyone but yourself? Ernestine is your namesake. You could at least be a little considerate of her." Aunt Ernestine was a stout, dour, old maid schoolteacher who had a wooden leg. I often wished Daddy had named me for any one of his six other sisters.

When I told Mr. Little I couldn't make the audition, he seemed disappointed but said he would try to work something out. And he did.

On Friday, the day before the competition, I arrived at Atlanta's Municipal Auditorium at 11:00 a.m., several minutes before the Atlanta Symphony's rehearsal break, to audition for Henry Sopkin, conductor of the Atlanta Symphony and sole judge for the competition. From backstage I heard a piano soloist playing with the orchestra, rehearsing one of the concertos by Brahms. The piece was so absorbing I almost forgot why I was there. A few minutes later, the musicians stopped, and I threaded my way through the chairs and music stands to the podium. I caught a fleeting glimpse of Mr. Little leaving the stage, but he didn't appear to have seen me.

"You must be the flutist Warren Little told me about," said the short, trim, bald conductor. "Let's get right to it. You can stand there at the front of the stage, beside the piano. I'll go out into the hall to listen." An encouraging smile softened the abrupt remarks.

"Oh, and I'm afraid I've forgotten your name," he said as he grabbed a clipboard and turned to leave the stage.

"Ernestine Whitman."

After Mr. Sopkin sat down midway between the stage and the back of the hall, I began to play. The first few notes sounded strange in the empty, reverberant hall, and I had to block out the sounds of people shuffling around on stage behind me as they left the stage and came back during their breaks. Mr. Little had pared the piece down for the five-minute limit, so the audition was over quickly. I thought I'd played well, but the unfamiliar sound of the hall made it hard for me to judge.

"That's very good," Mr. Sopkin said as he made his way back to the stage. "We'll post the results tomorrow after the others have auditioned. If you win, someone will contact you."

I hurried off to join my mother, who'd been waiting backstage. To her left was a short, kind-looking man, not quite as bald as Sopkin. He looked right at me as I walked toward Mother.

"My dear, that was very impressive," he said, in a foreign accent. "You must never stop playing your flute." Then he hurried onto the stage.

"Do you know who that was?" Mother asked, clearly excited.

"No, I assumed he played in the orchestra," I said.

"He's playing *with* the orchestra, as their guest piano soloist. That was Sviatoslav Richter!" Mother said.

The name meant nothing to me, but Mother said he was a great Russian pianist, right up there with Horowitz, whose name I knew well.

"Just think, Richter thought you played well." Mother looked more pleased than I'd seen her in a long time. Seeing her happy would be the high point of my weekend—probably hers too.

The following Monday when I got home from school, Mother was waiting for me. "Mr. Sopkin called this afternoon," she said. "You're going to play with the Atlanta Symphony, sometime next October!"

"Wow, I didn't expect that," I said, grinning. "I'm glad it's not soon. I'll have to know that piece inside out to play it with an orchestra."

When I told my father and then Mr. Little about winning the audition, their reactions were, predictably, strikingly different. My father's lack of interest still disappointed but no longer hurt; Mr. Little's enthusiasm made up for it.

A few weeks later, right before I went to Brevard, my flute lesson went almost ten minutes overtime. When I got to the car, my father exploded.

"This is ridiculous!" he shouted, deafening inside the car. "Tell Mr. Little if he can't let you out on time, you won't be taking any more lessons."

I retreated, silent, struggling not to break down in front of him. I knew he wouldn't physically harm me, but the threat of taking away the flute lessons terrified me.

Chapter 6: Expanding Horizons

Reveille? My groggy brain gradually identified what had awakened me. Apparently, our days began and ended with bugle calls of reveille and taps, the latter signaling lights out in all student cabins. A lovely smell of damp foliage greeted me, along with the mundane sounds of flushing toilets and running showers. I glanced down the row of bunk beds, one to my left, eight to my right, each with two footlockers in front of it, leaving a narrow aisle from the far end of the cabin to the bathroom, close to my end.

Last night I'd discovered a perk of having the upper bunk: my head was close to the screen that ran the length of the cabin on both sides, filling the narrow space between the upper bunks and the pine wood ceiling. Though anxious about being at a music camp, knowing no one, I'd quickly fallen asleep with a light breeze on my face and the soothing sound of crickets.

After swinging my legs over the side of the upper bunk, I descended the short ladder, grabbed clothes out of my footlocker, and rushed into the crowded bathroom. I'd mistakenly assumed there'd be more room to change in the bathroom than between bunks. Beneath the harsh fluorescent lighting, I hastily washed my face and threw on plaid Bermuda shorts and a white sleeveless blouse, trying to ignore the spiders on the walls and dead bugs on the gray concrete floor. I ran to the mess hall, eager, not for breakfast, but to see the ensemble assignments that were posted on lists outside the mess hall.

Several students, some elated, some disappointed, had to move away from the bulletin board before I could read the assignments. On the basis of the auditions yesterday, instrumentalists were placed in one of the two bands or the orchestra, the most coveted three spots. I grinned when I saw my placement: first chair in the top band. After wolfing down a piece of toast with some orange juice, I hurried back to the cabin to brush my teeth and grab my flute. Rehearsal started promptly at 8:30 a.m.

The rehearsal was in a large, square, open-air shelter that had a wooden floor. At one end was a podium with sixty or so chairs arranged in semicircular rows around it. After introducing myself to the flutist next to me, I looked through the music quickly, scanning to see if there were any hard solo parts. There weren't, which was both a relief and a disappointment. I assumed the tall, gangly man with the halo of white hair atop his high forehead was an old guy until the conductor leaped onto the podium with the agility of a twenty-year-old.

"I'm Doctor Guy Fraser Harrison," he said, "and I'm delighted to be working with
        you for the next eight weeks. Let's start with careful tuning, shall we?" He gestured to the principal clarinetist, occupying the other outside chair of the front row. She and I were the bookends of the row of flutes and clarinets.

"Do you have a tuner, young lady?" he asked her. She shook her head. "That's okay, but you must invest in one; it should be part of your practice. Here, use this for now." He pulled a small tuner out of a battered brown satchel. Dr. Harrison spent the next fifteen minutes tuning the group, starting with the lowest-pitched instruments, the tubas, and working his way up, instrument by instrument. He admonished anyone who played a note other than the tuning note. "This is not the time to practice your concerto," he said. "You must focus on this one note." If the section as a whole sounded out of tune—as they all did that first day—he started with the first chair and heard each player, frowning until the player matched the clarinetist's B-flat perfectly, when he would smile and move on to the next person.

At first, I was exasperated. In my high school band, the most thorough tuning we ever did was to tune the brass and woodwind sections separately. We certainly didn't spend fifteen minutes on it. But as soon as we played the first bar of Percy Grainger's "Irish Tune from County Derry," I understood. Never had I been part of such a warm, resonant sonority. Careful tuning greatly improved the quality of the band's sound, the first of many revelations that summer. Dr. Harrison set high standards and a fast pace for his rehearsals. I later learned that his main job, September through May, was conductor of the Oklahoma City Symphony Orchestra, and that he'd been born in 1894, making him sixty-eight that summer. In Harold C. Schonberg's book *The Great Conductors*, the famous music critic describes Harrison perfectly: "commanding presence, infinite dignity, fabulous memory, vast experience, high temperament, and serene wisdom."

When I arrived at Brevard in the summer of 1962, I knew little about serious practicing. One afternoon while I was practicing in my favorite spot—halfway up the grassy hill behind our cabin—a girl walked up the hill toward me. She appeared to be older than I, maybe because she walked with such confidence.

"Hey," she said, "you sound good. I'm Janet Gay, by the way."

"Hi, I'm Ernestine Whitman, and thank you. You're a clarinetist, right? I've noticed you practicing outside, a lot."

"Right on both counts. My goal is four hours a day." I tried to hide my shock. I thought two hours was pretty good.

"You must be in the orchestra, since I didn't see you in the concert band," I said. "Where are you from?"

"Michigan. During the school year, I attend Interlochen Arts Academy."

"Wow, that's amazing, no wonder you're so good." I'd heard about Interlochen, the excellent high school in Michigan for young musicians from all over the country; Interlochen seemed like another world, far removed from mine. I was flattered Janet had noticed me. We chatted for only a few minutes, but meeting her forever changed my standards for daily practice.

Each week, students attended several concerts, including at least one by the Brevard faculty orchestra. Although my parents often listened to the classical music radio station—Mother's preference—I'd never paid much attention to orchestral repertoire. It took a while for me to appreciate the concerts. I remember thinking Richard Strauss's *Ein Heldenleben* was long and boring. (I was right about the length.) But the constant exposure to great orchestral repertoire gradually beguiled me. In the third week of camp, when the faculty orchestra played Beethoven's Seventh Symphony, the expressive slow movement transported me.

Some of the concerts' appeal was the setting—an outdoor amphitheater at the edge of a lake, surrounded by the outline of the Blue Ridge Mountains. The most important thing, however, was being part of an attentive audience of young people, all of them serious musicians. After a few concerts, I learned to listen carefully, and became a tentative fan of classical music. The interest faded a bit when I returned to high school life. I still used my allowance to buy 45' recordings of the Beatles,

Elvis, and Ray Charles. I wouldn't fully appreciate orchestral music until I'd experienced it from the inside, as a player.

In addition to performing in ensembles and attending concerts, students took private lessons on their instruments. The flute teacher at Brevard, Charles Delaney, taught with humor and gusto. His colorful personality inspired students to do zany things, such as serenading him with "The Stars and Stripes Forever" piccolo solo, played outside his cabin at 6:00 a.m. by fifteen piccolos.

One of the pleasures of Brevard was practicing outside. The summer of 1962 was a rainy one, but I grabbed my flute and went outside the instant it stopped raining. By summer's end, the tarnished flute looked more black than silver. My tattered copy of Mozart's *Concerto in G Major* shows the effects of leaving it on a music stand during a light rain. When I look at that shredded part, I see the lush green hill behind our cabin and smell the fresh mountain air. Sensual treats for a city girl. For years the smell of wet foliage brought back the excitement I felt discovering the world of serious musicians and profound orchestral repertoire.

When I returned from Brevard Music Camp at the end of the summer, I walked into a different house. In July, my parents had moved into a modest house on Emory Road, built in 1929. My father, at age fifty-three, had finally moved out of faculty rental housing. Years later, I found out he was forced to take this step because the Andrew Circle houses were going to be razed. Despite being an economist, he was so averse to debt that he didn't want to take on a mortgage.

"So, how about this," Daddy said, with an uncharacteristic, sweeping gesture. Mother, though quiet, looked pleased.

I knew my father was proud of the house, but as soon as I stepped into the living room, I felt claustrophobic. It was smaller than the Andrew Circle house, with no side yards. The houses on either side, unlike ours, were two stories, which blocked out natural light. Because of its square shape, the house also felt squashed from front to back, in contrast to the elongated shape of our old house. Here, you could easily see the back of the house from the front door. At sixteen, I didn't know the sound economic principle of buying the smallest house in a very nice neighborhood, but I would come to appreciate the grander homes a few blocks away, with bigger yards and more trees.

"It's really nice," I said.

"Your room is straight back here," Mother said. I followed her down the short hall into my room and set down my suitcase.

"Melinda chose the bedroom with the bathroom, so you get the room with all these nice windows," she said.

"Yes, the windows are great." The two on the wall to my right were a driveway's width from the neighbor's windows, and I could see right into their kitchen. The other two, opposite the head of the bed, looked out upon a small, mostly dirt backyard, with one scraggly tree. I looked down the short part of the L-shaped hall and saw Melinda's bedroom on my right, the kitchen straight ahead.

"Oh wow, the kitchen's big," I said, finally able to express genuine enthusiasm. Mother beamed. The dark green linoleum floor, a marked improvement over the old rust-red floor, blended nicely with the pale yellow of the cabinets. The countertops were covered with small brown and white tiles. Despite the generous dimensions of the room, cabinet space was limited by the multiple doors: one connecting to the hall, another leading to the basement, a third leading into a tiny breakfast room, and finally the back door. All the doors opened inward. The one small window looked directly into a neighbor's dining room. "This is so much nicer than the other kitchen," I said. Mother smiled.

The house had two bathrooms. With her own bathroom and some distance between her room and the other two bedrooms, Melinda had gained some physical separation from the rest of us. I, on the other hand, was now closer to my parents, with a small bathroom separating our bedrooms. As I assessed the house and surrounding neighborhood, I thought how lucky I was to grow up in the old house. On Emory Road there were no places to play—no spontaneous games of kickball, no little girls gathering on the grass to make daisy chains. Mothers had to arrange playdates and drive kids to playgrounds. But my parents were pleased, and that made it much easier to like the house.

After eight inspiring weeks at Brevard, I was eager to practice. As soon as I unpacked, I took the flute out to get started on my new regimen of practicing longer and more carefully. I no longer had to practice while sitting on my bed; this room had space for a chair and music stand.

After two notes, my excitement evaporated. With sheer, flimsy curtains and an old, threadbare Oriental rug, the room was too reverberant, making me sound better than I was—great for performance, terrible for practicing. I thought longingly of the back porch on Andrew Circle. This house also had a screened-in porch, but it was in the front of the house, and because the houses were so close together, I'd be serenading the whole neighborhood if I practiced on the porch.

It took me several months to discover the solution. Dominated by a huge, ancient furnace that resembled a grotesque, gray snowman, the partial basement had barely enough space for me and a music stand. But the acoustics were perfect. The unevenness of the red clay walls, as well as the layer of soot on the concrete floor, soaked up sound, encouraging me to breathe deeply and develop my flute tone. And, except for Daddy's nightly trips to add water to the furnace, the space was all mine.

The basement did have its drawbacks. In the summer it smelled like mold, in the winter it was chilly, and the worn, wooden stairs leading to it were treacherous—widely spaced, no banister. The place was ugly, dusty, and located directly beneath the living room, where my parents watched TV or listened to the radio every evening. Fortunately, the house was well-built, so when I concentrated hard, I could block out the overhead noise.

Andrew Circle and Emory Road were at opposite ends of the Emory University campus. In both neighborhoods, several Emory faculty members (all male, of course) lived within a block or two of our house, and most of my friends were children of faculty. These things shaped the values I absorbed: being Southern did not mean opposing civil rights, a young woman's goal could be something other than getting married, and academic achievement was more important than pursuing wealth. While in high school, my friends didn't smoke, rarely drank, and, as far as I know, never experimented with drugs. All of us went to college.

If I could go back and add one element to my childhood, it would be to have a friend who loved classical music. As the only music nerd in our high school, I would've bored my friends if I'd talked about my excitement over discovering Beethoven and Brahms. Before I went to Brevard, I had no idea there were teenagers who liked anything other than popular music.

In fall of my junior year, Mr. Little suggested I try out for the Atlanta Community Orchestra. After three years of weekly flute lessons, I doted on Mr. Little's attention and praise, and when it came to flute advice, I would do anything he asked. I auditioned for the orchestra conductor on a Friday afternoon and went to my first rehearsal the following Monday night.

Community orchestras, unlike professional ones, are composed of adults who have regular day jobs and pursue music as an avocation. It's not unusual to find doctors, lawyers, and schoolteachers (occasionally, music teachers) in such groups. In a big city, the orchestra might be very good, as it was in Atlanta. The principal bassoonist in the group was a physics professor at Georgia State University, but he played as well as many professional musicians.

The Atlanta public schools had no string programs in the 1960s. Because I'd not been in a high school orchestra, I had no idea what to expect. When I walked into the huge rehearsal room at the Atlanta Jewish Community Center, I immediately felt disoriented. From attending orchestra concerts at Brevard, I knew the flutes sat somewhere in the middle of the group (as opposed to the front row in a band), so I timidly ventured into the mass of chairs and music stands. An older lady saw my flute case and pointed to a chair. I sat down, opened my flute case, and looked at the music on the stand: Howard Hanson's "Romantic" Symphony, flute 1.

As soon as I put the flute together, a well-dressed middle-aged woman told me, rather sharply, to move over two chairs. Embarrassed to have taken her seat, I moved down to a seat in front of a flute 2 part. Surely, she knew I'd made an honest mistake. She frowned at me and said nothing more. I wondered if flutists in community orchestras were even more competitive than those in high school bands. Maybe this wasn't such a good idea.

Shortly after I slunk down into my chair, another middle-aged woman and a young man sat down, one on either side of me. The person to my left shared the flute 1 part with the unfriendly woman playing principal flute. To my right was another of Mr. Little's students. I'd heard about the talented Neal Causey, who was also a high school junior but attended Westminster, a ritzy private school in Northwest Atlanta. I shyly introduced myself to him; he had also heard of me. Sitting ahead of him, I wondered if I had again picked the wrong chair, but he never complained. It was several rehearsals before I realized Neal and I were the only teenagers in the group.

After tuning to the oboist's A, we began the rehearsal. Right away I was struck by the conductor's joy. When Mr. Sieber lifted his baton to give the first downbeat, he looked as if he were about to devour the best meal he'd ever tasted. The three band directors I'd worked under previously, even my idol Mr. Barron, had never exuded such enthusiasm. Just gazing at Mr. Sieber's face reassured me.

But nothing prepared me for The Sound—the lavish richness of the string sections all around me. I'd never heard anything as beautiful. It's one thing to listen to orchestral music from a distance, quite another to sit in the midst of it. Enthralled first by the sound of the violas, seated in front of me, I was next drawn to the higher-pitched warmth of the violins. And then I heard the most enticing sound of all, the deep, expressive resonance of the cellos. In the midst of this magnificent aural tapestry, it took all my self-control to focus on playing the second flute part. The hostility of the principal flutist no longer mattered. That night, I discovered the flute spoke most powerfully to me as a voice in the orchestra. From then on, I wanted nothing more than to be part of that wondrous orchestral sound.

In a list of best pieces for luring impressionable teenagers into the world of orchestral music, Howard Hanson's "Romantic" Symphony would surely be near the top. Written in 1930, when most composers were turning away from such music, the piece is unashamedly accessible. Hanson said his aim was "to create a work young in spirit, Romantic in temperament, and simple and direct in expression." The piece showcases the rich sonority of the strings.

The "Romantic" Symphony's three movements flow together and are closely linked thematically. No matter how many times we rehearsed the work, several passages always thrilled me. One of them, about four minutes into the first movement, features a glorious horn solo intertwined with the upper strings in a voluptuous melody while the timpani and lower strings provide a pulsing rhythm underneath. The same theme appears in the last movement. My favorite moment comes two minutes from the end of the piece, when the timpani heartbeat is even more prominent.

A surprising thing happened after I'd been in the orchestra a few weeks: I reconnected with a lighthearted side of myself that had been dormant for years. During rehearsal, when the conductor was working with only the string sections, I began joking around. Neal, my audience of one, tolerated my banter, occasionally adding wisecracks of his own. (We were quiet, careful not to disrupt the rehearsal.) It's not that I'd been humorless before—I'd giggled as much as most girls—but my sense of fun had receded as I got older and felt the sting of my father's disapproval.

Sometimes a passage in a book prompts an *aha!* moment because it describes precisely what you feel but cannot find words to express; so it was with Hanson's symphony, which voiced my teenage yearning perfectly. The heartbreak of my first love, the disappointment of not being in the popular group, the aching desire to please my father but knowing I never would—it was all there in Hanson's passionate music. Most teenagers remember the moment they first fell in love; that night I fell in love with the orchestra, a love that has lasted a lifetime.

"Start halfway through the third variation," Mr. Little said at a lesson in early October.

In two weeks, I was scheduled to perform Briccialdi's "Carnival of Venice" with the Atlanta Symphony, as the featured soloist on their Young People's Concert. My stomach did flips each time I pictured playing on the huge stage of the Municipal Auditorium. I'd be accompanied by the entire Atlanta Symphony—the professional orchestra Mr. Little played in. Unlike a piano accompanist, the orchestra wouldn't be able to smooth things over if I had a memory slip. After I'd played a few measures, Mr. Little stopped me.

"Play it again, but this time stop after three measures and count five bars in rhythm, then come in where the orchestra would be if you had dropped out." I followed his instructions—playing, then waiting, then coming back in at the right time with the right notes.

"I think you're in good shape," Mr. Little said. "Don't worry if you have a memory slip. If you do, you can get back in quickly, but I bet you won't have any slips."

My teacher had prepared me carefully. As October 24 approached, my confidence increased and excitement over playing with a professional orchestra banished my anxiety. Most of it, anyway.

Ten days before the performance, a US spy plane flying over Cuba spotted and photographed a Soviet missile being assembled in Cuba, within striking distance of the United States. The Cold War had been a constant presence in my life. For most children raised in the 1950s, a sense of foreboding lay beneath our childhood innocence; as we grew older, that vague uneasiness coalesced into a specific anxiety about nuclear war.

My father stocked bottled water and canned foods in the basement, and at school we had regular nuclear attack drills where we scrambled under our desks and covered our heads with our arms. Atlanta attempted several practice evacuations; cars followed escape routes for various neighborhoods, resulting in colossal traffic jams. No one talked about the futility of such measures.

The intensity of the Soviet threat waxed and waned. In 1959, I had reached a place of relative calm, mostly because Daddy seemed less worried. Then the film *On the Beach* came out. After seeing the apocalyptic story of nuclear annihilation, my fear of a nuclear attack increased. I'm sure that film affected many teenagers' views of the future.

Nikita Khrushchev's rise to power heightened the threat. Khrushchev seemed capable of rash and dangerous behavior, especially after the incident at a United Nations meeting in 1960, when he'd angrily removed his shoe to pound the table with it repeatedly.

On Monday, October 22, 1962, I rehearsed "Carnival of Venice" with the Atlanta Symphony. I played well and was in sync with the orchestra, and I left feeling good about the upcoming performance. But that evening, on all radio and television stations, President Kennedy addressed the nation. His solemn remarks made clear the imminent danger of a nuclear confrontation.

"It shall be the policy of this nation," Kennedy said, "to regard any nuclear missile launched from Cuba against any nation in the Western Hemisphere as an attack by the Soviet Union on the United States, requiring a full retaliatory response upon the Soviet Union."

As soon as the address was over, my father checked the basement stock of water and food. None of us said much the rest of that evening, nor in the days that followed. Being a large city well within the missile's range, Atlanta was an obvious target. The sinking feeling in the pit of my stomach, usually caused by Daddy's anger, was a constant presence that week.

On Wednesday, standing backstage right before the performance, I felt both calm and anxious—calm about the performance, which seemed trivial, but anxious about the future. I've no idea how well I played. Afterward, Mr. Little, the conductor, and several other orchestra members complimented me, but it all seemed part of a fanciful dream, of little consequence compared to the nightmare that was reality.

Four days later, Kennedy and Khrushchev reached an agreement, ending the crisis. The food and water supplies remained in our basement, however, and the duck-under-your-desk school drills continued.

"Ernestine, phone for you," Mother called down to the basement, where I was practicing. By late April, the basement had transitioned to its damper, moldier summer smell.

"Who is it?"

"It's Mr. Little."

My heart started pounding, though I couldn't have said why. It seemed odd for him to call on Wednesday; the few times Mr. Little canceled a lesson, he'd called on Friday. And he talked to Mother, never asked to speak to me.

"Hello?" I said.

"Ernestine," he started, and it was amazing how good it felt just hearing him say my name, "I have a job for you."

Did I hear that right?

"There's a pickup band for a show at Rich's Friday afternoon. It's mostly Symphony players, and I wondered if you'd be interested in playing the flute part for it."

It took a few seconds to find my voice. "Yes. Of course I would."

"You'll probably want to look over the parts before Friday." *No kidding!* "I can drop the folder off at your house tomorrow night."

"Sure, I'll be here. It's 1533 Emory Road," I said, a bit breathless.

"I don't know what time I'll be by, but it won't be too late."

"That's okay." I'd happily stay up all night waiting for him.

"It's background music for a fashion show that starts at 4:30," he said, then rang off. A grunt job for adults, exciting for me.

The next night, I waited in the living room while my father read the paper and listened to the radio. Mother was in her platform rocker reading one of her self-help books. The later it got, the more my father stewed over the inconvenience of waiting for Mr. Little. He didn't say anything—his frowns and fidgeting said it all. About 9:45 p.m. the doorbell rang. I opened it, and there was Mr. Little, framed in the doorway to our house, with a big smile on his face.

He handed me a black music folder, wished me luck, and left.

"About time," my father muttered. "You can't practice tonight; it's too late." I considered pointing out that both he and Mother would still be up for an hour or so, but I didn't say anything. Better not add to his irritation.

I took the music to my room. There were over a dozen pieces in the folder, a few of them familiar to me—excerpts from *West Side Story* and *The Music Man*, plus "Bugler's Holiday" and several other pops standards. I wanted to spend all day Friday practicing the music, but Daddy wouldn't let me skip school. Mother was against my getting up early, insisting I needed sleep. We compromised: I got up thirty minutes early, rushed through breakfast and getting dressed, and spent what little time I had on the passages marked solo. I hoped my sight-reading skills would carry me through the rest.

Mother dropped me off at Rich's at 4:15 p.m. I would take the bus home after the show. On the second floor I found the makeshift stage, which was surrounded by five or six semicircular rows of folding chairs, already more than half filled. A clarinetist and a violinist, both middle-aged, were on stage warming up. As I mounted the three steps to the stage, my sweaty hand almost dropped the flute case. The clarinetist greeted me warmly and showed me where to sit in the small group, essentially a pit band. Each music stand held a piece of paper listing the order of the pieces. The rest of the players got there only a few minutes before we started, with barely enough time to arrange the music in the correct order. At 4:29 p.m. a tall, white-haired man took the area where a podium would have been, asked for the oboe A, and gave the first downbeat promptly at 4:30 p.m.

To provide constant background music for an hour-long show, we had to move quickly from one piece to the next. The conductor glared at me when I fumbled the music, switching from the first piece to the second, but I quickly figured out the technique. As soon as I played the last note of a piece, I licked the thumb of my left hand, slid the previous piece quickly to the left side of the music stand, and returned my left hand to the flute as I took a breath to play the first note of the next piece. The hour rushed by. I remember very little other than a big hole I created in one of the melodies of *West Side Story*. The passage was a one-bar solo, played in succession by bassoon, clarinet, and flute. Except there was no flute, only silence. I was lost.

When the show was over, I felt shaky, mortified that I had missed a solo. After several compliments from the other players, I felt better. Apparently, they didn't expect perfection from a seventeen-year-old. I took a picture of the fifty-dollar check, which I later framed. My first gig. If my father had his way, it would also be my last.

———

The flute piece I spent the most time with junior year was *Poem*, by Charles Griffes, one of the few American composers to write in the impressionist style of Claude Debussy and Maurice Ravel. I loved the sad, haunting theme at the beginning of *Poem*, and the quick, sometimes subtle mood shifts. My favorite passage, the flashy section that begins con fuoco (with fire) and builds to vivace (lively) and culminates in a frenetic presto, was a great outlet for anger. I'd play it as loud and fast as I could, enjoying a feeling of power as I expressed the hostility and aggression I could never express verbally. Composers seldom use the flute to express rage, but fast, loud, articulate notes in the flute's high register can sound quite furious.

In the spring of my junior year, I again auditioned for the Georgia Power Company scholarship to Brevard. I was disappointed when trombonist Jim Kraft beat me, but I won another scholarship, from the Atlanta Music Club, so I returned to Brevard that summer.

My second year at Brevard, I was thrilled with the audition results: principal flute in the student orchestra. But the thrill was mixed with anxiety. I'd heard lots of stories about the intimidating Dr. Pfohl, director of the camp, and conductor of both the student and faculty orchestras. When I took my seat in the middle of the stage and looked out over the huge, open-air auditorium, I felt very small. It didn't matter that I'd performed band concerts on that very stage the previous summer. Dr. Pfohl, a middle-aged, portly, humorless man, made it clear from the first downbeat that he expected perfection from the players. A few minutes into the rehearsal I got flustered and missed a note in Smetana's *The Moldau*. When Dr. Pfohl scowled at me, I crumpled, convinced I had been misplaced.

"You really should've gotten principal flute," I said to the girl playing second flute. When I suggested we switch parts, she quickly agreed. A missed note and a glare from Dr. Pfohl had exposed the fragility of my self-confidence. Without Mr. Little's support, belief in my musical abilities vanished. Two weeks later, however, I felt much better, for nonmusical reasons.

Once I got over resenting Jim Kraft for beating me at the Georgia Power audition, I grew to like him. About five foot ten, with expressive brown eyes and a quiet, gentle manner, Jim made me feel so special that I didn't need the validation of first chair. By the time we both won the camp concerto competition, we'd become serious sweethearts, ending three years of grieving for Ken. Strict curfews and the separation of boys' and girls' cabins forced us to settle for walking around the lake and stealing moments in a large practice room that had an old couch. At seventeen, my hormones raged, intensifying the excitement of being in love.

Chapter 7: Hope

When I returned to the community orchestra after the summer break, I learned that the grumpy woman had left, and I was principal flute. I loved my new role. I wasn't going to relinquish it, as I had at Brevard. Because of the position, I got more individual attention from Mr. Sieber. Prior to playing principal flute in the orchestra, I'd been more of a wallflower than a prima donna, but I was changing. I relished being in the spotlight, and the feelings of inadequacy that had plagued me for years disappeared. When I played principal flute, I again experienced the freedom and joy I'd felt as a little girl, singing on the swings in our backyard— completely immersed in music and happy to be me.

Mr. Sieber played a major role in my growing self-assurance, which expanded as my passion for the orchestra intensified. Whenever he praised me, I felt elated, treasured. At the time I didn't connect these feelings with yearning for paternal attention. I would've been unable to disentangle the threads that, woven together, made me so devoted to the orchestra. Where did need for male approval end and love for playing in the orchestra begin?

The orchestra also gave me a sense of belonging. Like many teenage girls, the trigger for my angst was the hurt from being excluded, whether from a relationship, the clique of popular girls, or a father's love. But in the orchestra, I was an integral part of creating something I believed in—profound music that was transformative. The symphonies of Beethoven, Brahms, and Dvorak inspired a deep sense of awe and gratitude, my version of a born-again conversion. Like the music students I'd met at Brevard and countless others, I began to dream of devoting my life to the extraordinary world of orchestral music.

Except for flute, Melinda was still better at everything. Whether intentionally or not, my father made me feel that being second-best was no better than dead last. My high school grades were unimpressive beside Melinda's 4.0 in college; National Honor Society was nothing compared to Phi Beta Kappa. Matching her GPA hadn't been difficult, but I dreaded taking the SAT test, where I'd surely fall short of Melinda's near-perfect scores.

The night before the SAT test in late September, the community orchestra performed a runout concert in Athens, a ninety-minute drive from Atlanta. We got back around 12:30 am. I lay awake most of the night, worrying that sleep deprivation would cause me to do badly on the test. The next day, as feared, fatigue and anxiety undermined my concentration during the test.

The SAT scores arrived in early November. My scores, though good, were considerably below Melinda's. In chemistry class the following day, I must've looked pretty dejected. Mrs. Gibson asked me to stay a few minutes after class.

"Now listen here," Mrs. Gibson said, in her no-nonsense way, "don't you go thinking those scores determine how smart you are. I know you look up to Melinda, but you're smart too. Don't you ever forget that." In addition to being an outstanding teacher who never called me Melinda, Mrs.

Gibson read people well. Her words lessened the shame and reduced doubts about my academic abilities.

"Daddy, could I talk to you about something?" I asked one day in early fall, after a particularly good flute lesson.

"Okay." Reluctantly, he put the newspaper aside. "What is it?"

"Well," I said, trying to sound confident, "Mr. Little's been talking to me about applying to music schools for next year."

"What? Oh, honey, you know that's a foolish idea," my father said.

"But he thinks I might have a shot at getting into a really good school."

"So what? Do you think we could afford to send you to a music school? And even if we could, what would be the point?"

I wondered if I should push it. At least he wasn't angry. Yet.

"Mr. Little said—"

"What does he know about *your* life?" he asked sternly.

"Well, he seems to think I could pursue a career in music."

"And pursue is all it would be," he said, frowning.

"Can't I just see if I can get in?"

"Why spend the money to apply when you're going to go to Emory? Just put that idea out of your head."

I backed off, hoping I'd planted a seed. Meanwhile, Mr. Little kept reminding me that musical talent is best developed at a music school, not at a liberal arts college like Emory University. A few weeks later, when I broached the subject again, my father's response was even more heated.

"Honey," he said, his tone making the word a reprimand, "what makes you think you could ever make a living as a flute player? Don't you think I know anything about economics?"

"Of course, but—"

"No!" he said, almost shouting. "It would be throwing money away. Don't you realize how stupid it would be to pass up a chance to attend Emory for free?"

There it was, the ultimate epithet: stupid. And he wasn't done.

"If you think you can make a living in music, you're kidding yourself. Mr. Little doesn't know what he's talking about."

Cowed by his anger, I acquiesced for a while to give my father—and me—time to recover from his anger before I triggered it again. Pursuing a career in music was completely foreign to my father's academic worldview. His disdain for musicians made me feel ashamed of my far-fetched, adolescent dream. But I persisted.

In November, Mr. Little told me about a regional audition in Atlanta for the Manhattan School of Music and encouraged me to take the audition just for the experience. Without my father's knowledge, I took the bus downtown and went to a hotel room in the Marriott to play for MSM's friendly, middle-aged director of admissions. After I played most of Griffes *Poem*, the director complimented me and asked about my plans for the future. Reluctant to describe my father's opposition, I simply said I was unsure. To my surprise, he offered me admission to the school, as well as a small scholarship, adding there might be more financial help once I formally applied. With no help from my father, I couldn't imagine earning enough money to live in New York City. But at least I had the answer to my question: Yes, I could get into a good music school.

In December, Mr. Little asked me to tell Daddy about the Curtis Institute of Music in Philadelphia, arguably the best music conservatory in the country and the only school that offered each student free tuition, along with room and board. Mr. Little thought that, without the financial worry, my father might let me attend a free music school. I hoped so, too, and begged Daddy to pay for a flight to Philadelphia so I could audition for Curtis. He refused. I kept asking. He kept refusing. Then he found out there would be over one hundred applicants for one flute opening that year.

"I'll pay for you and your mother to fly to Philadelphia," he said, "so you can audition for Curtis. If you prove to me by winning the audition that you are the best high school flutist in the country, then maybe you're good enough to go to a music school, but if you don't get in, you will go to Emory and major in something sensible."

Daddy wasn't worried about my actually enrolling at Curtis—he knew my chances were slim—but his willingness to pay for the trip surprised me. Financial anxiety made him wary of anything risky, and this plan was statistically an unwise investment. Mother must've advocated for me, and maybe Daddy was tired of my begging and simply wanted to settle the matter.

With the late February audition only six weeks away, I figured I'd need four hours of daily practice to be ready, but I couldn't do that and keep up with homework. I decided to drop AP English, with its heavy reading assignments. The English teacher, who often called me Melinda, was a humorless woman with a thick southern drawl. When I switched to the lower class, she reminded me almost daily that I'd made a foolish decision.

"You know," she said, her index finger wagging in my face, "Melinda would never do this." But neither she nor my father could dampen my spirits, because I could now practice as intensively as I wanted.

For the audition Mr. Little selected the virtuosic third movement of Jacques Ibert's 1939 Flute Concerto, a piece harder, both to play and to memorize, than anything I'd previously tackled. I loved the dramatic cadenza, which covered the entire range of the flute, from low C to high D-flat, and I relished the musical challenge of making the repetitious middle section of the piece interesting. For the main sections, I spent countless hours practicing the fast triplets (three-note groups) in different rhythmic patterns to get them perfectly even. It took me weeks to work up to the suggested metronome mark of 176, which equals nine notes per second.

Each day I descended the crude wooden stairs to the gloomy, musty basement. The only light came from a single bulb with a pull chain. I memorized Ibert's Concerto while staring at dirt walls and the ugly furnace. But the drab surroundings didn't lessen the joy of working toward the goal of getting into Curtis.

I began practice sessions with long tones (sustained, single notes) to focus on breathing deeply and developing a fuller sound. After about twenty minutes, I opened the flute part to the Ibert Concerto. Once I'd memorized the piece, I didn't need to use the music, but by then looking at the cover page and turning to the difficult third movement had become a ritual, one that aroused feelings of pride, hope, and excitement.

By practicing so intensely, I made significant improvements in tone and technique. Only one passage in the Ibert gave me fits: the tremolo passage at the top of page two. Mr. Little had two other students auditioning for Curtis. At one of my lessons, when I was struggling with the tremolo, Mr. Little said, "You know, Virginia never has trouble with that passage." His comment stung. In the five years of weekly lessons, Mr. Little had never said an unkind word to me. I dealt with the hurt by practicing harder.

Two days before the audition, I descended into the basement for the last time before leaving for Philadelphia. After

warming up, I played through several beautiful vocal melodies—anything that came to mind, from opera to popular
music—and tried to imitate the rich sound of great singers. I
then turned to the orchestral excerpts Mr. Little had assigned,
pieces he thought might be on the sight-reading part of the
audition: Debussy's *Afternoon of a Faun*, the scherzo from
Mendelssohn's *A Midsummer Night's Dream*, and Prokofiev's
Classical Symphony. For the Ibert, instead of working with the
metronome notch by notch, as I'd done for weeks, I played
through the piece slowly, focusing on tone. Fluent technique
isn't simply playing fast; it's playing runs with your best sound
on each fleeting note.

The next day, Mother and I flew to Philadelphia and
checked into the cheap hotel my father had found, in the
Curtis neighborhood. Mother wanted to sightsee, but I
refused. Instead, I practiced in the closet of our small room,
hoping the clothes we'd hung up would muffle my sound so
I wouldn't disturb other hotel guests.

On the morning of the audition, after weeks of intense
preparation, I felt ready to play for the great William Kincaid,
solo flutist with the Philadelphia Orchestra. The odds against
me were staggering, but I didn't care; I had done all I could to
prepare for the audition. Thirty minutes before my assigned
time of 10:45 a.m., Mother and I arrived at the elegant old
building in Rittenhouse Square that housed the Curtis Institute of Music. After warming up for twenty minutes in a small
practice room, I joined Mother, who'd been sitting on one of
the metal folding chairs that lined a hallway by the audition
room, similar to the setup for the Brevard scholarship, my
first audition. We were one of a dozen or so pairs of anxious
parents and hopeful flutists, each awaiting the ten minutes that
might decide their future. Through the door to the audition
room, I could hear the person before me playing the scherzo

from Mendelssohn's *A Midsummer Night's Dream.* His tempo for the scherzo wasn't any faster than my tempo. To my surprise, he didn't sound any better than I did.

When the door opened, my predecessor emerged—a skinny, dark-haired boy who walked by looking quite pleased with himself. Moments later a short, middle-aged woman (another ubiquitous feature of auditions) ushered me into a classroom and introduced me to Mr. Kincaid, who was sitting behind a small table placed about thirty feet from the music stand in the middle of the room. With his bushy white hair, big red nose, and toothy smile, he looked more like an unkempt grandpa than the highly esteemed principal flutist of the Philadelphia Orchestra. I wondered if my nerves would hold up under the scrutiny of this famous musician.

I performed the third movement of Ibert's Concerto well—no memory slips, fast tremolos, smooth triplets, and impressive cadenza. When I finished playing the piece, Mr. Kincaid smiled and said, "You must have worked very hard on that."

Mr. Kincaid got up from his chair and placed a piece of music on the stand, the orchestral excerpt I was to sight-read. Instead of the Mendelssohn scherzo, the stand held an excerpt from Beethoven's *Leonore* Overture No. 3. As I stared at the unfamiliar excerpt, the nerves I'd managed to control until then engulfed me. My hands started to shake. My sight-reading skills vanished. I butchered the passage.

"Why are you so nervous?" Mr. Kincaid asked.

Too distraught to hear the kindness in his voice and too crushed to reply, I stared at the floor in silence. I'd blown my one chance of becoming a musician. I would have to attend Emory University in the fall. My father had won.

Chapter 8: Resignation

Returning to the humdrum life of a high school student headed for college a few blocks away, I drifted through several weeks numb and rudderless. After focusing so intensively on one goal, nothing else interested me. At my first lesson after the audition, Mr. Little asked how I'd played. When I told him about the sight-reading, he immediately got out his copy of Beethoven's *Leonore* Overture.

"Okay, I think this is the part you had to play," he said. I nodded. He gestured for me to play through it, which I did, stumbling only slightly on one of the runs.

"So, that really wasn't hard, was it?" he asked.

I shook my head. No smiles that day, no words of encouragement. He was annoyed and impatient with me. I remember nothing more about the lesson except the dreadful feeling of having disappointed him.

Monday night rehearsals with the community orchestra revived me. Even if I had no future as a musician, until the end of the year I could savor each moment of playing principal flute in an orchestra. I also looked forward to participating in the All-State Orchestra, scheduled for later that spring.

Meanwhile, though far less important to me than music, I'd developed an interesting dating life. Jim Kraft left town the previous fall to enroll at Florida State. We'd made no binding commitment to each other, and in early November I went to a Delta Tau Delta party at Emory University, where I met Freddy Miller, a cute economics major.

"I set out to dance with the prettiest girl at the party, and here you are," he said, with a teasing grin. Despite the obvious pickup line, I found Freddy suave and mature compared to high school boys. I liked his easygoing manner and the kindness in his eyes, and I found his southern Mississippi accent charming. He looked a bit ridiculous (didn't we all?) dancing to "Surf City" and "Shout," but when we slow-danced to "Blue Velvet," I loved leaning into his broad chest.

"What's your major?" I asked during a break in the dancing.

"Economics. Wait . . . didn't you say your last name was Whitman?"

I grinned.

"Okay then, I'd better take good care of my professor's daughter. Just so you know, I'd made mostly As until I had your father," he said. "But I won't hold the Bs against you."

As a college junior, Freddy must have found my weekend curfews quaint, but my father's rules were strict. Regardless of who I was with or how big the occasion, I had to be back by 12:30 a.m. On the dot. To avoid my father's anger, I tried hard to be home on time.

In early February, roughly our fifth date, Freddy and I went to another Delt party, where we imbibed the typical drink of that era in Atlanta: rum and Coke. In 1964, the legal drinking age in Georgia was eighteen; I'd been legal for about a week. Always the southern gentleman, Freddy made sure I didn't drink too much. After leaving the party, he drove to our usual spot for parking. Even in February, we generated plenty of heat to keep the car warm. Freddy's kisses started chastely and progressed gradually. His slow accelerando aroused me to the point where I lost track of time—almost.

"What time is it?" I asked suddenly, pulling away from him. Fear of my father's wrath trumped physical desire.

"About 1:15," Freddy replied.

"Oh, *shoot*. Why didn't you say something? You know how strict my father is," I said.

"Don't worry, little lady, I'll get you home as fast as I can."

"Okay, but please hurry."

As promised, Freddy drove to my house quickly, arriving in the driveway at 1:20 a.m. In addition to worrying about the curfew, another mood killer was the blinding spotlight my father had installed over the driveway, shortly after my sister began dating, to discourage any romantic end-of-date moves. After walking me to the screen porch door and giving me a quick hug, Freddy followed my instructions, letting the car roll silently down the driveway, headlights off. I unlocked the door as quietly as possible, tiptoed past my parents' bedroom, and breathed a sigh of relief when I entered my bedroom. My father had not awakened.

Now I faced another hurdle: the bathroom was connected to my parents' bedroom and had creaky doors. Using the bathroom would surely wake up my father. If I put on my nightgown, I could pretend I'd just gotten up in the middle of the night, but Daddy had a sharp BS detector and I was a lousy liar. I didn't want to risk it. Could I make it till morning? I tried for a while, becoming increasingly uncomfortable.

I attempted to open the two windows farthest from my parents' bedroom. They didn't budge. The other two, right beside my bed, faced our neighbor's driveway. I got one of them open only to find the screen stuck. After what seemed like hours of tugging, the screen finally gave way. Still a bit tipsy, I stuck my fanny out the window, mooning our very close neighbors as

I anointed the azalea bushes that were right below the windows. I would go to great lengths to avoid my father's wrath.

———

The fall of that same year, Melinda, after barely a month in the PhD mathematics program at Stanford, had phoned to tell my parents she was giving up her National Science Foundation fellowship to return to Atlanta and marry Phillip Certain, a chemistry major in his senior year at Emory. This news caused great turmoil in our little family. I was excited, Daddy was furious, and Mother was conflicted, torn between romantic dreams for her daughter and loyalty to her husband. My father's anger and disappointment created a tense atmosphere in the house. I overheard Daddy yell at Mother, "What if Melinda's pregnant?" I couldn't hear Mother's soft voice, but I knew she was trying to calm him down. She was probably a bit worried too. More than once Mother had said to me, "If you ever get pregnant, don't come here, because you would not be allowed in this house." Cruel but typical of white middle-class families in the early 1960s, at least the ones I knew. Far more than the pregnancy itself, my mother feared friends' and neighbors' censure. Maintain the facade of perfect composure, no matter what is behind that facade.

Convinced Melinda was throwing away her future, Daddy fussed and fumed the entire week between the phone call and Melinda's arrival back home. Taking advantage of an offer of a round trip to anywhere in the country for ninety-nine dollars, Phil had ridden a Greyhound bus out to California to propose to Melinda; they rode the bus for the weeklong trek back to Atlanta. By the time Daddy met Melinda and Phil at the bus station, Daddy had accepted her plan as inevitable, but weeks passed before he was cordial to

Phil. Daddy's disapproval didn't bother Melinda in the least. She was too much in love to care.

I was excited about being the only bridesmaid in my sister's wedding, until I found out the date: March 20, 1964, the same weekend as All-State Orchestra. When I'd made All-State the previous year, I'd gotten sick the night before and had to withdraw. With no school orchestra, I'd played only in the Atlanta Community Orchestra. Though good players, those adult amateurs, especially in the backs of the string sections, weren't as outstanding as the top high school players in the state, brought together for one glorious weekend performance. Because I was so passionate about the orchestra, it saddened me to think I'd graduate never having played in that select group, especially frustrating because I thought I had a shot at first chair.

The day before the wedding—the first day of All-State weekend—I was trying to focus on chemical equations when I heard my name over the classroom speaker, summoning me to the school office. As I grabbed my books, my mind skittered from one catastrophe to another: A car accident? My father having a heart attack? The bridesmaid dress gone missing? Mother was waiting in the office. After checking to make sure I had my flute with me, she rushed me to the car and off we went. As she sped downtown (not her usual careful pace), she explained. Mr. Sieber had just called to tell her that the schedule of the All-State Orchestra was not what it had been in previous years. Instead of having the culminating concert on Saturday night, opposite Melinda's wedding, the concert had been moved to late afternoon on Saturday. If I could get there in time to make the Friday afternoon rehearsal, I could play. That would mean missing the wedding rehearsal dinner, but my sister's wedding was small, the rehearsal dinner a casual affair. Melinda had always supported my music dreams; I knew she wouldn't mind my missing the dinner.

As soon as we arrived, I was ushered into a small office in the Municipal Auditorium, to play for the All-State conductor. In addition to parts of *Griffes Poem*, I sight-read selections from Borodin's "Polovetsian Dances," then was rushed into the rehearsal room, displacing a very unhappy girl from her first chair position. In addition to "Polovetsian Dances," the concert included Mendelssohn's *Reformation Symphony*. An unaccompanied flute plays the opening phrase of "A Mighty Fortress Is Our God" to usher in the symphony's last movement. It's an exquisite moment for one lone flute.

At the concert the next day, I played the solo with as full and confident a sound as I could, trying to convey strength and conviction. I played it well, and although I didn't see him, I knew Mr. Sieber was in the audience, smiling. It removed a bit of the shame I still felt about the Curtis audition. As soon as the last note of the concert sounded, I rushed off the stage, raced back to the Emory chapel (Daddy driving this time), changed into a turquoise bridesmaid dress, and walked down the aisle to my sister's brilliant choice for the processional music, an arrangement for organ of the majestic theme from the finale of Brahms's Symphony No. 1.

It wasn't until later that I appreciated Mother's role in making the All-State Orchestra experience possible. The day before her older daughter's wedding, Mother responded quickly and eagerly to facilitate her other daughter's opportunity. She could easily have decided she had enough to worry about that weekend. Mother's passivity with Daddy irritated me, but she was decisive in supporting my musical interests that weekend, even the day before Melinda's wedding. I wish I'd thanked her for that

In April, when the Atlanta Symphony performed Stravinsky's *Symphony of Psalms*, I played with the symphony a second time, not as a youth soloist this time but as a member of the flute section. The piece's striking orchestration omits violins, violas, and clarinets, but features two pianos and an unusual number of winds, including five flute parts, which meant hiring two extra flutists. The text for the choir comes from Psalms 38, 39, and 150, sung in Latin. At the first rehearsal, my awe over playing in a professional orchestra was compounded by hearing the Latin text set to Stravinsky's haunting, often transcendent music.

From the first movement's opening staccato (short) chords and woodwind arpeggios, I noticed how clear and spare the music sounded without any violins or violas. After a few measures, the choir enters with a melody comprised of a mere half step, the smallest interval in tonal music; the text is *Exaudi orationem meum, Domine* (Hear my prayer, O Lord). Stravinsky makes this simple, half-step melody very expressive through his ingenious use of rhythm and orchestration.

The second movement opens with solo woodwinds, each instrument stating the theme of a fugue (instruments entering at different times with the same theme, overlapping each other). The principal oboe states the theme first, then the principal flute, then flute 3, the part I played. The flute 3 passage starts on low C, one of the flute's most challenging notes. For a high school student, I had a pretty good low C, but it was a stressful note to begin my debut with a professional orchestra. Although Mr. Little was playing during the solo, I knew he'd be listening for my entrance at the first rehearsal.

When it was time, I took a deep breath and played the strongest low C I could muster. A few measures later, when the conductor stopped the orchestra to work with the chorus, Mr. Little turned his head and smiled at me. Reassured my low C was good enough, I relaxed and enjoyed the week of rehearsals and concerts.

The third movement opens with the choir singing a simple, lovely "Alleluia," a passage that returns in the middle and at the end of the movement. The section I found the most moving was the long, sustained coda, where the choir seems to float as it quietly sings *Laudate Dominum* (Praise God), bringing a solemn, reverent end to a remarkable piece.

A few weeks later, the Atlanta Community Orchestra had its penultimate concert, which always featured one of its members as a soloist; this year it was me. Mr. Sieber had asked me to play *Poem*. Acutely aware my time with Mr. Sieber was coming to a close, I wanted my performance to be perfect. Since I'd played the piece the previous summer with the Brevard orchestra, I should've felt confident, but I was very nervous at the first of the three rehearsals. When I missed an entrance, my stomach plummeted, but Mr. Sieber was unfazed. He calmly stopped the orchestra and turned to me.

"Don't worry," he said gently, "this is why we have rehearsals." His kind, encouraging manner reassured me, as it always had. The rest of that rehearsal and the other two were fine.

The night of the concert, I felt confident and excited. One of the great things about being a female concerto soloist is that you get to wear a gown. I didn't want to worry about tripping over a long skirt, so I'd bought an elegant, calf-length dress of pink satin with a black lace overlay for the concert.

After the overture, which I did not play, I walked on stage. As the audience applauded, I bowed, then focused on Mr. Sieber's calming presence.

The performance went well, flawless up to the cadenza that happens toward the end of the piece. At that point, adrenaline, and maybe a bit of showmanship, made me push the tempo. It sounded great and then, a memory blank. *Damn!*

But I didn't stop. I faked it, playing a fast conglomeration of notes that vaguely resembled the final run. Mr. Sieber had no trouble following my improvisation, leading the orchestra back in at the right moment. When it was over, Mr. Sieber smiled and winked at me.

The audience applauded enthusiastically, calling me back for a third bow. The only reference to my slip came from Neal, the second flutist. "Interesting cadenza," he said, but kindly.

The remarkable thing about the performance was that I didn't feel like a failure. I was, in fact, proud of my poise in covering the mistake so that almost no one noticed. Of course, it would've been much worse if the slip had knocked the orchestra out of sync with me. Years later, I would look back on this concert and marvel at my complete lack of embarrassment. The reason was Mr. Sieber's warm support, which I knew would be there even if I played poorly.

The cavernous hall of the Municipal Auditorium was filled to capacity, the large choir spread across the spacious stage, the orchestra squeezed into the makeshift pit, all to perform Carl Orff's *Carmina Burana*, a massive piece, using massive forces. Because of the shoebox shape of the pit (the area between the front row of seats and the stage), the orchestra had an odd setup: winds and percussion sat to the conductor's right and the strings to his left, except for a few spotlighted violists right in front of him, wedged into the narrow space between the podium and the stage—close quarters for the orchestra.

In the days leading up to the concert, my excitement had been mixed with sadness. End of senior year, last orchestra performance, last time I would play the flute. Like an impassioned high school athlete who can't continue her sport in college, I couldn't imagine life without this activity, which had transformed my sense of who I was.

Carl Orff's pulsing, theatrical piece features driving rhythm, expressive vocal solos, boisterous choruses, and bawdy poetry. When I encountered *Carmina* later as an adult, its repetitions seemed tedious; as a teenager, I found the work thrilling. What I loved most, of course, were the numerous flute solos and duets, especially the lovely flute solo in the third section of Part 1.

When the lights went down, seated barely a foot from the front row, I could feel the expectant hush of thousands of people. Then, an explosion of sound: the timpani and low strings on the downbeat, followed by the chorus and full orchestra with three short phrases, all fortissimo. (*"Oh fortune, like the moon, you are changeable,"* sung in Latin.) The pattern repeats four times, followed by a sudden drop to pianissimo. A dramatic start for a powerful piece.

My moment to shine came later. There are longer, more ravishing flute solos in the orchestral repertoire than the eight-bar solo in the third section of *Carmina*, but I relished playing that passage. Maybe its virginal seductiveness suited me. Its poignancy was heightened by the close connection I felt with Mr. Sieber, and the knowledge that this was my final performance. I remember how each note in the solo felt that night.

All those people—on stage, in the pit, in the audience— listening to one solo flute. I'd memorized the solo, but when it was time to play it, I liked looking at the notes on the staff, which were like old friends. A quick glance at Mr. Sieber's smiling face as I took a deep breath, and then I was off. Floating. Nothing existed but that moment, every cell in my body focused on sound and phrasing. Ah, close to perfect, but I wanted to get just a little more lilt in the third note—and I *did*, thirty seconds later when the solo is repeated. Yes! That was *exactly* the way I wanted to play it. Such a rare thing, to play each note precisely the way you wanted.

But right after the solo, I felt bereft. So, I thought, this is the end of my seven years with the flute—from the capricious decision to try flute in the sixth grade, to the pivotal relationship with Mr. Little, and then with Mr. Sieber, and finally, the highs and lows of senior year. I could no longer center my life around the flute, the one thing that had given me a sense of purpose and accomplishment.

As much as I would miss playing in the community orchestra, leaving Mr. Little and Mr. Sieber was even harder. I adored Mr. Sieber. His love for orchestral music had sparked the same passion in me, and his interest in my musical development, along with Mr. Little's support, had enabled me to blossom as a musician. My interactions with Mr. Sieber had been minimal—weekly rehearsals plus a few extra rehearsals and the concerts—yet I was as attached to him as I was to Mr. Little. Perhaps because I'd had five years of one-on-one lessons with Mr. Little, I felt less sorrow about leaving him. With Mr. Sieber, the longing had only intensified the closer we got to the end of the school year. When the last notes of *Carmina* sounded, I desperately wanted to extend the last interaction with him. Packing up my flute as slowly as possible, I waited for the crowd around Mr. Sieber to disperse, but after the other musicians left, I felt conspicuous.

Assuming Mr. Sieber would eventually take the staircase down to the dressing rooms, I ran down the stairs, skipped the last two, and threw myself onto the hard floor in a pretend fall. I lay there motionless for about ten minutes, hoping Mr. Sieber would find me. Neither he nor anyone else came by. The memory of that desperate action still embarrasses me.

Although I didn't make the connection at the time, I was acting out my junior high fantasy about the junior high band director. Six years later, about to enter college, I still yearned for attention from a caring older man. As always, the fantasy played out only inside my head. I never saw Mr. Sieber again.

The next day, I wrote Mr. Sieber a long poem, describing my experience in the community orchestra, from the first rehearsal on the Hanson "Romantic" Symphony to the final performance of *Carmina Burana*. It was corny but heartfelt. About a week later, I received the most precious letter I've ever gotten. Mr. Sieber said he'd received many effusive compliments about *Carmina Burana*, but none had moved him as much as my poem. He went on to praise my unceasing efforts to keep improving as a flutist. The comment I most treasure was, "I can only hope that one of my kids will grow up to be an Ernestine Whitman." I carried that letter in my purse for years. I regret its loss; it was proof that, for two years, someone was proud of me.

Chapter 9: College

The summer after high school graduation, the flute stayed in its case for the longest time in seven years, adjusting to life without me. By the time I moved into Harris Hall dormitory at Emory University, the pain of separation (for me, I can't speak for the flute) had receded to a dull ache.

It took a while for me to view Emory as anything more than my father's choice, a punishment for failing to get into Curtis, but I knew I was privileged to be at such a good school. The courses were challenging and well taught, and living on campus provided a respite from my father's domineering presence. Daddy had agreed to pay for one year in the dormitory; I savored each day of independence and small, daily pleasures, like eating whenever and whatever I wanted. (My mother never made chocolate cream pie.) When my first paper was due, I discovered the adrenaline rush of staying up all night. With the study room all to myself and unhealthy snacks in the vending machines, I relished having intellectual insights at 3:00 a.m.

Except for making jokes in orchestra rehearsals, for the past two years I'd been a serious teenager, too caught up in the world of classical music to spend time with friends my age. Living on campus changed all that. I reconnected with Anne and Xenia, childhood friends who went to Emory, and met new friends, beginning with Alice, my cute, funny, mostly compatible roommate.

Alice and I bonded immediately. When we were unpacking the first day, we discovered we had *three* sets of identical pajamas, hers purchased in Tampa, Florida, mine in Atlanta. She did, however, have one annoying habit: she disliked the study lounge and insisted on studying in our room well into the night, with the bright, overhead light on. At first, I put a pillow over my head; when that didn't work, I put my mattress under the bed frame and slept there. Not bad unless I bumped the underside of the bedsprings while turning over, which stirred up lots of dust.

That fall I took Bible 101, the only required course, plus a basic history course, and Chemistry 101, the first course in my proposed major. The only music option at Emory was a music history major, but if I couldn't attend a music school, I wanted to pursue the other field where I'd encountered a caring, charismatic teacher—Mrs. Gibson, my high school chemistry teacher. The Emory chemistry professor, however, was terrible—my only bad course in four years. Despite the easy A, I had no interest in taking more classes in that department.

Once again, I traipsed after my older sister and switched to a math major. My father's hierarchical view of fields of study placed math and the hard sciences at the top, along with economics, which included enough math and hard data to elevate it far above other social science fields. Music ranked at the bottom, if it even had a place.

As the sadness over not attending a music school lessened, I decided music didn't have to be all or nothing. Midway through the first quarter, I joined the Emory Chorale and the Emory Chamber Orchestra, both under the odd but engaging leadership of Dr. William Lemonds. Tall, portly, with longish blond hair, Dr. Lemonds was a good but perpetually flustered conductor. His office in the decrepit Temporary Fine Arts Building, a repurposed WWII Quonset hut, always looked as chaotic as I imagined his mind was, though he was very focused in rehearsals. Students adored him and enjoyed quoting his head-scratching sayings, such as, "Remember, everyone is indispensable, but no one is irreplaceable."

Because there was only one dreary practice room in the TFAB, I often practiced in Dr. Lemonds's office at night when he wasn't there. I got to know several three-inch cockroaches who seemed to like my flute playing.

After deciding that I would, in fact, be playing the flute, I took a few lessons from Mr. Little, even though college life left little time for practicing. The lessons were awkward. Perhaps Mr. Little was disappointed in me for not working harder, but without my dream of being a musician, my motivation was gone. I stopped after the third lesson. Resigned to my fate as an Emory student, I focused on coursework, fraternity parties, and the joys of living away from home.

About three weeks into the fall term, Anne came running down the hall, yelling, "Ernestine, you won't believe this!"

"What, what?"

"When I came back to the dorm just now, guess who I saw in the lobby?" Nonresidents were allowed only in the small waiting room by the front door. Anne was breathless with excitement.

"I've no idea."

"Oh, come on, just guess," she said.

"Nat King Cole?" Highly unlikely.

"No. Someone less famous."

"Then why are you so excited about it?"

"Because it's someone we both know but would never imagine in Harris Hall."

I remained clueless.

"Okay, I guess I'll have to tell you." Dramatic pause. "It was Mr. Little!"

"No, you've got to be kidding. What on earth was he doing here?"

"But Ernestine, that's not even the best part. Guess *why* he was here."

"I can't imagine, but he must've been meeting someone, probably someone who lives here. Maybe a residence hall counselor?"

"Not even close, it's someone we both know—or at least used to know."

"I still don't—"

"In band."

I thought back, way back, to sub-freshman year. Even in my naivete, I vaguely remembered sensing something. Then it dawned on me, and my grin widened. "Lenore?"

"Yes! Can you believe it? They walked out the door, Lenore hanging on his arm. It didn't look like they were about to have a flute lesson," Anne said with a mischievous grin.

"I'm surprised Lenore's at Emory," I said. "What's she doing in a freshman dorm?" In high school, we'd dismissed Lenore as sort of an airhead, and a bit cheap.

"She must have one of the rooms reserved for nontraditional students. I wonder how long they've been going out."

"God, he's got to be twenty years older than she is."

"At least she's four years older than we are," Anne said.

"Okay, so only sixteen years, but still . . ."

The disruption of generational boundaries shocked us. We remembered, barely five years ago, fantasizing about Mr.

Little as a father, and here he was in our dorm, with someone who'd been in our high school band flute section. Anne's revelation made me think back to my third year of lessons with him, when I sensed some discord between Mr. Little and his wife. By the end of that year, Mr. Little had moved his teaching studio from his home to a small, windowless room at a music store in Buckhead.

"Hmm, I wonder if this had something to do with why he moved his studio to Ritter Music," I said.

"You mean so he could make passes at students?"

"Oh God, no!" I was horrified. "I meant maybe he moved because his marriage was in trouble and he wanted to get away from Mrs. Little."

"Or maybe she kicked him out." Anne raised her eyebrows. "Do you think he and Lenore messed around in the room at the music store?"

"Oh, gross," I said. Anne agreed, but we continued to speculate.

Though we were eighteen, our excitement about Mr. Little appearing in the dorm resurrected the crush and mindset of our early teen years. There's something about being with a friend you've grown up with that encourages occasional regressions to earlier emotional states.

After telling me about seeing him with Lenore, Anne forgot about Mr. Little. She had quit flute lessons after a year, but it was harder for me. Mr. Little was my hero. Knowing he'd betrayed his wife, and with a woman we thought of as cheap, disturbed me.

———

During spring of my sophomore year, I received an intriguing phone call. The second flutist in the Atlanta Symphony told me she was leaving and wondered if I might be interested in taking the audition for her position. I called Mr. Little, whom I hadn't seen in over a year, to ask if he thought taking the audition would be a waste of time. My call surprised him.

"I guess, if you want to," he replied, in a voice devoid of enthusiasm. "Sure, why not."

I took his indifference to mean I didn't have a chance. Instead of being discouraged, I decided taking an audition would be interesting. Living away from home had chipped away at my automatic acceptance of someone else's opinion. My courses weren't too intense that spring, so I had time to practice. Also, no chance of winning meant no pressure.

In 1966, the Atlanta Symphony ranked as one of the top fifteen orchestras in the country. As was true of most orchestras in that era, only a few of the highest-paid musicians (concertmaster, principals in the wind sections) came close to earning a living wage. Of the forty-six applicants for the second flute position, mostly from Georgia and the surrounding states, I was the youngest. The audition consisted of a solo piece chosen by the applicant (good old *Poem* for me) and eight orchestral excerpts, most of which I'd studied in high school. With no expectations, I walked into a small classroom on the campus of Georgia State University and played for four men: the conductor, two strangers, and Mr. Little. After playing reasonably well, I forgot about the audition and started getting ready for a fraternity dance that evening.

Late in the afternoon, the personnel manager of the Atlanta Symphony called and offered me the position. Initially suspicious, then ecstatic, I didn't think to ask about salary or even to tell him yes, I would accept the position. Too stunned to say more than an ambiguous okay, I hung up the phone.

Weeks earlier, a friend had asked me to go to a fraternity dance that night, a chance to hear saxophonist Cannonball

Adderley live. That evening, however, I barely noticed Adderley's rich sound and energetic improvisation. I kept trying to take in the staggering news that I'd be part of the orchestra I had admired for years, sitting beside my idol, Mr. Little.

Arriving home late, I waited until the next morning to tell my parents. Despite my father's low opinion of musicians, I thought winning the audition would impress him, that maybe he'd even be excited for me.

"Daddy, I have some great news." As in most scenes from my past, I don't remember if Mother was even in the room.

"What's that?" he asked.

"The personnel manager from the Atlanta Symphony called and offered me the second flute position!"

"He did? You must have played pretty well," my father said. "What did you say to him?"

"What do you mean?"

"Did you accept?" he asked.

"No, I guess I didn't. I was too shocked."

"Have you thought about whether you can do this and still go to Emory?" he asked.

"No." Should I point out it had been less than twenty-four hours since the phone call?

"Honey," he said, irritation creeping into his voice, "you're doing well at Emory, but you can't possibly go to all those rehearsals and still maintain your GPA."

"I—"

"Why would you throw away your college education just to play in the symphony?"

I didn't have a good answer for that. I was stuck on the phrase "*just* to play in the symphony."

"Don't their rehearsals conflict with classes?" he asked.

"No, they rehearse each weekday from 4:00 to 6:30 p.m."

"If you insist on doing this," he continued, "you'd better ask the dean for permission to take an underload, although I can't see him allowing that if all you're doing is playing flute in an orchestra. Do you even know what your salary would be?"

"No, I didn't ask," I said.

"Probably very little since you don't have any experience. And what about job security?"

"I don't know."

"You need to find out because you might not last more than a year," he warned.

As they had countless other times, my father's words left me tongue-tied and deflated. I left the house to get away from him. I wanted this to be my decision, but he did have a point: I would be extremely busy. Could I practice a lot, spend hours each day in rehearsals, and still keep up my grades? Maybe I should focus on my studies and forget silly dreams.

I walked from Emory Road to Oakdale Road, then all the way down to the Byway. It was a lovely April day. The further I got from our house, the better I felt, enjoying the beauty around me. Atlanta's spring is a colorful tapestry of dogwood, azaleas, hydrangeas, and flowering fruit trees. A large house at one end of the Byway had a magnificent flower garden, always stunning in April.

If I did join the symphony, I would spend less time at home and a higher percentage of my time practicing in the basement—therefore less time interacting with my father. By the time I returned from the walk, I'd decided: I would join the Atlanta Symphony in the fall.

Development, Part I

The development is the dramatic section of sonata form, the place where both themes are altered. Sometimes the themes become intertwined, one serving as a countermelody to the other. There are no set rules for the development; the only certainty is that the themes will change.

Chapter 10: Dream Job

In September of 1966, I walked onto the stage of the old, musty-smelling Municipal Auditorium for my first rehearsal as a member of the Atlanta Symphony. I was twenty years old—the same age, I found out later, Warren Little had been when he joined the orchestra in 1948. The previous week, I'd picked up the concert dress a seamstress made according to the ASO's dress code—all black, floor-length, long sleeves, no décolletage. I'd worried it would resemble a nun's habit, but the brocade bodice, sheer sleeves, and flowing A-line skirt looked elegant. That was the easy part; now I had to see whether I could meet the musical requirements.

I had performed on the same stage three times in high school, the last time two years ago for the *Carmina Burana* concert, when the orchestra was seated in the pit. Today the stage seemed enormous. With a dry mouth and wildly beating heart, I wondered what the heck I was doing at a professional orchestra rehearsal. When I spotted an oboist warming up, I knew my seat had to be in that row of chairs, but I hovered at the back of the stage until Mr. Little arrived a few minutes later. After walking to his chair, he gestured for me to come sit in the chair to his right. No welcoming smile. No word of encouragement. I might be sitting beside my former teacher, but I was on my own. Like a professional.

Unable to obtain the second flute parts before the rehearsal, I hoped nerves wouldn't rob me of my sight-reading skills. When I opened the large black folder with *Flute II* embossed in gold on the front, I saw that the first concert featured Beethoven's Symphony No. 6, the *Pastoral Symphony*, a piece with no difficult second flute parts. Gradually, my pulse slowed to a reasonable pace.

Playing in the community orchestra had not prepared me for the demands of a professional orchestra. The pace is quite different: A community orchestra rehearses only once a week and has three to five concerts a year, devoting weeks of rehearsal to each program. A professional orchestra rehearses every day and presents a new program each week. The community orchestra is composed of individuals for whom the orchestra is an avocation, not their profession. In addition to attending all rehearsals, professional musicians usually practice several hours a day.

The hierarchy in a professional orchestra is also different from a nonprofessional group. The conductor is the autocratic leader in both, but in the woodwind and brass sections of a professional orchestra, the second chair players defer to the principal, or first chair, of their section. The musician's contract specifies each position—mine was second flute and piccolo. Upward mobility in an orchestra is almost unheard of except, occasionally, in the string sections.

My first month as a professional was equal parts terror and exhilaration. Non-musicians assume wrong notes are what musicians fear, but in a professional orchestra, correct notes are assumed; it's the subtle variations in articulation, style, and blend that distinguish pros from amateurs. I quickly discovered how precise my rhythm and intonation had to be: being just a millisecond late or a cent sharp elicited a frown from Mr. Little. But when I got it just right, I saw a hint of his smile. At age twenty, I had no sense of where my role as former student ended and the new role as Mr. Little's colleague began. A second chair player must match the first chair in sound and pitch, so I expected Mr. Little's criticism and direction. For a while, that worked just fine.

To perform each day at the level of a professional orchestra, I had to practice three or more hours each day. By living at home, I avoided restricted practice hours and didn't waste time on dorm floor parties or worrying about meals. I eliminated inessential things, such as dating and getting a full night's sleep. After studying past midnight, I would get up at 6:00 a.m. to practice for an hour and a half before classes. Within a few weeks, I felt confident enough to relax and enjoy rehearsals. Concerts were far less scary than rehearsals, because the only ones who could judge whether or not I belonged there were the musicians on the stage.

By October I realized the ASO's schedule, including weeklong tours, would make it impossible to take the lab courses I needed for a math major. Although majoring in English or philosophy tempted me, the only practical solution was to major in music, which in 1966 was essentially a music history degree. At least the music professors were sympathetic to my missing classes due to symphony tours. Daddy made no comment on this switch to a music major; I think he was relieved I was earning money, whatever the source.

During my first season with the symphony, the city was building a new performing arts complex that included Symphony Hall, which would be the permanent home of the ASO. Although we performed in the Municipal Auditorium, we could not get the hall for many of the rehearsals. That year we used various school gymnasiums and a large band room at Georgia State University. But when winter arrived, we had our own, strange place—the locker room of the Atlanta

Braves. Their season didn't dovetail perfectly with ours, but for several months during their offseason we occupied the long, narrow, and—fortunately—carpeted room in the bowels of the recently built Atlanta Stadium. The room was shaped like a shoebox. Maestro Robert Mann chose to spread us out width-wise, which put the flutes very close to the podium, the basses and last stands of the other string sections way off in left or right field, so to speak. The *Atlanta Journal* ran a feature article that year on this bizarre pairing of baseball with a symphony orchestra. It included only one picture, of two people—me holding my flute to my lips, and the lavishly dressed, politically incorrect Chief Noc-A-Homa, posed in the semblance of a war dance.

The higher musical standards of rehearsals were juxtaposed with surprisingly crass behavior. As I quicky discovered, professional musicians are used to this odd combination of inspiring music and bawdy humor. Sitting beside Warren—as I got used to calling him after a few months—I was subjected to a steady dose of his witty, often sarcastic commentary during rehearsals. Lots of cracks about crude brass players and inept conductors. "What's the difference between an orchestra and a bull? In an orchestra, the horns are in the back and the ass-hole's up front." And, of course, viola jokes, the musicians' version of ethnic jokes. "How can you tell when a violist is playing out of tune? His bow is moving."

Wisecracks weren't the only distractions. Sometimes, when the conductor worked with the string sections, Warren used whisper tones to play a ridiculous countermelody to the string passage: "Ta-ra-ra-boom-tee-ay," or "Tea for Two." The principal oboist was a hand-fart virtuoso who could play any rhythm and a few simple melodies with his talented hands. Sometimes he and Warren had funny little duets going, all *sotto voce* (very quiet). Only the players seated around them heard it. I quickly realized

Warren was respected as both one of the best musicians in the orchestra and one of the more outlandish jokesters.

Warren even stooped to using a whoopee cushion. At the beginning of a concert, when the orchestra stands for the conductor's bow, Warren slipped the cushion onto my chair. In the post-applause silence, as we sat back down for the beginning of the program, a crass sound would come from my chair. The first time he did it, my heart pounded and my face turned red. It sounded so loud to me, I thought the conductor and even the front rows of the audience could hear it. A few players sitting close by grinned, but if the conductor heard it, he ignored it. With impeccable strategic planning, Warren waited, sometimes months. Then, as soon as I got out of the habit of checking my chair after the bow, he used it again, four or five times during that first year.

One day, just as I sat down for a rehearsal, Warren reached into his flute bag and pulled out a small black thing. He looked at me, smiled, held it up, and *ZING*, a large shiny blade popped out. He chuckled as he began cleaning his fingernails with the switchblade knife, a striking image. But maybe not so bizarre—his fingernails were often quite dirty.

As with the whoopee cushion, Warren's sense of humor could be crude and repetitive. If my music folder was shut when I returned from a rehearsal break, I knew he'd inserted a cartoon or picture in the folder, ranging from merely funny to mildly suggestive to borderline pornographic. I don't think any of this behavior was malicious; it was simply part of the culture—a collection of mostly men who did silly things when they were bored.

At first, this behavior astonished me. Far from offended, I was delighted by the incongruity between my lofty pre-conception of professional musicians' behavior and the zany shenanigans they indulged in. Yes, much of it was corny and juvenile, but the absurd contrast between the formal setting and the campy humor struck me as very funny.

When I joined the ASO, longtime music director Henry Sopkin had just retired; Robert Mann, the former assistant conductor, took over, but most concerts were led by guests who were auditioning to be the symphony's new director. None of the candidates excited the players. In early March, we heard that the orchestra board had contacted Robert Shaw, the internationally famous choral director and assistant conductor of the Cleveland Orchestra.

Robert Shaw first garnered national attention when he prepared the choir for Arturo Toscanini's 1948 NBC Symphony performance of Beethoven's Symphony No. 9. After the performance, Toscanini remarked, "In Robert Shaw I have at last found the maestro I have been looking for." The Robert Shaw Chorale, founded that same year, quickly became the best professional choir in the US and beyond. Their international tours included more than thirty countries, and they made numerous iconic recordings with RCA Victor.

Shortly after the rumors of Shaw's appointment were confirmed, we learned that Mr. Shaw's contract gave him permission (overriding the musicians' union rules) to audition every member of the orchestra. Barely a week later, months before Shaw's first rehearsal with us, the auditions began.

Because Shaw didn't group auditions by instrument, I played two days after Warren. I'd been battling the flu and had a temperature of 103. Somehow, I got through the audition successfully, with only one daunting moment. Shaw, at that time mainly a choral conductor, asked me what the highest note in the flute orchestral literature was; I told him high D. He then asked me to play the D pianissimo (as soft as possible), crescendo to fortissimo (as loud as possible), then back down to pianissimo. This was the same exercise Mr. Little had given me in high school, but never on high D. In the flute range, the higher the note, the harder it is to play softly. (Conversely, very low notes on the flute are hard to play loudly.) High D requires such a strong thrust of air to get the note out that it is impossible to play softly. After an ugly attempt, I told Shaw what most orchestral conductors know: composers write only fortissimo high Ds. Shaw then asked me to do the exercise on C. Even C is tough, but I played it with at least a modest dynamic range. The next day, Warren asked me what note I'd played. When I told him I'd first tried high D, he laughed. "I told Shaw the highest note on the flute was an A." High A is *much* easier to play softly than high C.

Though many musicians grumbled about having to audition, most of us were excited about working with Robert Shaw. The auditions were only the first of many changes Maestro Shaw initiated. I predicted (accurately, as it turned out) Shaw's rehearsals would be intense and demanding.

Now that my contract with the ASO had been renewed, Daddy agreed with my decision to buy a used car to drive myself to rehearsals. I would pay for it with ASO money I'd saved, but Daddy knew much more about cars than I, so when he offered to select the car, I accepted. My one request: any color but white. When Daddy said he'd found a used 1965 Mustang, I jumped at it and wrote a check for it right away. Two days later, Daddy drove the car into the driveway—a white car. At least the interior was red.

"It suits you," Mother said, sensing my disappointment, "reserved and traditional on the outside, fiery on the inside." *What?* I thought I'd protected her from all my inner turmoil. Once I got over the shock, her comment did make me feel better. And boy, was it fun to drive: V-8 engine, four on the floor, and peppy as a puppy.

Many southern girls in the early 1960s grew up assuming a coed's primary goal in college was to find the man of her dreams. That mindset was part of my childhood only in the sense that all the mothers of my friends were housewives. But I'm grateful Daddy never subscribed to that, probably because his two eldest sisters, one of them my namesake, were unmarried schoolteachers. Daddy believed any graduate of a good school like Emory would be able to make a living. As with most of my father's strongly held beliefs, I assumed he was right, so I enjoyed casual dating, without worrying about finding a husband.

Shortly after buying the car, I went on a double date the night before my parents drove to Chicago for an economics conference. Because I was excited about the Mustang, I drove my car on the date, very unusual in that era. When I returned home, I parked the car in our driveway behind my parents' car and left my keys on the kitchen table so Daddy could move it in the morning. When I turned twenty-one, my father extended the weekend curfew to 1:30 a.m. That night I'd stayed out much later. I knew Daddy wouldn't wait up for me since he was leaving early the next morning. I'd slept only a few hours when my father came storming into my room.

"Do you know what I found in your car?" he yelled, shoving something in my face.

I tried to make sense of Daddy's anger. I was still relatively inexperienced and didn't recognize the cute little foil package in my father's hand. Hungover, sleep-deprived, and genuinely puzzled, I asked, "What *is* that?"

The question enraged him.

"You mean to tell me you don't know what this is? *It was in your car,*" he said, shaking the thing in my face. Suddenly, I realized what it must be.

"Where did you find it?" I asked.

"I told you, in your car."

"In the back seat?"

"What the hell difference does that make?"

"We double-dated. It must have fallen out of the other guy's pocket."

"YOU EXPECT ME TO BELIEVE THAT?"

I mumbled something. The louder he shouted, the quieter I got, even at twenty-one.

"I don't see how your mother and I can leave you here by yourself if you're going to go out with people like this."

"But Daddy, I honestly think it fell out of John's, not Robert's, pocket, and I swear I've never seen one before."

My befuddlement gradually convinced Daddy. He calmed down, admitting the object in question could have belonged to the other guy. Perhaps he should've worried about *un*protected sex, but that never crossed his mind. I think, like most middle-class parents of that time and place, he assumed I would be a virgin until my wedding night.

When I sat down for the first rehearsal with Robert Shaw in early September, the woodwind section was almost unrecognizable. Except for Warren, the principal winds were missing. Well, not exactly missing: the principal oboe had been demoted to English horn, the first bassoon moved to contrabassoon, the principal clarinet to bass clarinet. (He quit a few weeks later.) The second chair players had disappeared, except for me. Shaw had fired or demoted players in almost every section. Only the flute section remained intact: Warren, me, and the piccolo player, Benson Prichard. Clarinetists Alan Balter and Bob Wingert, and bassoonists Russ Bedford and Lynette Diers were all from the Cleveland area, graduates of Oberlin Conservatory and the Cleveland Institute of Music. For the principal oboe position, Shaw chose a rising star, Joe Robinson, who after leaving Atlanta would become principal oboist with the New York Philharmonic.

From Shaw's first downbeat, the rehearsal atmosphere sizzled with the focused concentration of ninety musicians. Right away, I noticed a warmer, richer sound in all the sections—each new member played both more in tune and with a better sound than the person they replaced. Other changes also happened immediately. Pranks and horsing around ceased. Warren quit drinking, the brass players stopped muttering off-color jokes, and the timpanist no longer listened to Braves games during long rests. No more funny stories.

A barrel-chested man with boyish good looks and a florid complexion, Shaw always wore a blue-gray corduroy shirt, with a white undershirt peeking out of the open collar. He usually had a small towel slung over his left shoulder, to mop up his sweaty face. The players sitting close to him soon learned to raise their music stands a bit to avoid the spray. Shaw masked his inexperience as an orchestral conductor by leading laser-focused rehearsals. He was often impatient— frustrated, perhaps, by his inability to communicate the phrasing he wanted (in contrast to his eloquence with choirs). And frustration worsened his stutter. Nevertheless, he could terrify players with his intense, blue-eyed stare. Despite his stuttering, spluttering manner, he was an excellent musician who gradually rose to the challenge of being a full-time orchestra director.

Robert Shaw's first concert with the symphony con-
cluded with Beethoven's epic masterpiece, Symphony No. 9.
On opening night, the Municipal Auditorium was packed—
orchestra, choir members, and audience all equally excited.

Shaw led the orchestra in a gripping interpretation of
the first movement of the symphony, followed by a scherzo
packed with Dionysian energy. After the scherzo, the principal
clarinetist had to disassemble his instrument and swab (clean
out the condensation). Shaw, eager to keep going, didn't
notice that Alan's clarinet was in pieces. The second clarinetist
gesticulated wildly to get Shaw's attention, but Shaw had his
eyes closed, preparing for the sublime opening of the slow
movement. The solo wind entrances that open the third
movement go from low to high; Alan's solo was the fourth
one. During the few seconds of the bassoons and second
clarinet entrances, Alan jammed his instrument together,
barely making his entrance. Whew. One of many dramatic
moments that night. All the others were musical.

After the haunting third movement, Shaw, a quick
learner, glanced at the wind sections to make sure they were
ready for the finale. Even after rehearsing the piece all week,
and in addition to the many times I'd heard the end of the
piece, the "Ode to Joy," I wasn't prepared for the electrifying
performance Shaw elicited from the orchestra, soloists, and
choir that night. The standing ovation following the performance must have lasted ten minutes. Shaw's debut had met
and surpassed our high expectations.

Mr. Shaw could be cruel, especially to singers. We first
witnessed it the week we performed a Handel oratorio. I'd
heard terrific recordings of contralto Florence Kopleff and
was excited to hear her in person. The one rehearsal the
orchestra had with Ms. Kopleff confirmed the rumors that
she and Shaw were more than colleagues. When Ms. Kopleff

walked to the podium to rehearse her aria, she looked upset. Her face was pinched, and she stared at the floor, a striking contrast to her usual proud diva persona. After a few measures, she stopped singing and ran off the stage, crying. Furious, Shaw buried his head in the score and continued to play through the entire aria, including the repeat of the first section—a waste of time without the soloist, but he refused to acknowledge her absence. His usual ruddy complexion turned several shades darker.

The choir was not immune to Shaw's sharp tongue, such as when he said, in a tone of exaggerated courtesy, "Ladies and gentlemen, if it isn't too much to ask, I would suggest that you spend more time focusing on the music, less time picking your noses." He would work meticulously with the choir on details of dynamic shaping and tonal subtleties, then come out with a creative zinger. For the "Dies Irae" (Day of Wrath) in Verdi's *Requiem*, he said, "Sing as if giant rattlesnakes are crawling out of your armpits."

What made Robert Shaw's choral performances so exceptional? It started with the quality of the sound he created with his choirs, reflecting careful attention to intonation, enunciation, and blend. But rhythm was what made his performances sizzle. He had an unerring sense of the perfect tempo for each section of the great choral works. Unlike most members of the orchestra, I had no familiarity with the Western canon's choral repertoire. It was intoxicating to discover and perform Bach's Mass in B Minor, the Brahms and Verdi requiems, and other choral masterpieces under the baton of arguably the best choral conductor of the twentieth century.

Although he had a brilliant mind and kept up with musicological scholarship, Robert Shaw was not a champion of Baroque performance practice. One could argue his Bach interpretations were a bit Romantic (style period, not romance), but I loved the expressive lyricism of his slow movements and the driving energy of his allegros. Bach was never plodding. I remember a performance of "Cum Sancto Spiritus" from his Mass in B Minor where all members of the orchestra and choir seemed to be dancing as one joyous, levitating unit.

In addition to his extraordinary work with choirs, Shaw was an inspired interpreter of the great nineteenth-century orchestral repertoire. Shaw's Brahms and Beethoven symphonies were profoundly moving, reflecting a spiritual depth few conductors possess. Perhaps it was partly his background — son of a minister and brother of a soldier killed in World War II. During performances, even in the most sublime passages, Shaw didn't close his eyes as many conductors do, but maintained eye contact with the orchestra, his face so earnest you became part of his intense reverence for the composer's work. His commitment was first and foremost to the music, not to his adoring public.

I discovered these masterworks from a privileged vantage point, surrounded by exceptional woodwind players. Joe's expressive playing in the second movement of Beethoven's *Eroica*, Alan's marvelous *Pines of Rome* clarinet solo, Russ's sultry bassoon entrance in *Bolero*, are but a few examples of the many times I was transported by the artistry of the players around me. And Warren? Perhaps because I was so familiar with it, Warren's playing struck me as quite good, but not as exceptional as that of the other woodwind players. They were all young, at the top of their game, and eager to play their best at every rehearsal and concert. Much later I would realize how exceptional it was to have so many gifted, not-yet-jaded players in one section. I was lucky to be part of it.

Chapter 11: Work / Study

Robert Shaw's high standards increased the pressure on us to learn music quickly and be note-perfect at every rehearsal. One of my most intense experiences occurred during Shaw's first year. We received the parts to Ravel's *Daphnis et Chloé*, Suite No. 2 on Friday, for Monday's rehearsal. The first page was almost completely black. I'd never seen so many thirty-second notes per page, all of them difficult runs. After I'd looked through the part, I focused on the beginning, which appeared to be the most difficult passage. Then I discovered an entire page of solo runs that alternated between first and second flutes later in the piece. I wasn't the only symphony member who would be practicing a lot that weekend; I was, however, the only musician for whom this difficult work was completely new. Why hadn't Warren warned me about this tough second flute part?

After devoting all of Saturday and Sunday to learning *Daphnis*, at Monday's rehearsal I could play or fake most of it, though I still struggled with the hardest parts. I wasn't the only one: the runs at the beginning of the piece between flutes and clarinets sounded more like potholed roads than gently rippling meadows. By Wednesday morning's rehearsal, the runs were smooth, including the ones that alternate between first and second flutes. That passage ends with one of Ravel's brilliant effects: the final run begins with the highest notes of the piccolo, descends through first and second flutes, and culminates in a solo for the low-pitched alto flute. When played well, with no seams, it sounds like one super-flute with a gigantic range. All those runs come right after one of the most gorgeous flute solos in orchestral repertoire. Even in the first rehearsal, Warren played it well, earning him a compliment from Shaw—rare for any player—and many others, including me. I wondered if I would ever get to play that luscious solo with an orchestra.

During rehearsals, Ravel's music kept jerking me back and forth between astonishment at the lush, seductive beauty of *Daphnis* and the pressure to play one of the most difficult parts I'd ever seen. I wanted to luxuriate in the sensuous sounds around me, but the flute part was almost nonstop—very few bars of rest when I could savor Ravel's ravishing music.

The exhausting week culminated in thrilling performances. The frenzied ending was electrifying, even at the third performance. *Daphnis* easily qualifies as a GSO, guaranteed standing ovation—works with rousing, extremely loud, and usually fast endings.

In December, following a decades-long tradition, the orchestra joined the Atlanta Ballet for numerous performances of *The Nutcracker*, including one show on Christmas Day. (Shaw assigned this tedious task to an assistant conductor.) The "Dance of the Reed Flutes" movement is a flute trio, with three equally important parts. The lowest part is played by the person whose contract position is piccolo/third flute. Benson Prichard excelled on the piccolo, but like many piccolo specialists, his low register on the flute was weak. He asked me to switch parts with him so I could play all the low Ds and C-sharps, notes that are difficult to play loud. Benson and I got along well, and I was comfortable playing either part. I consulted Warren and he agreed the switch made sense. Things were fine during the rehearsals and most of the performances.

For some reason, during the month of December Warren had been in a foul mood. At the final *Nutcracker* rehearsal, when I glanced at my watch, Warren glared at me.

"Are we keeping you from some hot date?" he asked, almost snarling. Unlike remarks he'd made before—casual chitchat or innocuous teasing—he sounded angry. Hours later, I wondered if I'd imagined his hostility. Then came the *Nutcracker* performance on Christmas Day.

"I don't know why you're playing Benson's part when you can't even play your own," Warren hissed as soon as we'd played the trio.

My pulse raced as I tried to think what I'd done to prompt Warren's rebuke. Had I played any differently than in previous performances? I didn't think so, but Warren kept scowling at me. After the ballet, I left the pit quickly and fought through the festive holiday crowd, a familiar feeling of dread making my stomach clench. If Warren thought I'd played poorly, I must be losing the ability to assess my own playing. A seasoned professional wouldn't have let one comment and some nasty looks shake her confidence. But Warren was the expert. I'd always trusted his opinion of my playing.

It was years before I thought about the timing of the change in Warren's treatment of me. When Shaw arrived, the intensity of rehearsals increased enormously. Struggling with doubts about my own abilities, I didn't think about the challenges Warren faced. He'd seen his buddies demoted or fired. Because of the changes, Warren was surrounded by strangers—young virtuosos handpicked by Shaw. Though we were all under increased pressure, Warren may have felt it more keenly as the lone survivor among the principal woodwinds. Whatever the reason, my former mentor now added to the stress of playing under a demanding conductor.

The change in our relationship coincided with increased academic pressure. By senior year, I'd fulfilled the requirements for a music major, so I took advanced courses in English and history. With heavy reading assignments and more time practicing, I was riding two horses going in opposite directions, one galloping down the path my father had chosen, the other struggling up the increasingly steep path I had chosen.

A few weeks after Christmas, we performed Beethoven's Symphony No. 7, with the haunting slow movement I'd loved since I heard it at Brevard Music Camp, when I was sixteen. The piece opens, however, with lots of prominent high Es played by first and second flutes. High E on the flute tends to be sharp, especially when loud and short, as in this passage. At the first rehearsal, I matched the pitch of Warren's high E even though I thought he was flat compared to the strings' pitch. Shaw's frown at us confirmed my suspicions, but was it wrong to tune to Warren? Two flutes playing slightly flat to the general pitch of the orchestra is much less grating than two flutes out of tune with each other on piercing high notes. And, as the second chair player, my job was to play in tune with Warren. Right after the passage, Warren turned his head and scowled at me, indicating the pitch problem was my fault.

From then on, if there was an intonation problem in the winds, Warren frowned at me. Most of the time I assumed Warren was right, but even when I knew the problem was in another section, I worried Warren's frowns would convince Shaw it was my fault. Robert Shaw had a great ear for intonation in choirs, but when he came to Atlanta, Shaw's inexperience in orchestral conducting made it difficult for him to tell who was out of tune in the winds. (Professional players constantly monitor intonation; a concert hall's change in temperature or humidity alters the pitch of some instruments.) Shaw never commented about my intonation; later I wondered if he knew Warren was blaming me unfairly and simply chose to ignore it.

In the weeks before and after the concerts featuring Beethoven's Symphony No. 7, I was busy preparing for a solo recital. Music majors at Emory weren't required to give recitals, but there were several solo pieces I wanted to perform, including Prokofiev's masterful Sonata for Flute and Piano (also a favorite of violinists, but the original version was for flute). I scheduled the recital in early February, before winter quarter coursework piled up. After four years of playing only orchestral music (interpreted by the conductor), working on solo literature, with me as the interpreter, was exhilarating. The Prokofiev sonata features exciting, virtuosic passages, but I loved the lyrical, melodic sections, where I could shape phrases using my own musical ideas.

To prepare for the concert, I took two lessons from Warren, which was a mistake. I don't know why I thought he'd be helpful; maybe it was simply force of habit. He spoke to me formally as if I were a new student, one he didn't particularly like. Warren was especially mean to me in rehearsals right after each of those lessons. Perhaps when he heard me play difficult solo repertoire, Warren realized that, over the past eighteen months, I had improved greatly with no help from him. That thought only occurred to me years later.

Despite the friction between us, I wanted Warren to hear the recital, and I repeatedly asked him to come. I still thought of him as my teacher and hoped he might be proud of me, as he had been years ago. During the concert, I searched and searched for Warren in the audience. By most measures, including the glowing review in the *Atlanta Journal*, the recital was a success, but his absence cast a pall over the whole evening. Pretending to enjoy the post-recital reception, I shoved aside my hurt and disappointment.

As the situation with Warren worsened, did I consider quitting? No, for two reasons. The Atlanta Symphony was a very good professional orchestra, and with Shaw at the helm, getting better each day. I knew my chances of landing another job of equal stature and pay were slim. Second, for a while the thrill of discovering great music offset the turmoil created by Warren. Sometimes just a short passage grabbed me. It first happened in the fall of Shaw's first year. Bizet's Symphony in C, composed when he was seventeen, is a simple, sometimes banal work, but the second movement features an extended, mournful oboe solo. From the first notes of the solo, the music overwhelmed me. Joe's beautiful sound and lovely legato shaped the melody so exquisitely that my heart ached with longing, and I momentarily forgot where I was.

Other times it was complete works that captivated me, none more than Bach's magnificent setting of the crucifixion story, the *Saint Matthew Passion*, performed Shaw's second year. One of the pieces that established Shaw's international reputation, *Saint Matthew* is a massive oratorio, written for solo voices, two choirs, and two orchestras. Shaw had translated the entire, lengthy German text. Performing the work in English added to its impact.

At various points in the text, Bach added chorales and arias. The chorales reflect upon the spiritual aspect of each part of the story; the arias focus on the emotional perspectives. Bach enhanced the arias' expressive texts by his imaginative addition of solo instruments. In a group of powerful arias, the one that moved me the most was the contralto aria "Erbarme dich" (Have mercy on me), with its ornate, expressive solo violin. Placed right after Peter's denial of Jesus, it describes Peter's agony and remorse over betraying his beloved teacher. Florence Kopleff, whose voice was perfect for the aria, sang the solo. Did the aria speak to me so intensely because I felt betrayed by my mentor? Or did I feel guilty for betraying Warren by questioning his criticism of me? At the time, I think the emotion I felt was less specific—I responded because it so eloquently expressed profound despair. I teared up every time Kopleff sang the aria, and it has remained a favorite of mine.

In my teens, I rebelled against the Southern Methodist religion my mother believed in, and by the time the symphony performed the *Passion*, I was agnostic. Performing Bach's masterpiece was the starting point for a gradual journey back to believing in God. Such powerful, spiritual music was at odds with my dispassionate agnosticism, and several times that week I found myself thinking, *I may not believe in God, but I sure as hell believe in Bach.*

***

The friction between my father and me had been at its worst during my last two years of high school, when our arguments— or Daddy diatribes—were about my pleading to go to a music school. Enrolling at Emory mollified my father, and although he was against my joining the symphony, I gradually proved to him I could maintain good grades while playing in the ASO. Living at home my last two years at Emory, I enjoyed being around my father for the first time in years. It happened to coincide with the period in which Warren increased his harassment.

I'd always been a night owl. At home, staying up late offered the rare opportunity to connect with Daddy. After Mother went to bed, Daddy and I watched Johnny Carson on *The Tonight Show*. I loved hearing Daddy laugh. Usually, it was his own jokes and stories that made him laugh, often at someone else's expense. But when we watched Johnny Carson, I saw—and shared—Daddy's genuine appreciation of someone else's wit. Watching television was the only way I could spend time with my father. Although I had no interest in football, I started watching college games on Saturday afternoons. It was okay if we didn't talk much. With Daddy's attention focused on TV, there was little danger of him criticizing me. And by then, Melinda had moved away from Atlanta, far less present as the perfect daughter.

Musical achievements meant nothing to Daddy, but we did share an appreciation of the absurd. My first year in the symphony, before Shaw's arrival, Warren and others provided me with lots of entertaining anecdotes. At the rare dinner parties my parents hosted, I would jump into the conversation with a bizarre story. In those brief moments, Daddy seemed pleased with me. If I couldn't make him proud, I could at least make him laugh.

On the night of April 4 in the spring of my senior year, I arrived home around 10:30 p.m. after a symphony concert. As soon as I walked in the door, I knew something terrible had happened. My parents had the TV on with the sound turned down, both of them apparently in shock.

"Martin Luther King was shot and killed tonight in Memphis," Daddy said, as I sank into the love seat by the front door. My father didn't know any details. Sitting frozen in silence, we waited for the eleven o'clock news to come on, but we didn't learn anything more that night. Mixed in with the sorrow and disbelief was the fear of a violent backlash. How could the Black community not react with anger when their beloved leader had been murdered?

Born and raised in Atlanta, Dr. Martin Luther King Jr. graduated from Morehouse, one of Atlanta's four Black colleges and universities, and then became the preacher at Atlanta's Ebenezer Baptist Church. Because of King's leadership and deep ties to the community, the city became the epicenter of the civil rights movement. That may explain, in part, why Atlanta was spared the serious disturbances that broke out in many cities after King's death. Years later, I learned that the close friendship between Mayor Ivan Allen Jr. and the Kings also helped. After spending many hours that night with King's wife, Coretta Scott King, Mayor Allen met with the presidents of the Black colleges. With both Black and white leaders urging calm, the city mourned peacefully.

The people I knew found the assassination of Martin Luther King deeply shocking, which reveals how limited our world was. My high school American history course never mentioned Jim Crow laws or the horrors of lynching in the South. I'd heard about lynching but assumed it had happened long ago, and only in Mississippi and Alabama.

My involvement with civil rights was minimal before Dr. King's death. That spring, I joined some friends from high school to participate in the big march after Dr. King's death. We also helped circulate petitions and raise funds for Andrew Young, Maynard Jackson, and other Black leaders—the easy things liberals did in those days, which may have made little difference beyond making us feel better.

Like most of my friends, I adopted my parents' social

and political views, which in our house meant Daddy's view. Although her own mother was a proud member of the United Daughters of the Confederacy—the group most responsible for erecting Confederate statues and memorials—Mother readily adopted my father's beliefs and values, probably by their third date. At the yearly Whitman reunions (our summer vacations), I gradually realized that the heated arguments between my father and his siblings were about the treatment of Black people. Because my father's seven sisters and one brother were all older, I've often wondered how and when Daddy became such a staunch supporter of civil rights, one of many things I wish I'd asked him. His brother never said much, but all his other siblings talked about "the coloreds" in ways even a child recognized as derogatory. Was it hard for my father to speak out against his older siblings and their equally prejudiced spouses? Probably not. By then he had developed the confidence in his own opinions—which he had in abundance—that overrode the Whitman family hierarchy.

During my sheltered childhood, I never questioned why Black people had to sit in the back of the bus, or whether it was right to have bathroom and seating areas in movie theaters "for coloreds only." My parents never talked to me about race. The only Black person who came to our house was Nellie, a young woman who did the ironing every Tuesday, when I was five years old. Despite Nellie's calm demeanor she intimidated me. I wondered why she ate lunch by herself after we had eaten, but I didn't realize that was because she was Black.

When I was a high school senior, a Black man named Sherry came to the house occasionally to do yard work. Although I didn't speak with him, I remember my father being very concerned about Sherry when he became ill. Knowing he had no health insurance, my father sent money to Sherry's family. I sensed Daddy thought it was unfair that Sherry had no insurance, but I was oblivious to the reasons. Like so many middleclass white children in the 1960s, I didn't have the opportunity to interact with Black people until I was an adult. I supported Black leaders, but I knew nothing about systemic — or even day-to-day — racism.

Many families suffer a lot of discord over political differences, but when it came to civil rights, compassionate support for the poor, and other social issues, I was, and am still, proud to be my father's daughter.

———

Although I yearned for approval and affection from older men, I had enough self-awareness to avoid dating obvious father figures; I was, however, drawn to men in positions of authority. That same year (senior year at Emory, second season with ASO), I developed a crush on Michael Palmer, the symphony's young, recently hired assistant conductor. Compared to college guys, Michael seemed lofty, erudite. He knew so much about so many things. At a dinner party he hosted, Michael served artichokes. After chewing an outer leaf for several puzzling minutes, I noticed how the other guests dismantled the weird vegetable. After removing the mangled leaf from my mouth as discreetly as possible, I sneaked it under the other leaves in the funereal pile.

Michael's excellent musicianship and culinary sophistication weren't his only assets. He was tall and thin, with remarkably thick, wavy, light-brown hair. But the magnet that drew me most strongly was his position as conductor — all that confidence, all that knowledge of scores. And what did he see in me? A young, attractive, single member of the orchestra who gazed at him with longing. After we'd gone out several times, I thought I was in love with him. That he showed not the slightest interest in anything other than casual friendship only increased my yearning.

In the spring of that year, shortly after the artichoke dinner, I used some of my symphony earnings to buy a stereo system. Daddy selected it (not the best, of course, but the best value) and helped me hook it up in my bedroom. When I bragged to Michael about the fidelity of the sound, he suggested we listen to Mahler's Fifth Symphony on the system. There were no chairs in my bedroom, so when he came over one night to hear the stereo, we sat on the floor with our backs leaning against the bed—fully clothed, bodies not touching. We'd heard about half of the first movement when my parents returned from a bridge club meeting. My father stormed into the bedroom and sternly told Michael to leave. Michael started to say something but changed his mind when he saw my father's angry face. Michael stumbled out quickly, almost forgetting his car keys. Then the shouting began.

"Ernestine, what the hell were you thinking, inviting Michael into your bedroom?" he asked.

"I wanted him to hear the new stereo."

"And you don't see how stupid that was?" The scowl in his forehead deepened.

"But we were just listening to music, with the door open."

"Do you think that makes it okay?" The shouting fueled his anger, and the anger made him shout louder.

"What if he had raped you?" he yelled, his face about a foot from mine. "Do you think a jury would believe you, since you let him into your bedroom? You wouldn't have a leg to stand on."

With breathtaking speed, my father had jumped from the innocent scene in my room to a courtroom drama. Reasoning with him was futile, so I let him rant about his imagined rape trial. But instead of reeling from the attack, as I usually did, I was struck by the extremity of his reaction. Why had this episode so upset my father? Did he still need to control me, a twenty-two-year-old? Maybe Daddy's anger was not so much my problem as *his*. This insight—really a paradigm shift—did not make me instantly immune to my father's outbursts. His anger still hurt, and I remained as eager as ever to get away from him. Only four more months of living at home.

When the orchestra season ended, Michael returned to his hometown for the summer to conduct a choir that was preparing for a performance of Bach's Mass in B Minor. The ASO hadn't yet performed the work, so I bought Robert Shaw's 1965 recording of it, hoping to impress Michael with my knowledge of the piece. He wrote to me infrequently, his letters filled with details about his choir rehearsals. No questions about my life, certainly no references to us. For Michael, there was no us.

Where is the line between healthy interest in a would-be lover's passions, and letting those passions obliterate one's own interests, ideas, self? I sometimes felt like an empty ship going from harbor to harbor, seeking the cargo I was supposed to carry. Though I detested the Cinderella complex—waiting for a man to rescue and define me—the myth remained embedded in me, sometimes overshadowing my drive to be a musician.

The distress of pining for someone unattainable was compounded that summer by academic pressure. Missing classes for symphony tours resulted in three terms of underloads; I needed three courses, including two science courses, to graduate. In the squeezed, eight-week summer term, students were advised to take only two classes, but postponing a course wasn't an option for me. In the fall, the symphony would move to a daytime rehearsal schedule, a crucial part of its new status as a full-time orchestra. I could've chosen geology courses, the easy way out, but something—probably Melinda's record—made me pick two physics courses, both with labs. Only science nerds take two physics lab courses at the same time. Idiots take them in the summer.

I also took a poetry class, which had a reasonable work-load, as did one of the physics courses. The other course was grueling. Taught by a young, good-looking man named Mr. Ohms (yes, real name), the course had difficult labs and word problems about baffling things like governors on steam engines. In letters to Michael, I described my panic about fail-ing the course: daughter of a distinguished Emory professor, sister of a straight-A alum, ruins the family name. My father would be furious, I'd be kicked out of Phi Beta Kappa, and in penance I'd have to quit the Atlanta Symphony.

None of that happened. Sacrificing what might have been As in the easier courses, I focused on the hard course and ended up with three Bs. After all that angst, I didn't care about the low GPA. By that time, my anxiety was about return-ing to the Symphony and facing Michael and Warren—one a reminder of my failings as a woman, the other, my failings as a flutist.

Two weeks after taking finals, I moved into an apartment with a couple of high school friends. Beginning in elementary school, where kids were seated alphabetically, Xenia Wiggins and I were destined to be good friends. Over a span of twelve years, Xenia sat behind me many times, as we progressed from giggly girls to teens with crushes to seniors cracking jokes in study hall. Because Xenia also went to Emory, we continued to see each other during college. The other room-mate, Susan, had been a member of the drill team, part of the popular crowd. Although I had nothing in common with Susan, when Xenia asked me to be their third roommate, I said yes.

In a northern suburb of Atlanta, near the Shallowford Road exit off I-85, a cluster of apartment complexes had sprung up around the freeway, forming a village of swinging singles. We chose Georgetown Apartments because the two-story units looked like red brick townhouses. Each complex featured loud, boozy parties around the pool on weekends, which my roommates loved. Annoying for me in the summer, fine during the year when I had evening concerts. Since Xenia and Susan were good friends, they shared the large bedroom; I had the one barely large enough for my double bed.

Chapter 12: Downward Spiral

The eventful summer ended with another big change—the Atlanta Symphony's move in the fall of 1968 to Symphony Hall, our own space in the newly built Woodruff Memorial Arts Center on Peachtree Street in midtown Atlanta. Rehearsals started at 10:00 a.m., long after the early rush hour, so I could whiz down I-85 from my apartment to Symphony Hall in seventeen minutes.

Walking from the parking lot into the arts center for the first rehearsal, excitement over seeing the new hall was mixed with anxiety about Warren. I wondered if he would greet me warmly or with the hostility he'd shown at the end of last season.

As I stepped onto the stage of Symphony Hall, the sheer grandeur of the space overwhelmed me, pushing aside all thoughts of Warren. The light-colored wood of the stage floor gleamed, the pale beige panels along the back wall towered several stories above the stage floor, and the three-tiered hall shimmered with the bright gold and crystal of the chandeliers, set against the deep, rich red of the velvet seats. It even smelled better than the musty old Municipal Auditorium—newly varnished wood with a hint of citrus. Symphony Hall was bigger than the auditorium, but because of the steeply banked seats, the audience seemed much closer to the stage, even in the second balcony. It felt both intimate and elegant.

Summoning the friendliest smile I could manage, I sat down next to Warren. He stared straight ahead, refusing to acknowledge my presence. Disappointed, for a few moments I failed to notice one of the best changes: the chairs for the musicians had the customary black seats and backs, but with more cushioning and a better ergonomic shape than the seats in the old hall. Well-designed for long hours of sitting. Perhaps in the comfortable seats of a new hall, Warren and I could start anew—no tension, no resentment, no fear.

The opening concert of Shaw's second season with the orchestra featured Mendelssohn's Symphony No. 4. When we rehearsed the first movement, we were delighted to find we could hear each other on stage, a rare but crucial feature of the acoustics in concert halls. My anxiety about Warren diminished as the rehearsal proceeded smoothly, conductor and orchestra savoring various aspects of our new home.

The next day, we rehearsed the symphony's last movement, an allegro with lots of rapid articulation in the woodwinds (like saying *tut-tut-tut* many times per second). Right before the first exposed flute duet, Warren gestured with the end of his flute as if he were going to come in slightly early, a subtle but definitive movement that almost made me jump in too soon. The question I'd repressed last year surfaced again: *Is Warren trying to sabotage me?* Years of trusting him made me dismiss the thought. Surely, it had been an inadvertent movement. Though rattled, I was eager to rehearse the lovely flute duet in the slow movement. We had played only two bars of the haunting passage when Shaw stopped the orchestra.

"We need more second flute," Shaw said, looking at me. "Both flutes are equally important here." When we resumed and I played louder, Shaw rewarded me with one of his rare smiles.

"Now you're too loud," Warren hissed as soon as the duet was over. "Can't you hear that?" His harsh tone felt like a punch in the gut. Should I acquiesce to the conductor or to my former teacher?

During the rest of the rehearsal, Warren glared at me several times. Was I still too loud? After the rehearsal, I left in a hurry, eager to escape Warren's disapproving scowls. On the drive back to the apartment, I tried to make sense of the conflicting directions from Shaw and Warren. Warren had played the piece many times in his twenty years with the orchestra, whereas Shaw had been mostly a choral conductor. Maybe there was something about the flute passage that Warren understood but Shaw didn't. Or were they both right—was I too soft at first, then too loud because I didn't hear the subtle difference?

When I got to the apartment, I tried to explain to my roommates what had upset me about the rehearsal, including doubts about whether I should even be in the symphony.

"Wait a minute," Xenia said, "if Mr. Little didn't think your playing was good enough, he wouldn't have let you into the symphony."

"Maybe I was good enough then, but the orchestra's a lot better now."

When Xenia referred to Warren as Mr. Little, I remembered the years of lessons with him, when he'd been unfailingly kind and supportive. As his student, I'd been confident in my skills as a flutist; as his colleague, my confidence was crumbling. If I started calling him Mr. Little again, would it bring back the comfortable teacher/student relationship? Did I want that?

"Besides," Susan jumped in, "it's just a rehearsal. You have another one tomorrow, right?"

"Yes, but - "

"Hey, it's Tuesday," Susan said brightly. "No one expects you to be perfect at the second rehearsal. That's what rehearsals are for." *True for the high school drill team*, I wanted to say, *but you understand nothing about professional orchestras.*

"I'm not talking about perfection," I tried again. "I'm talking about which boss to obey when one tells me to play louder, the other says softer."

"Oh, Ernie," Xenia said, "don't worry about it. Playing music is what you've always wanted to do. Just enjoy it."

Xenia didn't know any more about classical music than Susan. She did, however, know me better, and she was right—playing in a professional orchestra had been my dream. But not like this.

The next two rehearsals were better. Warren glared at me a few times after exposed flute passages, but at least he didn't say anything. Thursday night at the first performance, three movements were fine, but in the final allegro, right before the last flute duet, Warren gestured with the end of his flute, a half-second early. Again, instead of reacting to the gesture, I came in precisely with him. After working with him for so many hours, my sixth sense about when he was going to play was more trustworthy than his slight movements. The other performances were without incident. Perhaps I'd imagined the whole thing.

Despite my father's confidence in his car selection, a few weeks after the concerts featuring Mendelssohn's Symphony No. 4, the Mustang's transmission gave out. Though only three years old, it had over 100,000 miles on it. Resigned to draining my bank account, I replaced the bald tires along with the transmission. My first trip in the restored Mustang was a Saturday night trip to Tallahassee for a flute lesson Sunday morning with famed flutist Albert Tipton, who had recently joined the faculty at Florida State University. After playing the first half of a symphony concert (no second flute parts on the second half), I started the four-hour drive at 9:15 p.m. I'd planned to be in the motel room by 1:30 a.m., enough time to sleep, eat breakfast, and warm up for my 10:00 a.m. lesson the next day.

For the first half hour, I sang along with a popular radio station — the Beatles, the Supremes, Marvin Gaye, the occasional Simon and Garfunkel. There was something brazen about leaving a symphony concert at intermission — a musician playing hooky — and I savored each mile in my well-cared-for Mustang. Leaving town also gave me a brief reprieve from the escalating problems with Warren. After struggling through rehearsals and concerts all week, I felt exuberant driving to Florida, by myself, late at night, in my cool Mustang.

About halfway to Tallahassee it started raining, and as I approached the Florida border, it became a deluge. I could barely see the poorly lit, two-lane road. As I went around a curve, two blinding headlights came straight at me. I swerved to the right, avoiding a collision, but the slick road put the car into a spin. It slid off the road, rolled over a couple of times down an embankment, and landed, right side up, in a ditch about twenty feet below the road. Thank God I had my seat belt on; it probably saved my life. Though I felt shaken, my injuries seemed to be minor. My lovely, sassy Mustang, however, was crumpled in heartbreaking ways, and I now had the problem of how to get to Tallahassee, still twenty miles away.

I put the flute case inside my raincoat, struggled out of the car, and grabbed my small suitcase. After slipping and sliding up the embankment, I reached the highway and stuck out my thumb. Perhaps if the wrecked car had been visible from the road, I might have gotten a ride quickly. Huddled into my raincoat, trying to keep the flute case dry, I waited for what seemed like hours. Finally, a beat-up truck pulled over, driven by an older guy wearing a rumpled plaid flannel shirt and dirty overalls.

"Where ya headed?" he asked, slurring his words, which accentuated his southern drawl.

"Tallahassee," I replied. "Can you take me there?"

"Sure, hop right on in."

Fully drenched, one hand clutching the flute to my chest, the other gripping the small suitcase, I climbed into the truck and wedged the suitcase by my feet. After a few miles, the driver pulled over and stopped the truck.

"Why are you stopping?" I asked.

Instead of answering, he put his arm around my right shoulder, pulled me toward him, and started kissing my neck, his breath a foul mixture of onions, tobacco, and alcohol. After trying to pull away, I finally yelled at him.

"I just wrecked my car! Can you please just take me to Tallahassee?"

He continued to paw at me until I burst into tears, a lucky move on my part because, for this guy, crying was a turnoff. He released me abruptly.

"How much money ya got?" he asked.

"Twenty-five dollars." A lie. A smart one, I hoped.

He grunted. "Gimme all your money and I'll take ya there."

Twenty minutes later, we came to a stoplight on the outskirts of the city. "Here's my house," I said brightly, pointing vaguely to a residential street. Another lie. I wasn't about to let this character know I had a motel room.

After dragging my suitcase a few blocks, I checked into the motel about 2:30 a.m. Relieved to have the ordeal behind me, I sank gratefully into a lumpy bed, expecting to fall asleep right away. But there was one last aggravation—a rowdy party next door. Even with a pillow jammed over my head I couldn't block out the loud music and raucous laughter, which continued for another hour. The next morning, extremely sore and sleep-deprived, I called my insurance agent to report the accident, then took a taxi to Mr. Tipton's house.

"Where's your car?" Mr. Tipton asked. After telling him the saga, omitting the advances of the drunk guy, he asked, "Are you sure you want a lesson?"

"I would hate to drive all the way down here just to wreck my car," I said.

The lesson went surprisingly well, but I still had to get back to Atlanta, and the only option available was a Greyhound bus. My sore neck and bruised body felt every bump on that eleven-hour bus ride. By the next day, the entire left side of me was a mural of blues, purples, and browns—not only painful but disappointing, because I'd bought a new bikini for the upcoming ASO trip to Florida (again). And sure enough, my colorful blue-and-green suit was upstaged by the far more colorful bruises.

The insurance company declared the Mustang a total loss. My father, who knew everything about the wreck except details about the truck driver, once again found a bargain: a four-door 1963 Plymouth Valiant, a grandma-mobile to replace my beloved Mustang. It did share one feature with the Mustang: it was white.

———

That fall, my third season with the symphony, Warren's remarks became increasingly derogatory. He didn't bombard me, opting instead for the occasional, well-timed insult after an important second flute part: "Is that your cheap Artley flute?", "Do you ever practice?", "You're not cut out for a professional orchestra." And the one that worried me the most: "I hope you know we usually change second flutists every two years."

Sometimes, with a look of absolute fury on his red face, Warren repeatedly grabbed his right knee (he sat immediately to my left), conveying the message that he was so annoyed by my playing he could hardly stand it. I can still see the prominent black hairs on the fingers of Warren's right hand, and the image still makes me queasy.

After one particularly difficult rehearsal, Lynette, the second bassoonist, caught up with me as I was walking to my car.

"Hey, Warren was really riding you today," Lynette said, looking concerned. I kept walking, eager to get away.

"I think I was too loud or something," I mumbled, opening the car door. Lynette didn't take the hint.

"No, you weren't. He's trying to undermine you," she insisted, moving closer. "I don't understand why he's doing this to you." I fought the tears that threatened my composure, embarrassing because I barely knew Lynette. Like the other musical hotshots Shaw had hired, she intimidated me.

"Oh, I'm so sorry, I didn't mean to upset you," she said.

"It's fine, I'm just . . . it's hard sometimes. But thanks." I slipped into the car and left.

As I drove to the apartment, I thought about Lynette's words. I decided she must have misheard. Warren wasn't trying to undermine me; he criticized me because my playing was getting worse. I would simply have to practice harder. For the hundredth time, I wished I could talk to someone who understood the situation, wished my roommates were musicians—or at least closer so I could tell them how upset I was.

A few days later, Michael asked me to meet him in the concert hall lobby during a rehearsal break.

"I wanted to suggest something to you," Michael said, as we sat down on one of the lobby's cushioned benches.

"Sure, what is it?" I asked.

"I think you'd benefit from seeing a psychiatrist," he said. He could be very forthright.

"What?" I frowned, not sure I wanted to hear more.

"I've been seeing a terrific guy. His name is Nathan Norton. I think you'd like him."

I didn't know what to say. On some level, I knew he was right—hadn't I just been wishing I could talk to someone? The fact that he was seeing this psychiatrist lessened the sting of his suggestion, but I was ashamed Michael had sensed my desperation.

"Look, don't take it the wrong way, but you seem . . . I don't know, different, more withdrawn. And the situation with Warren isn't helping. Here's the number," he said, handing me a small piece of paper as he got up to leave.

I sat in shocked silence. I'd tried so hard to hide my anxiety and self-doubt. Did Michael recommend a therapist because he thought I was about to be fired? Whatever his reasons, I decided to follow his advice.

After one meeting with Dr. Norton, he suggested I see him as a patient in the Psychoanalytic Institute, where he was in training to be an analyst. To be admitted, I filled out a lengthy application form and was interviewed by a panel of supervising psychiatrists. When they selected me, I felt relieved and slightly insulted. Though time-consuming, the cost was minimal: four sessions a week, $3.50 per session, patient lying on a couch, analyst listening. It would have been five sessions, but I had two rehearsals on Wednesdays. I didn't know much about psychoanalysis, other than the importance of dreams in getting to the root of whatever problems the patient experienced.

Dr. Norton rarely said anything beyond, "Our time is up," but I suppose voicing my feelings was helpful. He encouraged me to explore the dynamics of my family of origin, so I spent a lot of time describing my father's disappointment in me, and how inferior I felt to my older sister, whom Daddy adored. I didn't see how this would help the tense situation with Warren, or my growing doubts about my playing, but at least I could talk to someone who listened. Despite his silence—or maybe because of it—I quickly transferred my yearning for a father to him. I spent countless sessions trying to get him to react. Whenever he uttered a few words, I seized upon them as if they were precious gems, turning them over and over in my mind.

As the weeks passed, while my feelings for Dr. Norton deepened, my doubts about being in psychoanalysis increased. As an analyst in training, Dr. Norton had to focus on childhood issues. But I had more pressing problems.

"This morning Warren's scowling was even worse than usual," I said during one of my sessions.

"And you think he was scowling at you," Dr. Norton said.

"Yes, as I've told you, his scowls are always directed at me."

"Why did he do that today?"

"I guess I must've been out of tune. It's strange, though, I really thought the intonation in the woodwinds was good. We were rehearsing the overture to Mendelssohn's *A Midsummer Night's Dream.* The opening chords are tricky to tune, but to me they sounded fine today."

"Is it his job to let you know when you're out of tune?" Dr. Norton asked.

"To some extent, but usually a principal player will say something like, 'I think you're a little sharp there.' Warren just glares at me."

Silence.

"In most sections, if there's a problem, players get together during a break and go over the passage. Whenever I ask Warren to do that, he refuses. Last week, his response was, 'It's your fault, you fix it.'"

More silence.

"I don't know what else I can do," I continued, though it felt like I was talking to myself. "I frequently work with a tuner, and I'm always listening carefully, trying to match his pitch."

No comment.

"When he keeps grabbing his knee, it's like my playing is driving him nuts."

"How do you know his gesture has anything to do with you?" Dr. Norton asked.

"I'm sitting next to him, and he always does it right after I play an important part."

"Could you be mistaken about why he does that?"

"I don't think so. The timing can't be coincidental. He just isn't happy with my playing. And neither am I."

Silence.

"He used to say I had a great ear, that my intonation was excellent."

"When was that?" he asked. Finally, a reaction.

"When I was his student, in high school."

"I see. You've said your father was very critical of you. Was that also in high school?" he asked.

"Yes, but I'm talking about what happened today, in rehearsal, just two hours ago."

Silence.

"You think I'm making this up, but I swear it's real, and it's happening more and more."

"Even if it is real, you might be making it more significant than it really is," he said.

"But in a professional orchestra, if I'm out of tune that means I'm not playing well, and that is significant. In that case, Warren should let me know, but when all he does is shake his head and grab his knee, it doesn't help."

"Our time is up. Next time, perhaps we can talk more about your father."

As usual, I left the session annoyed and confused, doubting my perception of things. I knew Dr. Norton had a valid point: Warren's behavior upset me more because of the distant (at best) relationship with my father. But Dr. Norton didn't understand that for years, when it came to emotional support, Warren *was* my father. All through high school, Mr. Little had provided the very things my father was unable to give—belief in my musical abilities and pride in my achievements.

In addition to not recognizing my dependence on Warren's approval, Dr. Norton didn't understand the tense atmosphere of professional orchestra rehearsals. Non-musicians assume rehearsals are fun, but each rehearsal is like a three-hour audition, with conductor and players constantly assessing each other's performance. Unlike string players, who can hide in their sections, wind and percussion players face constant scrutiny.

Whenever Warren's insults made me doubt I was good enough to be in the orchestra, Dr. Norton suggested I'd imagined or exaggerated Warren's behavior. I didn't know whose opinion to trust—the therapist who thought I was overreacting, or the former mentor who thought I should be fired.

Later that fall, we played a program that included an arrangement of Bach's *Brandenburg* Concerto No. 4 that featured Warren and me as soloists, along with pianist Peter Serkin, the guest artist. For the performances, Warren and I stood beside the piano at the front of the stage, adding to the pressure. When we rehearsed the *Brandenburg*, Warren muttered demeaning things, just loud enough for me to hear. He said I was playing too loud; when I played more softly, Mr. Shaw sternly told me to play louder.

"I don't know how I'm going to get through these performances," I said to Dr. Norton on Tuesday. "Today's rehearsal was awful. Can you give me something to calm me down for the first concert?" I begged.

Silence.

"Look, maybe psychoanalysis doesn't usually involve drugs, but surely there are exceptions."

"You haven't asked before," Dr. Norton said.

"I've never been a featured soloist with Warren before. He hisses at me to be soft, then Shaw tells me to be louder. Plus, the glaring," I said.

"If you're both soloists, isn't looking at you part of staying together?"

"No, it's not like that. We stay together by watching Shaw."

"How would a pill help?"

"Nerves make it harder to breathe deeply. Can't you, just this once, prescribe something to at least take the edge off?" I asked again.

Silence.

"This is *not* about my father. I wish you could see that." Time was up. I left frustrated. And very anxious about the performance.

At the beginning of the concert Thursday night, my breathing was shallow and my fingers trembled. The *Brandenburg* was second on the program, after the overture to Wagner's *Die Meistersinger*. Maestro Shaw had programmed the spare, delicate *Brandenburg* to follow Wagner's triumphant, bombastic overture. I liked that order. Playing the Wagner calmed me down.

Right after the overture, the wind players left the stage so stagehands could move the piano and reset the stage for the smaller Bach orchestra.

"I've really enjoyed working with you two," Peter Serkin said, as we were waiting backstage. He made a point of looking at me as well as at Warren.

"It's been an honor to play with you," I said, surprising myself. We then walked on stage and took a bow. Before the flutes' first entrance, I had a wonderful insight: because we were at the front of the stage, in the spotlight, Warren couldn't harass me during the performances. With that reassuring thought, I relaxed and played well, all three concerts.

At our first rehearsal the next week, I felt pretty confident. Despite Warren's efforts to undermine me, I'd played well. While I was putting my flute together, right before the rehearsal started, Warren shattered my good mood with a devastating comment.

"I'm going to get you fired, and if you even think about filing an appeal with the union board, remember, I am the president." Warren was a powerful person in the Atlanta music community; I took his threat seriously.

The Atlanta Symphony rehearsals were two-and-a-half to three hours long. Each week we had five rehearsals and three performances; a typical week included about thirteen hours of rehearsals and six to seven hours of concerts. It may not sound like a lot, but each of those hours I was sitting less than two feet from Warren. Every week I considered quitting. The dream job had become a nightmare.

The unrelenting problems with Warren would have been easier to handle if I'd had a therapist who understood the situation better, or a trusted friend to confide in, or even better, a loving relationship. Months of yearning for Michael convinced me I would never attract anyone desirable. The destruction of my confidence as a musician seeped into my self-assurance as a woman: I may have thought I wanted a loving relationship, but deep down I felt unworthy of one. Instead, I had one-night stands with a couple of men in the orchestra and a few I met at the apartment complex—men who sensed my willingness to have a casual sexual encounter. Physically satisfying sex left me feeling desolate, triggering only partly controlled weeping. Perhaps the physical release brought a sudden, sharp awareness of how meaningless, how *un*loving the sex was, and how degraded it made me feel. I quickly learned to postpone the weeping until I was, again, alone.

The previous summer, when I'd listened to Bach's Mass in B Minor in my attempt to impress Michael, I'd been drawn to Florence Kopleff's poignant rendering of the *Agnus Dei*. When cheap sex and Warren's abuse threatened to overwhelm me, I turned to that music, playing Kopleff's *Agnus Dei* over and over while I sobbed, pleading with a God I didn't believe in to take away my misery.

After weeks of therapy, I gave up trying to explain the problems with Warren to Dr. Norton. Bowing to his direction, I focused on my father's preference for Melinda and his contempt for me when I chose music as a career. Becoming estranged from my roommates and with no friends in the orchestra, I turned more and more to Dr. Norton for emotional support. He didn't say much, but at least he was always there—even during concerts. Dr. Norton had season tickets to the symphony—Friday night, front row loge, stage left, very close to the string bass section. It was disconcerting to see him, with his wife and two young daughters, so close to the stage.

One Friday night, the second piece on the concert had no second flute part. Instead of waiting downstairs in one of the musicians' warm-up rooms, I stood backstage, peeking through a crack in the stage scaffolding where I could see Norton and his family. While I watched, the most extraordinary thing happened: Norton's younger daughter, about seven years old, crawled into his lap and laid her head against his chest—my fantasy, played out before my eyes. The longing that engulfed me was so powerful I gasped.

As I watched, I became more and more distressed. How could he allow his daughter to do that? I was never allowed to sit in my father's lap even at home, much less at a concert. I desperately, obsessively wanted to be that little girl. Watching them made me nauseated and disoriented, but I could not tear myself away from that peephole.

The image of Norton's daughter in his lap haunted me all weekend. In Monday's therapy session, I didn't want to confess what I'd done, so I skittered from topic to topic. Finally, at the end of the session, I admitted I'd spied on him and that I'd seen his daughter sitting in his lap. I felt shamed, as if I'd broken into his home and stolen something. Dr. Norton was silent until I opened the door to leave, when he said, "You seem to think you've done something wrong."

He said it—or did I imagine this?—gently, almost tenderly. For days I mulled over that comment. It was, after all, at the heart of my problems: Was longing for physical affection from a father wrong? Could I admit to myself how much I wanted a father who cared for me, who was demonstrative, who took an interest in my life—even in my musical life? I pushed away the painful thoughts, frightened by the intensity of the longing.

As winter approached, my depression deepened. I became more and more isolated, avoiding even the briefest interactions with people. My attachment to Dr. Norton weakened when he failed to understand the effects of Warren's behavior. Repeated attempts to talk to my roommates simply underscored how little we had in common. And day after day, my former mentor disparaged me. My world shrank until only one thing seemed real: Warren's contempt for me. I was a failure as a flutist. I was a failure, period.

One Friday evening in mid-December, I struggled to focus on playing my part during a performance of Robert Shaw's lovely Christmas choral program. Most members of the orchestra had been delighted to replace the traditional *Nutcracker* with Shaw's inspired program of Christmas music featuring his extraordinary choir. But I'd barely made it through last night's performance without breaking down. I still had to play the rest of tonight's and Sunday afternoon's concerts.

Christmas. Loving families giving presents to each other, sharing holiday meals. I hadn't been part of a happy family for a long time, and the increased intensity of Warren's attacks made this Christmas especially hard. Music had always been my solace, a way to both express and escape from emotional turmoil. Far from comforting, music was now the source of the pain. Tonight the pure, sweet voice of the boy soprano singing Mozart's "Laudate Dominum" chipped away at my composure. Then, the beautiful sound of the choir engulfed me during the haunting selection from Berlioz's *L'enfance du Christ*, "The Shepherds' Farewell to the Holy Family."

Family. I hated that word. It meant belonging. Had I ever felt like I belonged?

Yes. Childhood Christmases—a sense of enchantment, decorating the tree and watching *Amahl and the Night Visitors* on our tiny TV, as a family. When my sister and I were little, each year Mother put aside marital and financial strife to create magical Christmases for us. But that was many years ago.

The walls of the hall closed in, squeezing me out. I couldn't stand seeing the happiness of others. I was the loner surrounded by groups: couples and families in the audience, singers together in the choir, friends in the orchestra—but not my friends. Warren had made it clear I didn't belong there. I was a fraud, a pretender. If not in the orchestra, where did I belong? Each note of the "Shepherds' Farewell" mocked me. The lush sound of the strings playing a slow, tender melody reminded me of my first orchestra rehearsal, six years ago, when I'd fallen in love with the orchestra. I'd wanted nothing more than to be part of that gorgeous sound. But tonight, that same beauty hurt. I wanted to run across the stage, screaming that I didn't belong, that an impostor was playing the second flute part.

I forced myself to play the rest of the program. As soon as the last note ended, I slammed the flute into its case, rushed off the stage, and drove recklessly to my apartment, running a red light at Fourteenth Street and edging the speedometer close to one hundred on the freeway. Tempting fate. Desperate to do something, anything, to avoid the incessant hours of Warren's ridicule. My father had been right all along: it was ludicrous to think I could be a successful musician. I could no longer maintain the facade, and I had no desire to do anything else.

I ran into the apartment. Not bothering to hang my coat in the front closet, I rushed up the stairs and shed my coat, shoes, and concert dress quickly. My roommates were at a late-night party; I had a couple of hours. In the small upstairs area, my bedroom was next to the bathroom. While the bathtub filled with hot water, the sobbing I'd held back all night began. Trembling, I took out a new razor blade and knelt on the tiled floor, almost touching the toilet a few feet away. Strangely, I thought about my roommates. I was careful to stay off the blue bathroom rug so I wouldn't stain it. To spare them the ordeal of dealing with my naked body, I kept my slip and underwear on, and draped my arms over the side of the tub. Surely it would work that way, as long as I kept my heart above my wrists.

With a savage, downward thrust, I sliced into my left wrist—straight across but deep. I screamed, more from despair than pain.

The blood was a shock, such a vivid contrast to the white tub and white-tiled floor. I watched it run down the side of the tub and flow into the water, then remembered to put my hand deeper in the water to increase the blood flow. As the tub filled, I became mesmerized by the gradual reddening of the water, wondering how dark it would eventually be. Resigned to my fate, now that I'd taken a decisive step, I pulled my weakened left hand out of the water and transferred the razor to that hand, ready to cut into my right wrist.

Then, something jolted me. Suddenly, I couldn't go through with it. I became obsessed with the what-ifs: What if I maimed myself but didn't die? What if I lost the use of one or both hands? Or, in the short term, what if I did just enough damage to prevent me from playing the concert Sunday? I couldn't let Warren know how weak I was; he would use a suicide attempt as proof I was unfit for the job. Either I had to make sure I ended my life or I needed to seek medical help right away. Perhaps the will to live took over. Or some shred of pride in my playing. Whatever it was, I stopped sobbing and switched my focus to covering up the failed attempt. After opening the tub's drain, I hurriedly wrapped a towel around my wrist, threw on some clothes, and drove to the Emory University Hospital emergency room.

When I arrived, a nurse quickly assessed the wound, rewrapped it more tightly in my bloody towel, and told me to keep my wrist elevated above my heart. After I'd waited about an hour, an exhausted intern stitched me up, ignoring the psychic pain other than to ask, "Is there someone you can call?"

"No, no one."

On the drive back to the apartment, I kept my left hand immobile—tricky with a stick shift. I arrived around 2:00 a.m., after my roommates had returned from their party and gone to bed. I lay awake, torn between disappointment and relief. Sometime after 3:30 a.m., the combination of blood loss and painkillers put me to sleep.

As soon as I awoke the next day, I tried bending my wrist. The pain and stiffness made it difficult, and I wondered if I'd be able to play the next day. Taking care to hide the bandage from my roommates, every hour I tried bending it a little more. Though it was painful, by the evening I was able to hold the flute, and by Sunday I had enough control back in my left hand to get through the concert. The long sleeves of the concert dress hid the bandaging. Only one person noticed.

"So, you botched that too," Warren said, with a derisive laugh.

I hid the suicide attempt from everyone—my roommates, symphony people, my parents. If I'd said anything to Mother or Daddy, they would've, like Warren, viewed the incident as confirmation that I was a failure. Besides, in our family you never talked about anything unpleasant. In therapy the following Monday, I wanted to talk about it but felt embarrassed because I hadn't gone through with it. How serious could it be? I waited till the end of the hour, then said, almost casually, "I got very depressed at the concert Friday night and cut my wrist."

Instead of asking more about it, Dr. Norton remained in his tight-lipped, distant analyst role. That hurt. I hadn't realized how desperately I'd wanted some overt support from him. I left the session almost as depressed as I'd been Friday night. In the following weeks, I often asked myself why I hadn't gone through with it; at other times I minimized the whole thing—just a little nick in my wrist, nothing really.

Was it a turning point? A year later, I recognized the attempt as the nadir, but at the time it didn't seem that way. Despite all the drama, nothing had changed; my former teacher continued to torment me.

It took several months to climb out of the pit of depression, a journey that included several setbacks when despair and self-doubt threatened to drag me back down, but those spells became increasingly short, and the periods between, longer. When I had recovered enough to be a more detached observer, I noticed that I wasn't the only target of Warren's ridicule. Although the majority of his grimaces were directed toward me, Warren also showed contempt for the outstanding musicians around him—the principal players in the oboe, clarinet, and bassoon sections, those very musicians I so admired. I knew his criticisms of them had no merit; perhaps it was time to question his censure of me. But for every three steps forward in reassessing my flute abilities, I took one step back. Sometimes two.

Chapter 13: Recovery

Professional orchestras have two kinds of tours—the one- or two-day runouts to neighboring towns, and longer tours ranging from a week to a month or more. Each season, the Atlanta Symphony typically had several runouts plus one or two extended tours. Unless the distance was longer than a seven-hour drive, we traveled by Greyhound bus. Most of the men in the orchestra, both young and old, were married; the handful of young women were single. There were several older women in the orchestra, all married. These mostly married men and mostly single young women were thrown together for long bus rides, mediocre hotel meals, stressful concerts, and late-night drinking, for days, sometimes weeks.

A typical tour day began with four to six hours' travel on the bus, followed by hotel check-in, a quick dinner, and the concert. Some nights we performed in a nice city auditorium, other nights in an aging high school gymnasium. On the buses people sat in groups that reflected the natural social divisions within an orchestra, divisions based on a combination of age and instrument. Sheer proximity in rehearsals meant violinists got to know one another, as did those in the woodwind section, etcetera. There were three married couples in the symphony; two sat with their spouses, while Warren and Jane did not.

During my first year in the orchestra, choosing a seat was awkward. Warren sat with his buddies—older players, mostly from the string sections, who had been in the orchestra for many years. Jane Little sat with her fellow bass players. After the first tour, I avoided Warren's bus. Being a little shy and knowing no one except Warren, I joined the loners in the front of the bus, the avid readers who ignored each other. When Warren's treatment of me worsened, I became even more withdrawn. Sitting by myself reflected the isolation I felt.

In the middle of my third year, as I recovered from depression, I began to interact with the recently hired wind players who were about my age. Before long I sat with them on tours. They welcomed me into their group, reawakened my sense of humor, and greatly accelerated my recovery. Our mostly woodwind bus group included two string players—Karen, the youngest member of the first violin section, and Judy, a violist in her late forties who was eager to befriend the new members of the orchestra. She and her husband, Tom (a non-musician), frequently invited young musicians to their dinner parties. Russ Bedford, the principal bassoonist, usually sparked conversation with his clever, wicked sense of humor, but we all joined in—puns, witticisms, and an abundance of double entendres, fired at rapid speed. On longer bus rides, we played made-up word games and worked together on *New York Times* crossword puzzles.

The group often went out for drinks after concerts. For the first time in my life, I got to unwind with friends who understood and shared the stresses and joys of playing in a professional orchestra. To alleviate the tedium of being on the road day after day, we occasionally did some zany things. One night during a weeklong tour, we performed in an excellent hall—reverberant but not echoey, with lots of wood. We played the best concert of the tour, one of those nights when everything clicked, conductor and orchestra perfectly in sync. The standing ovation must have lasted six or seven minutes. Even Warren seemed pleased. At the Ramada Inn bar, in our post-concert exuberance, a few of us exceeded our usual single-drink limit, though alcohol was redundant—we were already high from the concert.

"Hey, you guys, I've got an idea," Russ said after his second martini. I'd opted for my usual gin and tonic and accepted Lynette's offer to split a second one.

"What's that?" asked Elwood, the lone brass player (French horn) in our group. True to brass-player form, he stuck with beer.

"Well," Russ said with a twinkle in his eye, "let's test the Magic Fingers," referring to the hotel bed's massage-for-a-quarter.

"Okay, I'm in!" said Lynette. "We can use my room."

"What exactly do you have in mind?" I asked.

"Let's see," Russ said, looking around the table, "there are eight of us."

"Here's the plan," he continued while we took the elevator, then filed into Lynette's room. "We'll create a pile of three layers of bodies, the three biggest on the bottom, three next-biggest in the middle, two smallest on top."

"I don't know about this," said Joe, by far the most reserved member of the group except for me, but I was changing.

"Wait, you haven't heard the goal of the experiment: we're going to see if the top layer—Ernestine and Lynette—can feel the Magic Fingers vibrations through two layers of bodies, a sort of princess and the pea experiment." Russ looked pleased; Joe looked doubtful.

"Oh, come on, Joe, it'll be fun," Lynette said.

Trying to keep giggling to a minimum, and with some clumsy maneuvering, we climbed onto the shiny blue-and-green bedspread and constructed the pyramid. As usual, we'd all changed out of our concert clothes; that night, fortunately, the women were wearing long pants. On the bottom, Russ had his quarter ready, and after a little shifting of bodies, slipped the coin in. The bed began to drone, loudly.

"I definitely feel movement," Russ said. "How about you, second layer?"

"There's . . ." pause for laughing, "definitely wiggling. Does that count?" Elwood asked. "How about you, top layer?"

Lynette and I, between fits of giggling, reported that the experiment had failed due to a design flaw: mattress vibrations were impossible to detect through bodies that were laughing. Shortly after disassembling the pyramid, the party broke up. I hadn't acted that silly or felt that happy in a long time.

The last night of the tour we stayed in a Howard Johnson's motel in Tallahassee, Florida. I expected Howard Johnson's to have a grungy bar, but the dark wood paneling and subdued lighting gave the small bar an air of intimacy. Best of all, no live band, only soft jazz in the background. Among the first to arrive, Lynette and I sat on barstools and ordered gin and tonics. The rest of the group trickled in, some joining us at the bar, others seated at tables.

"What's wrong?" Lynette asked a few minutes later.

I raised my eyebrows and tilted my head slightly to my left, where Warren had sat down. Definitely not part of our group.

"Shoot," Lynette said, "do you want to move?"

"Maybe, in a bit," I said, wondering why Warren had chosen to sit there. I turned to take a sip of my drink.

"So here we are," Warren said, with something between a smile and a smirk. Lynette turned away to talk to Russ.

"Yes, we are. I thought the concert went pretty well," I said, an attempt at normalcy.

"Except for the trumpets," Warren said. "Out of tune, as usual."

"You mean in the third movement of the concerto?"

"For starters. It was even worse in the Beethoven," he said, referring to the *Eroica Symphony*. "So, what are you drinking? Looks like a G and T. Appropriate for a southern girl."

"More than Kentucky bourbon?" I asked, eager to move away from the topic of who had played poorly. At least he hadn't criticized me—yet.

"More a man's drink," Warren said, lifting his glass of amber-colored liquid. His smile seemed less sneery.

"I guess you're right. My father has a glass of Evan Williams every night when he gets home from work."

We proceeded to have a faux normal conversation. As soon as I began to relax my guard, Warren put his hand on my left thigh, then snaked it up my back and around my right shoulder. Before I grasped what was happening, he pulled me close to him.

"You know," he whispered, "there is one way your troubles could all go away."

I jerked away from him, got up, and walked toward the farthest table.

"Or you could just be fired," he added in a loud voice as I moved away from him.

In 1969, few people talked about sexual harassment. But even if I'd known the phrase, it wouldn't have mattered. One pass/threat had little effect on me; it was the daily denigration of my playing that destroyed my confidence. I was more surprised than offended.

―――

Not long after the tour, we played a program that included Béla Bartók's imaginative, virtuosic Concerto for Orchestra. Just as a concerto for an instrument showcases that instrument,

Bartók's work puts the spotlight on each instrument in the orchestra, with challenging parts for everyone. The work is filled with exposed flute duets that require the second flute to be as loud as the first flute. Warren didn't like that. Two years ago, this would've prompted the familiar seesaw of Warren shushing me, Shaw asking me to play louder, and me getting flustered. But I'd discovered an effective coping strategy, one I wouldn't have had the guts to do even a few months ago: ignore Warren. Shaw certainly liked it. Instead of constantly asking me to play louder, Shaw nodded and smiled after the prominent duet passages. This did not improve things in the flute trenches.

Early in the first movement of the Concerto, there's a short, expressive flute solo. The first time Warren played it, I tapped my hand on my left knee in approval (the musician's quiet alternative to clapping). I did not do it hoping Warren would treat me better; I knew that was unlikely. I did it because he played it well. Regardless of how he treated me, Warren was a very good flutist. I liked the way he shaped not only that passage but also the cadenza at the end of the fourth movement. I tapped after that one too. Maybe Warren thought I was doing it to curry favor, or maybe he was annoyed because Shaw had smiled at me. Whatever the reason, the frowns, headshaking, and complaints about my being too loud continued the rest of the week. At the end of the last rehearsal, as we were putting our flutes away, Warren made a strange comment.

"You and I will never get along because you have the same birthday as my wife," he said with some vehemence. I was bewildered. Why did he compare me with his wife, and how the heck did he know my birthday?

During my five years of weekly lessons, when I was so attached to Mr. Little, I never thought about his love life. That changed suddenly freshman year when Anne told me about seeing Mr. Little with our schoolmate Lenore. Anne and I had found it both shocking and funny. Here was our idol, someone who'd seemed far removed from our teenage world, appearing in the small, drab lobby of the freshman dorm. But now it didn't seem so funny. Now I wondered if Lenore was an isolated case, or one in a series of affairs. Had Jane been the first one to cheat on their marriage? It seemed logical; she was much better-looking than her husband.

When I told Lynette about Warren's strange comment, she had a theory. Lynette and I had become much closer since we'd been roommates on several tours.

"I think Warren is attracted to you," she said.

"Oh, come on, that's ridiculous."

"Why is it ridiculous? How many pretty young women does he know, much less sit beside each day?" she asked.

"If that were true, though, why would he try to sabotage me?"

"I don't know exactly. But I bet there's a connection, even if it's just subconscious."

"During all my years of private lessons, Warren never said or did anything inappropriate."

"I'm not saying he thought about you that way when you were a kid, or even a teenager, but since you joined the symphony, he's seen you every day, for years now. And when you think about it, there's some resemblance. Both you and Jane are short, petite, pretty brunettes. Maybe you remind him of Jane when she was younger, when the two of them were in love."

Lynette was a wise woman, two years older and with far more experience in the world. I trusted her instincts, but I thought her theory far-fetched. Whether as a teacher or a section leader, Warren was the one with the power, the one I had to please. The suggestion that I had something he wanted didn't line up with my perception of things. Whether or not

Warren found me attractive, one thing was clear: Warren's marital problems added to his unhappiness during the years I was in the orchestra.

———

That spring I noticed an ad in the musicians' union paper about the Florida International Music Festival with the London Symphony Orchestra (LSO), an eight-week program where students were coached by members of the LSO and played in their own orchestra of advanced students and young professionals. (The ASO's season ran from September through May.) Based on my résumé and a tape from my senior recital at Emory, I was accepted. I hoped getting away from Atlanta would accelerate my recovery.

The first day of the festival, each of the seven participating flutists played for Geoffrey Gilbert, former principal flutist with the Royal Philharmonic Orchestra and occasional guest principal with the LSO. Mr. Gilbert helped direct the program, gave flute master classes, and conducted woodwind sectional rehearsals. I might have approached the audition with confidence; after all, I was probably the only flutist there who played in a major symphony orchestra. But I hid that fact, embarrassed, assuming everyone would think, as I did, that I'd sneaked into the ASO—a fluke, explained by my having been a student of the principal flutist.

Mr. Gilbert gathered us all in one room, so we heard each other's auditions. Listening to the other flutists play, I thought each one sounded fabulous. By the time Mr. Gilbert turned to me to play, I was a wreck. My sound tightened up, my fingers shook badly, and my brain couldn't make sense of the sight-reading. The audition results confirmed my worst fear: I was placed last chair.

The rest of that first day, I sank back into despair. The progress I'd made since December seemed to evaporate, and for the first time since the suicide attempt, I felt hopeless. I thought about calling Dr. Norton, but what could he say? He'd never understood the competitive music world nor how damaging Warren's attacks were for me. He had no basis for judging my ability as a flutist. Today an objective assessment had been made by an expert flutist: I was the worst flutist there. I thought of looking for a place where I might slip into the ocean unobserved, but the temptation was brief, and unlike last December, I didn't stay in that dark place very long.

The next day, I recognized my self-destructive pattern of thinking and reminded myself that the audition hadn't represented my level of playing. And perhaps being the worst flutist in a competitive summer program didn't mean I was terrible. I soon learned that of the seven, I was both the only flutist in a major professional orchestra and the only one without conservatory training. The rest were from Eastman, Juilliard, and other top music schools. Sitting last chair to such pedigreed players didn't seem so shameful. Eager to improve Mr. Gilbert's opinion of me, a few days after the audition, I asked Mr. Gilbert if I could take a couple of private lessons from him.

"Before I take you on as a student," he said, "you need to deal with your psychological issues."

His words stung. Once I'd gotten over the initial shock, however, I found his comment oddly comforting. At least he had noticed. I'd held the negative thoughts inside for so long, it was affirming to have someone acknowledge their severity.

By the end of the week, after adjusting to the disgrace of sitting last chair, I woke up to the world around me. There it was—the ocean! In the late 1960s, Daytona Beach was much less crowded than it became a few years later. I gazed at the vast expanse of sky and sea, listened to the sounds of the waves and seagulls, smelled the salty air, and felt the sun on my face. I regained my equilibrium and didn't even mind the cheap, un-air-conditioned motel, where one large room housed over twenty women students, each with a footlocker and a single, uncomfortable cot.

Every few days we heard fabulous concerts given by the London Symphony Orchestra, under the sexy direction of André Previn. Occasionally, we glimpsed the glamorous stick figure of his wife, Mia Farrow. Previn conducted the student orchestra for our first performance. I played very little, merely doubling the second flute part in loud passages. Compared to Shaw, Previn struck me as very adept—certainly cleaner baton technique than Shaw—but not inspiring. Flashy and slick rather than impassioned.

Early in the second week, during a rehearsal break, a cute young man walked up to me and introduced himself. Gazing into his remarkable turquoise eyes, I wondered why I hadn't noticed him before. He was the timpanist, not really in my line of vision, but at the next rehearsal I turned in my seat to watch him. Few things are sexier than a good-looking guy playing the hell out of a big timpani part. (We were playing Britten's *The Young Person's Guide to the Orchestra*.) Rusty Simmons and I enjoyed a hot summer romance, facilitated by his having a car. Most of us had flown in from out of state, but he attended Stetson University in DeLand, Florida. Rusty's 1959 Ford Fairlane had a conveniently long and wide back seat.

Geoffrey Gilbert led woodwind sectional rehearsals for the student orchestra, and often targeted a group (flutes, oboes, etc.), going down the line of players to hear each person play a selected passage. He was making sure all of us had learned our parts, even the parts, like mine, that nobody would hear. During the weeks of the festival, Gilbert shuffled the flutes around, and in the fifth week assigned me the principal flute part for Prokofiev's *Lieutenant Kijé Suite,* a piece with lots of exposed flute parts, including one extensive, difficult solo.

The concert that week was conducted by the legendary Jascha Horenstein. Born in Russia and trained in Vienna, Horenstein first conducted the Vienna Symphony in 1923, at the age of twenty-five. He gained international fame through his recordings with many of Europe's leading orchestras and was best known for his interpretations of Mahler's symphonies. With his reputation as a tyrant, plus a Russian accent, bushy eyebrows, and ferocious stare, Maestro Horenstein inspired both awe and fear. When he worked on *Lieutenant Kijé,* most of his scathing remarks were for the brass players. At the first rehearsal, unhappy with the high French horn part toward the beginning of the final movement, he abruptly cut the orchestra off and, with a deep frown, pointed to the second chair hornist. "You, play the solo." The student hesitated, expecting Horenstein to lift his baton to rehearse the whole orchestra. "Now!" Horenstein shouted. When the rattled second chair hornist flubbed a note, Horenstein shouted, "Next!" and the third chair took a shot. One by one he went down the section of six, not happy with any of them. The poor guy who was principal ended up playing it, but Horenstein glared at him each time he played that solo. I was sorry for the horn player; I knew all too well how that felt. The rest of the brass were good, the principal trumpet, exceptional. Much to my relief, Horenstein never gave me or the piccolo player, who also had a number of solos, anything but encouraging smiles.

The summer that had begun in such a dismal way ended up not only restoring but adding to the confidence I'd regained since December. The ocean, wonderful music, working my way from last chair to first, and a summer romance. Now, alas, I had to return to Atlanta.

Chapter 14: Better Days

The fall of my fourth year in the orchestra had the opposite trajectory of the previous fall. Instead of a steady descent into depression, I felt better and better, building on the progress I'd made in reclaiming my self-assurance. For starters, Xenia and I moved into a three-bedroom apartment with Lee, a high school friend I felt closer to than Susan. In the smaller apartment, I often heard Susan and Xenia laughing in their bedroom, well into the night, which reinforced my feeling of being excluded. Separate bedrooms eliminated that.

A few weeks into the symphony season, Lynette invited me to join a woodwind quintet with several players in the symphony. After saying yes, I wondered if I'd be able to keep up with the group. All hired by Maestro Shaw, they were excellent players who had attended prestigious music schools where they had performed lots of chamber music. The horn player, Elwood White, had played in a quintet with all the first chair players (though he was assistant principal), but that quintet had fallen apart due to personality conflicts—mostly with Warren. My paltry quintet experience consisted of two summers at Brevard Music Center camp, way back in high school.

They'd scheduled a program in about a month that would feature Samuel Barber's *Summer Music.* When I saw the flute part for *Summer Music*, I almost backed out. The piece is beautiful but full of gnarly flute runs and passages with complicated rhythms (mixed, uneven meters). I was lucky the symphony music during those weeks was relatively easy, giving me plenty of time to conquer the fast runs in *Summer Music*.

One October afternoon, as I climbed the steep, carpeted stairs to the second floor of an old house, my heart raced as though I were about to walk on stage for a big solo performance instead of a casual first rehearsal of a chamber group. Bob Wingert, the clarinetist, and Elwood shared the top floor of an elegant Victorian house in Ansley Park. Lynette and Sandy Arenz, the oboist, were already there.

"Hey, Sandy, what did you think about Joe's Rossini today?" Lynette asked, as we put our instruments together. A few hours earlier, we'd played our first rehearsal on the week's symphony program, which included Rossini's *The Italian Girl in Algiers*. The piece opens with a long, lovely oboe solo.

"I thought he sounded great," Sandy said. "He was grousing about reeds, but geez, I don't know why, when he plays like that." We all agreed. To me, Joe always sounded terrific, but Sandy, a recent Indiana University graduate, had a keener ear for the finer points of oboe sound.

"Warren sounded pretty good too," I said. Unlike the principal oboe part, which has both slow, expressive solos and technically challenging ones, the flute has only very fast solos.

"It's nice of you to say that, given the way he treats you," Bob said.

"You know, he's been almost nice this week," I replied.

"Yes, because there aren't any important second flute parts," Lynette said. "Darn it, he shouldn't get away with all the stuff he does."

I switched the subject, returning to the discussion about the music the symphony was performing that week. Lynette had started the relaxed chitchat, which calmed me down. I suspect she'd planned that. Lynette's generous heart and fierce support of her friends became more and more apparent the better I got to know her.

"Well, shall we start with the hard one?" Bob asked, putting the clarinet part to *Summer Music* on his music stand.

"Sure, might as well tackle it while we're fresh," Elwood said.

When I missed an entrance in *Summer Music*, I was sure the others were wishing they had asked Anne, the flutist who played extra with the symphony, instead of me. I felt better after Elwood missed an entrance too.

"Hey, we got through it!" Bob exclaimed later, after he and I successfully negotiated the difficult runs that alternate between flute and clarinet. He looked at me and smiled. After that I relaxed and savored the new experience of playing chamber music with fine musicians. I was so in awe of their playing, I had to restrain myself from bombarding them with compliments. The atmosphere was one of congeniality and respect, the rewards of chamber music versus orchestra, where a conductor (or Warren) can humiliate you in front of ninety other musicians.

As I became more comfortable in the group, I gradually regained that fundamental joy of creating a beautiful sound simply by taking a deep breath and blowing into a silver tube, bringing an inert thing to life. Pretty weird when you think about it. In a woodwind quintet, I was surrounded by different but equally rich sounds, all made by using the breath. Although playing any instrument engages the body, it's more personal when you create the sound with your breath. Maybe that's why I love listening to great singers.

Playing chamber music is an intimate experience that includes breathing together, as well as making lots of eye contact during a performance. The flutist in a woodwind quintet usually leads the group when it begins to play, gesturing with a physical motion, or upbeat, that indicates the tempo. (Because flute is the only instrument held horizontally, it's easier for others in the group to see a subtle motion from the tip of the flute.) This little act of leadership added to my sense of being an equal member of the group.

At the time I didn't appreciate how exceptional the quintet was—not only good musicians but, more importantly, people who enjoyed each other's company. For every successful chamber music group there are dozens that split up over personality conflicts. Usually, one egotist in the group considers his (less often, her) ideas more valid than anyone else's, which destroys the natural give and take of collaborative rehearsals. In our rehearsals, we exchanged ideas freely, with no subtexts of power or hierarchy. All in our twenties, all except me (because of Warren) glad to have a job with a fine orchestra, we were a happy group.

For the concert I put my long hair in a French twist and wore my first miniskirt—a sleek, sleeveless crimson dress with a gently plunging neckline—with black sheer pantyhose. The gold and ruby (fake, but sparkly) choker necklace and dangling earrings completed the ensemble, garnering me appreciative comments backstage from Elwood (a whistle) and Lynette. But the elegant dress wasn't what gave me confidence; it was the welcoming acceptance into this group of excellent musicians. The Barber runs were flawless.

When we realized how compatible we were in rehearsals, the four of us who were single formed a dinner group. Monday through Thursday, one of us cooked for the other three. When it was my night, I cooked in Lynette's apartment, which was much closer to Bob and Elwood's house. Sharing good food and lively conversation, night after night, deepened our friendships.

It is impossible to overstate how much these friends bolstered my self-confidence. Their support was an antidote to Warren's constant denigration.

———————

During the weeks when the quintet was preparing for its concert, the ASO embarked on a ten-day tour. The concerts featured Igor Stravinsky's *Firebird Suite*, a five-movement work excerpted from the ballet of the same name. Written in 1909 for Sergei Diaghilev's Ballets Russes, it was the first of several collaborations between Stravinsky and Diaghilev. The excitement of the "Infernal Dance," the lovely gracefulness of the "Round Dance of the Princesses," and the beautifully paced buildup of its majestic finale make the *Firebird Suite* a favorite of symphony audiences. The second flute part has several charming solos in the slow movement, but the one flutists worry about is the first solo, which occurs at the beginning of the piece. Against a hushed background of low strings, the second flute enters in its low register, stating the foreboding theme. The solo goes down to low C-sharp, almost the lowest note on the flute, which is hard to project. I was relieved Shaw asked me to play louder only in the first rehearsal. After that he seemed pleased.

The night before the tour began, we played the third of our three concerts at home. When I arrived at the hall, the personnel manager rushed over and told me I'd be playing principal flute, that Warren had called in sick. I had ten minutes to go through the part. I didn't have time to be nervous. Because I'd heard the first flute part all week, I knew which passages to fake, which to leave out. Benson played my part. (Alas, the low-register solo was too soft.) The two fast movements weren't perfect, but I was pleased with the solos. Afterward, several woodwind and brass players told me I sounded as good as Warren. (String players didn't seem to notice the change.) That was the first of only two times Warren missed a concert. The other program featured Prokofiev's *Classical Symphony*, which is difficult but was less scary because I'd studied it in high school.

On our first tour concert, in Tallahassee, Florida, I again received positive feedback on my playing. Right after the concert, a young man ran up onto the stage and rushed over to me.

"Ernestine, your low register sounds fantastic! I was sitting in the back row of the hall, and it just boomed out," said Albert, a former flute student of Warren Little who was now a flute major at Florida State. (A few years later, he won the piccolo position with the National Symphony.) He was referring to the solo in the opening of the piece. The unexpected compliment from a fellow flutist made me feel pretty good.

The concert hall in Tallahassee was a great place to play; alas, it turned out to be the best venue of the tour. Days later, the fourth concert took place in one of our least favorite venues—an old city auditorium with terrible acoustics.

The next morning, inhaling the familiar diesel fumes, a smell I actually liked, I boarded the Greyhound bus. Though relatively new, the bus had the familiar dreary, gray-speckled linoleum floor and brown, fake-leather seats. As I walked toward the back, I saw an empty seat beside Alan, the principal clarinetist.

"Hi, Ernestine, have a seat," Alan said. "How are you this morning?"

"Probably about as well as you," I said with a smile, as I stowed my black flute bag in the overhead rack and sat down.

"Yes, we did stay out pretty late last night," Alan replied, stifling a yawn. We departed from Jacksonville that morning at 8:00 a.m., with a five-hour drive to Miami that day. I'd gotten up too late for the Holiday Inn breakfast. I'm sure others had also chosen sleep over weak coffee and stale bagels. "Much as I've enjoyed partying, I'll be glad when this tour is over," I said.

"Me too. Last night's concert was depressing. It's hard to play in a hall like that," Alan said.

"No kidding, it was like playing into a pillow."

After a few minutes of silence, Alan said, "I don't know how you stand it."

"You mean playing in a crappy hall?"

"No. Sitting next to Warren. I've often been tempted to yell at him to stop it." Unsure how to respond, I kept quiet. After a moment, Alan added, "He treats you much worse than he treats Joe and me."

"What do you mean, Joe and you? I never noticed him making faces after your solos. With me, though, it's part of his job."

"I disagree. Being principal flute doesn't give him the right to mutter insults," Alan said.

"You heard those?"

"Most of them. And I saw him turn his head and scowl at you after your solos. It's been a while since he's done that with me. The last time was after the long solo in *Pines of Rome.*"

"But you sounded terrific on that piece," I said.

"Thanks. Apparently, Warren didn't think so."

"Well, I don't know why he frowns after your solos, but in my case his criticism is probably justified."

"What do you mean? The better you play, the more he harasses you," Alan said, turning in his seat to face me squarely.

I just stared at him. I couldn't make sense of his words.

"Last night was a perfect example. Your solos in *Firebird* went well, yet he was shaking his head constantly."

"Wasn't I out of tune?" I asked.

"Gosh no. If anything, Warren was the one out of tune. Why don't you complain to Marty?" Marty was the personnel manager.

"Like I said, Warren's often right."

"No, he isn't. I'm surprised you don't see that. Look, maybe because Warren's older, or because he's been in the orchestra longer, he intimidates you, but he's certainly not trying to help you sound better. Your playing is fine. *He's* the problem."

"Huh. I'll have to think about that." Alan didn't know Warren had been my teacher—my only teacher—and I wanted to keep it that way. Warren was on the other bus, sitting with his older buddies. Despite the way Warren treated me, talking about him behind his back made me feel like a traitor. "Hey, y'all," Russ said in a mock southern drawl, "let's do a crossword together." I welcomed the distraction. Alan's comments disturbed me in ways I couldn't sort out.

Although I wasn't sure I believed Alan, that conversation was another important step in my recovery. Perhaps his words carried weight because Alan was a principal player, or perhaps I paid more attention to what he said because Lynette had voiced similar thoughts. I'd thought of Alan simply as a terrific clarinetist, and had been a little intimidated by him, but after that exchange he and I became frequent seatmates, finding lots to talk about during the long hours on the bus.

Smart, sophisticated, with deep-set dark eyes and luxuriant brown hair, Alan exuded the confidence of a man much taller than his five-foot, seven-inch frame. Even when he was simply telling a funny story, Alan projected an intensity that drew me to him. The first thing I had noticed about Alan, however, was not his appearance but his musicianship. Alan's expressive clarinet playing combined a rich, dark sound with the smooth legato and exquisite phrasing of a great singer.

Toward the end of the tour, we were housed in another Holiday Inn, this one next to a Baskin-Robbins. As soon as we checked in, about twenty of us showed up at the ice cream shop for an afternoon treat, much to the chagrin of the one, frazzled woman serving us. After she'd served about nine people, she looked at me.

"Single scoop of burgundy cherry, waffle cone," I said — or rather, we said. Alan, standing directly behind me, had answered in perfect unison with me. Out of all the possible flavors. We just stared at each other.

One look. Everything shifted. For the final two days of the tour, we sat together as usual, but now an electric current sizzled whenever our shoulders touched. Although I'd known Alan for over a year, falling in love with him happened suddenly, in that shared look at Baskin-Robbins. The clarinetist whose playing I admired was now the focus of my every thought. Because Alan was married, I thought the pull toward each other would disappear once the tour ended. But at the first rehearsal after the tour, we shared a look of longing that said otherwise.

Assuming we'd never be lovers, I simply enjoyed the craziness of being in love, fantasizing about Alan and belting out love songs in my car — "Something," "I'm in Love with a Wonderful Guy," "If I Loved You." Even my roommates noticed the change, though I refused to tell them the reason for my unrelenting cheerfulness. Alan was married, nothing would happen, what was there to tell?

With the undercurrent of desire, rehearsals were exciting. I sat where I'd always sat, but now I was acutely aware of Alan, a few feet behind me, watching me. Warren's attacks, no matter how vicious, didn't faze me. Post-concert parties had the added enticement of seeing each other, surrounded by people yet alone together. Determined to keep our attraction a secret from both our friends and Alan's wife, we mimicked normal conversation, though we'd passed the point where we could talk easily as casual friends.

This unspoken dialogue of mutual yearning continued for two months, until the day in mid-November when we were the only ones who showed up for an after-rehearsal group lunch. Now that we were finally alone, we were stunned. Speechless. Neither of us ate. We could only stare at each other. Desire. Exhilaration. Fear.

Eventually, I broke the silence to tell Alan where I lived. He very gently told me he could never leave his wife and asked me to think about what we were about to do. He could have cautioned me for hours; it would've made no difference. Too inexperienced to care about consequences, I welcomed love's engulfing power.

We drove to the apartment and went upstairs to my bedroom. As we sat on the edge of the bed, Alan took my face in his hands and softly asked once again if I was sure I wanted to do this. Oh yes. Even more gently, he asked if this was my first time. A slight shake of my head to indicate no. We undressed each other slowly, gently. After imagining this for so long, we were careful, tentative, almost reluctant to end the anticipation. When tenderness finally gave way to the passion we'd held back for so long, the intensity was as much emotional as physical. Delirious with desire, we devoured each other. After coming together quickly, we pulled apart several inches so we could look into each other's eyes—speechless, yet saying so much. When we made love again, we held on to the tenderness longer.

Two weeks after Alan and I first made love, I casually mentioned to Dr. Norton that I'd fallen in love with a married man, then skipped to another topic. Dr. Norton tried to bring the conversation back to Alan, but I resisted. My happiness was complete; analysis would only threaten it. Dr. Norton would presume I'd chosen someone unattainable and therefore safe, but falling in love hadn't felt like a choice; it seemed instead like the inevitable result of getting to know each other so well after many hours of talking on the tour buses.

I had little experience for comparison—eighth-grade puppy love, a couple of serious, adolescent boyfriends who were never lovers, and the recent crush on conductor Michael Palmer, fueled more by his position of power than by physical attraction. But this was different. Alan was not an authority figure. I had no fantasies about him simply holding me. And no illusions that he would rescue me and we'd sail into the happy-ever-after. He'd made it clear that even though his marriage was in trouble, he would not leave his wife. It didn't matter. Alan desired and cherished me in a way I'd never experienced. His reflection of me gave me confidence and joy that were, for once, independent of any achievements. I felt loved.

Due to the concert schedule of Thursday evening performances, the symphony rarely rehearsed on Thursday afternoons. Alan and I settled into a pattern of his coming to the apartment on Thursdays for lunch (while my roommates were at work). But it was never routine. Long after the intensity of the first few times together had waned, we continued to crave each other's company. Whenever one of my roommates was in the apartment during the day, we ate lunch at restaurants close to parks and spent the afternoon walking, talking, laughing, and embracing. In addition to classical music, we shared other interests, from Hermann Hesse and Kurt Vonnegut to Joni Mitchell and Blood, Sweat and Tears. We were among the nerdy BS&T fans who discussed the trumpets' sound quality.

The second week of December brought a rare gift: a week off with full pay. Robert Shaw had programmed the version of Handel's *Messiah* closest to Handel's original orchestration, which had neither flute nor clarinet parts. The luxury of being together five days in a row made us wish every week were like that.

Knowing he would never leave his wife, I was content with what we had—proximity in rehearsals, Thursday afternoons, occasional nights together on tour, and, on the few occasions when his wife was out of town, lovely, leisurely complete days and nights together. Although I didn't fall for Alan because he was unattainable, I'm sure the limits imposed on our time together heightened the intensity of the affair.

We continued meeting until the symphony season ended in late May. During the early part of the summer, Alan played in the Blossom Music Festival, near Cleveland. The months apart seemed endless, but Alan rented a postal box in Akron and we exchanged love letters two or three times a week, then had to stop after he returned to Atlanta and I left for the Tanglewood program in Massachusetts.

When a single woman falls in love with a married man, one of two things usually happens: she begins to demand more, hoping her beloved will leave his wife, or he decides to stop seeing her and save his marriage. In early November, one year after we became lovers, Alan ended the affair. I understood and respected his decision, but seeing him every day in rehearsals made it tough to get over the longing. Sometimes I think I never will.

In the wake of such an intense affair, I had no interest in the single men I met. Alan had shown me what it's like to feel loved, and I no longer slept with men I didn't care about. Had the timing been different, I might've fallen for the good-looking symphony cellist with the curly, slightly scruffy, red beard. While we were dating, I willed myself to fall in love with him. It didn't work.

During my fourth season with the symphony, guest conductor Gunther Schuller—brilliant musician and president of the New England Conservatory in Boston—presented a program that included Schuller's imaginative piece, *Seven Studies on Themes of Paul Klee*. The piece is effective even if you don't know Klee's paintings, though seeing them adds to the piece's allure. To prepare for the concert I listened to the Boston Symphony recording of the piece and was captivated by the offstage flute solo at the beginning of the fifth piece, "Arab Village." The glorious flute sound belonged to James Pappoutsakis, second flutist with the Boston Symphony, and principal flutist with the Boston Pops Orchestra.

Like every aspiring young flutist, I had listened to a variety of flute recordings, but on Schuller's piece, Mr. Pappoutsakis projected a sound unlike any other flutist I'd heard, live or recorded. It's difficult to describe the aural phenomenon of a particular flute sound compared to other flute tones, though they are obvious to a trained ear. Richer, rounder, more colorful? Inadequate and subjective language. The beauty of his sound on this recording was especially impressive because the solo was played offstage, therefore somewhat muted. Once I'd heard the solo, I wanted to sound like that. I played the one-minute passage repeatedly; between repetitions I grabbed my flute and played the solo, trying to imitate the Pappoutsakis sound. I vowed I would find a way to study with him someday.

My chance arrived a few months later, during the week when Leopold Stokowski was the ASO's guest conductor. Excited to be working with this legendary musician, we were disappointed and shocked when, during rehearsals, Stokowski made only one comment to the orchestra.

"Do beddur," he said, over and over, a phrase that entered the lexicon of classic ASO jokes.

That week I called in sick for two rehearsals (the only rehearsals I ever missed) so I could fly to Washington, DC, and audition for Tanglewood, the Boston Symphony's summer program for gifted graduate students and young professionals. Mr. Pappoutsakis, I had learned, taught at the New England Conservatory during the year, Tanglewood during the summer. If I got into Tanglewood, I could study with him that summer.

The audition material consisted of orchestral excerpts, the ubiquitous Mozart Concerto in G Major, and "a contemporary piece." Knowing the competition would be stiff, I picked the most difficult contemporary piece I could find, Persichetti's 1965 *Parable* for solo flute. *Parable* has complex rhythms but no time signature or delineated measures. I developed my own crazy rhythmic shorthand to represent fractions of seconds for various rests and spent an obsessive amount of time making sure each note was precisely the right length.

The audition took place in a classroom at Catholic University. Doriot Anthony Dwyer, principal flutist with the Boston Symphony and one of the first women to win a principal position with a major symphony orchestra, judged the flute applicants. Ms. Dwyer greeted me formally and nodded as I went through the repertoire. After I played the Persichetti, she seemed more interested and looked at my application form.

"Tell me," she asked, "why do you want to go to Tanglewood? I see here that you play in the Atlanta Symphony, so you must be missing a rehearsal."

I admitted I was, in fact, missing two rehearsals. Then, like an idiot, I told her the truth.

"When Gunther Schuller conducted in Atlanta, we played his *Seven Studies on Themes of Paul Klee*. I heard James Pappoutsakis on the recording, and I want to study with him to work on my sound."

My answer was both clueless and tactless. I had no idea Dwyer and Pappoutsakis had been enemies for years. How little I knew of orchestral politics, despite my daily experience with Warren. Dwyer and Pappoutsakis were as adversarial as Warren and I. She visibly stiffened after that damning response.

I didn't get in, but I did study with Mr. Pappoutsakis the following summer, as a participant in the less competitive Tanglewood Institute. While there, I learned about the jealous rivalry between Dwyer and Pappoutsakis; only then did I understand the extent of my colossal blunder.

———

Several weeks after the program with Stokowski, one of our concerts featured Dvorak's Symphony in G Major. I'd been looking forward to playing it, not because the piece has great flute parts but because it contains two of Dvorak's most gorgeous melodies; one of them, played by the cellos, opens the piece. The other, presented by the violins, is the main theme of the scherzo. Hearing these themes in a concert hall is thrilling; sitting on stage surrounded by that sound, transporting. When I played the piece my first year in the community orchestra, I practically swooned each time the strings played those passages. The Symphony in G Major has several exposed flute duets, but none are difficult. Because I knew the work so well, I thought I could relax and enjoy the rehearsals. Finally, a stress-free week.

The last movement of the Symphony is a theme and variation, with a fast, flashy variation that is all flute solo, the biggest moment in the piece for the principal flute. The first part of the two-section solo starts on an easy note, the D above the staff, but descends rapidly to much lower notes, where projecting the sound is difficult. Warren had many strengths as a flutist; a strong low register was not one of them. The second half of the variation goes into the high register, with runs that are technically difficult, especially at the fast tempo Shaw would likely choose. Warren had flawless technique; the second half of the solo would be fine.

In the first rehearsal of the flute variation, Maestro Shaw, as predicted, asked Warren to play the low notes louder. The orchestra started again; after the flute solo, Shaw frowned but didn't stop the orchestra a second time. In subsequent rehearsals, Shaw motioned to Warren, wanting more sound on the low notes. As usual, Warren took his frustration out on those around him. The three principal woodwind players found his scowls and headshaking simply annoying. Although I'd gained a lot of confidence in the past two years, his attacks still rankled me. Not a hassle-free week after all.

The slow second movement opens with a passage for strings that ends very quietly, a hushed moment where nothing happens. At the end of this bar of silence, the first flute plays three pickup notes that lead to a flute duet on the next down-beat, accompanied only by quiet oboes. When we rehearsed it, I was careful to tune my C to Warren's C an octave higher. Years of sitting beside him had made me an expert in following the slightest change in Warren's intonation. Trying to make me sound out of tune, he often changed his pitch, leading me on an intonation chase. Sometimes I even enjoyed this subtle game, but only if Shaw didn't notice.

After four days of rehearsals filled with Warren's grimaces, the first performance started out well. The cellos played the opening melody beautifully, Warren sounded fine on his first solo, and the rest of the movement went smoothly.

When we started the slow movement, I didn't bother to count the measures of rest before I came in; I knew the passage well, and besides, Warren came in first. I was about to pick up my flute when suddenly I heard Warren playing—one measure early. During the quick second of Warren's pickup notes, my mind raced.

What the hell is he doing? Do I go with him or wait and play my part in the right place? But his part will sound wrong without mine underneath, and mine will sound even worse if I play it after instead of with him.

Making the snap decision, I slammed the flute to my chin and came in barely on time. In the ensuing confusion, the oboes didn't play their parts underneath the flutes, but in the next bar, with a frantic cue from Shaw, the clarinets came in one bar early so their part sounded right, relative to the flutes. The rest of the orchestra adjusted quickly to the fact that we'd skipped a bar. Whew.

The same passage comes back toward the end of that section. I picked up my flute two measures early. I was ready for anything. When we came to the quiet bar that Warren had omitted before, it sounded just as it should and then . . . nothing. He didn't come in. There was absolute silence.

How can he screw up the same entrance twice? Now what do I do?

I decided to wait. The entire orchestra was frozen in suspended animation; one empty beat stretched into a whole bar. Four seconds felt like four minutes. Finally, Warren came in and the entire orchestra had to adjust, this time adding a bar. For those in the audience who didn't know the piece well, nothing sounded amiss, but for the players—especially me—it was a bizarre, nerve-racking performance.

After the shock wore off, I began to wonder if Warren had made those mistakes on purpose, to trick me into playing my part late in the first entrance, then early when it comes back. If so, even though it failed, it was a brilliant and gutsy strategy. Because of the tension between us, I couldn't simply ask Warren, "What the hell happened?" I'll never know, but he certainly gave me yet another reason to be on high alert during performances. That Warren wasn't fired or demoted for those mistakes is a testament to how much power he had in the orchestra.

My favorite ASO concerts were the choral masterpieces we performed with Robert Shaw, including a stunning interpretation of Brahms's *Ein deutsches Requiem*, which we performed in the spring of my fourth year. Instead of writing a traditional requiem—the Catholic Mass for the dead—Brahms chose scripture passages that present a nondoctrinal reflection on mortality, with no references to Jesus. We performed the work in English, which added to its immediacy. Some of the unforgettable highlights were the powerful opening of the second movement when the choir sings, "For all flesh is as grass that withers," the poignancy of the baritone solo in the next movement, "Lord, help me to know the measure of my days on earth," the haunting eeriness of the choir on the text "And we shall all be changed," and the sweetness of the lyrical soprano in the fourth movement, "How Lovely Is Thy Dwelling Place."

Except that, in the first performance, it wasn't so lovely at the beginning.

Before the soprano enters, the principal flute and clarinet begin the movement with A-flats an octave apart, totally exposed. At the first performance, Warren played an A-natural. Instead of a mellow, consonant octave, the piece started with a screeching minor ninth, a very dissonant interval. The mistake was less puzzling than Warren's entrances in the Dvorak symphony, but much more jarring for the listener. Was it simply coincidental that just as I was gaining more confidence, he seemed to be making more mistakes?

That summer, Lynette, who'd gotten into the main Tanglewood program, drove with me to the beautiful Berkshires in western Massachusetts for the Tanglewood Music Festival. We started out at 2:00 a.m. in my old Plymouth Valiant, to avoid paying for a night's lodging, and arrived on the Tanglewood grounds at dusk. The dorm room was hot, the mattresses lumpy, and the one shelf—our pantry—just large enough for a stash of jelly and peanut butter jars. I lost my roommate the second week when Lynette moved into a tent with clarinetist Frank Cohen (whom she later married). The luxury of a little more space in the room was offset by loneliness. Lynette introduced me to one of Frank's friends, a cellist he'd known at Juilliard, but his good looks didn't make up for his self-absorption.

Tanglewood Institute was a fancy name for two privileges: lessons with members of the Boston Symphony and free admittance to concerts. Unlike those admitted to the main program, Institute students had no performing groups. Other than attending concerts, led by conductors such as the famous Leonard Bernstein and the not-yet-famous Michael Tilson Thomas, I ate, slept, and practiced, all in my hot little room, subsisting on Cheerios and PB&J's. I spent lots of practice time on simple exercises designed to focus on sound quality. A boring summer punctuated by moments of joy when I got the sound I was seeking.

The previous spring, when Lynette had asked me to be her roommate, I'd resisted. She reminded me too much of my sister—someone so gifted that everything came easily for her. I'm grateful she didn't give up, because moving in with her that fall was one of the best decisions I ever made. Having shared an apartment with friends who never understood my passion for classical music, I loved living with a musician, one who practiced as much as I did. Though my former room-mates didn't intend it, I always felt like an outsider, the odd one who didn't share their musical tastes and carefree weekends. It was such a relief to walk in the door of our house and not have to worry about offending roommates if I practiced for three hours without saying a word to them. Even more important, I could talk to Lynette about whatever Warren had done in rehearsal that day. She sat in the row behind the flutes and could see what Warren was doing to me, and also to Russ, the principal bassoonist. Though not as frequently as he attacked me, Warren insulted the other principal woodwinds, shaking his head derisively after their solos.

Lynette was an extraordinary person. I admired her gorgeous hair, slim body, effortless bassoon playing, and, especially, her eternal optimism. Despite her many accomplishments, she never triggered my lesser-sister comparison baggage, partly because she was so supportive of me. Her constant insistence that I was as good a flutist as Warren reinforced Alan's comments, and gradually changed my perception of the situation with Warren.

In the kitchen of our house on Courtney Drive, which we moved into after we got back from Tanglewood, Lynette put up a bright purple-and-yellow Snoopy Be Happy poster. Having grown up in an academic household, I sometimes found her frequent declarations of "It was a gas," or "That's so-o-o groovy" annoying, but most of the time I loved her unrelenting joie de vivre. We got a kick out of the fact that the Snoopy poster was above the Robertshaw oven.

When Alan ended our affair that fall, talking to Lynette helped immensely. She was the one person who knew just how deeply in love I was. Whenever I think of Lynette, I see her wide, mischievous grin and the sassy way she tossed her lustrous, thick brown hair. She was also the most supportive, understanding friend I've ever had.

The one time I stood up to Warren was in the fall of my fifth year, during a week of children's concerts. Like most professional orchestras, each year the Atlanta Symphony devoted one week to children's concerts; for us, it was the second week of November. Junior high students were bused in from various schools in Atlanta. Non-musicians might think this would be a low-pressure week, but in fact much of the repertoire geared toward young audiences—*Peter and the Wolf, The Carnival of the Animals, The Sorcerer's Apprentice*—is coincidentally some of the most technically challenging repertoire, especially for flute. The typical schedule was to have one rehearsal, then play two shows daily, Monday through Friday.

When I arrived for the only rehearsal, I saw that in addition to all the second flute parts, my music folder contained the first flute part to a suite from Bizet's *Carmen*. As soon as I sat down, I asked Warren why I had the part.

"Because there's a piccolo duet in the third movement. I'm playing all the first flute parts, of course, but you're going to play the piccolo part," Warren said.

"But there's no piccolo in the second flute part," I said, after quickly looking through the music.

"That's why you have a copy of my part. The second piccolo is written in the first flute part," he said.

"Then you should play it."

"I don't want to, so you're going to play it," he said.

"But—"

"I don't believe you're in a position to object," he said sternly.

Reluctantly, I took my piccolo out of its case and spent the remaining few minutes warming up on it, rather than on flute. The rehearsal felt like a gallop through a field of fast flute and piccolo runs, but at least we had the weekend to practice before the first two concerts on Monday. Since second flute parts rarely call for piccolo, I normally spent very little time practicing that instrument. In the rehearsal, the piccolo duet went pretty well, mostly because Benson always sounded great.

At the Monday morning concert, Warren missed a couple of notes on one of the many runs in *Peter and the Wolf.* He'd played the piece on dozens of kiddie concerts, but that day his fingers simply got tangled up. No doubt he hadn't practiced the music as much as he would have for a regular subscription concert, especially since Robert Shaw was not conducting. At the afternoon concert, *Peter and the Wolf* went well, but Warren frowned at me pointedly after the piccolo duet, which was my only exposed passage on the concert.

Tuesday's concerts went well except that, again, Warren shook his head and scowled after the piccolo duet. On Wednesday morning, he frowned and muttered, "Christ," right after the duet. Instead of simply taking his abuse, as I had for years, I resisted.

"Look, I don't want to play piccolo," I said to Warren when the concert was over. "Neither do you, but it's in your part. Since you're so unhappy with the way it sounds, you play it. I'm not going to this afternoon or the rest of the week."

I tried to sound confident, but as soon as the words were out of my mouth, my heart started pounding. This was new territory. During the hour-and-a-half lunch break, I drove to a McDonald's where I knew I wouldn't run into anyone from the orchestra. I needed to think about whether to carry out this plan. If Warren refused to play piccolo, did I have the chutzpah to just sit there, not playing, during the piccolo duet?

Warren no longer made me question my musical ability, but he still intimidated me. Even seated, he was a head taller than I was—large male versus petite female. That was but one of several unequal pairings: first flute/second flute, middle-aged/ young, orchestra veteran/relative newbie. And the most difficult and rare one, former teacher/former student. But this time I rebelled against the power dynamics. I knew I could not be fired for refusing to play something written in Warren's part.

At the afternoon concert, I didn't take my piccolo out of its case. Neither did Warren. The concert proceeded as usual until we played the third movement of the *Carmen* suite. When we came to the piccolo duet passage, it was a piccolo solo, without the harmony underneath. The conductor immediately looked at me, more startled than angry. A few other heads jerked around. Everyone knew this piece well—we'd just played it five times—and, I admit, the part sounded peculiar without the second piccolo part. I tried not to look guilty. Even though I'd not played a note, my hands were shaking. When the concert was over, the personnel manager rushed up to me.

"Why didn't you play the piccolo part?" Marty demanded.

"I was playing the part as a favor to Warren," I explained. "The second piccolo is written in the first flute part, not in my part. He's been muttering insults, indicating he doesn't like my piccolo playing. This morning I warned him I wouldn't play it this afternoon."

Marty turned to ask Warren about it, but he'd left in a hurry.

"Tell you what," he said, "I'll call Warren tonight and remind him that you're doing him a favor. If he backs off, will you play piccolo the rest of the week?"

I hesitated just long enough to make him uncomfortable. Even though I had a legal right to refuse to play the part, my refusal would only make matters worse in the long run.

"Okay, but tell him to stop muttering under his breath," I said, knowing Marty would never have the guts to say that to Warren.

Warren did indeed back off, making no more derisive comments, and I played the piccolo part for the Thursday and Friday concerts. Only Warren and I appreciated the significance of my rebellion: for four kiddie concerts, I had forced him to treat me well. After the radical piccolo part boycott, I hoped things might be different between us, but the exhilaration I felt was short-lived. The next week, Warren resumed scowling and muttering insults.

One week we had the honor of working with guest conductor Max Rudolf, music director of the Cincinnati Symphony, for a program that included Beethoven's Symphony No. 6, *Pastoral.* During the first rehearsal, Warren, as usual, was grimacing and throwing me accusatory looks. At the break, Maestro Rudolf came over to us and addressed Warren.

"Why are you so unhappy?" he asked, sounding genuinely puzzled. "We are playing such beautiful music, and here you have this lovely young lady sitting beside you." In a disarmingly casual way, Rudolf had confronted Warren's disruptive behavior.

As stunned as I was, Warren said nothing, merely shook his head and looked at the floor. For the rest of that week, Warren behaved so well it was almost like my first few months in the orchestra, and I could immerse myself fully in Beethoven's bucolic music. Max Rudolf had the guts to do what no other conductor had attempted. And it worked because, as much as he would like to deny it, Warren had a grudging respect for the man on the podium.

———

"Boy, you sounded so much better than Warren on those runs!" Anne exclaimed after a performance of Tchaikovsky's Symphony No. 4. Anne occasionally played with the orchestra, when a piece had four flute parts. She was referring to the exposed runs in the second flute part. She failed to notice Warren standing off to the side, well within earshot.

"Thanks, Anne." I smiled and tried to look gracious, but already a knot had formed in my stomach. I'd been dreading our upcoming tour for many reasons; now I had another. After hearing her comment, Warren would increase his efforts to sabotage me every time we played that piece.

The first movement of Tchaikovsky's Fourth Symphony follows the typical sonata form structure, with two main themes. In the second theme, there is a moment when a short run is played in succession by three solo woodwinds, the second flute solo coming just before the first flute plays the same notes, an octave higher. Since the passage occurs four times, there were four little solo passages where Warren played right after me.

Anne McFarland made that remark after a concert in January, right before we departed on a monthlong tour that would culminate in performances at Carnegie Hall and the recently opened Kennedy Center. Long tours are always exhausting; high-pressure concerts at the end made this one exceptionally grueling.

The tour route from Atlanta began in Baton Rouge, proceeded up the Mississippi River to western Illinois, east to New York City with stops in Chicago as well as lots of smaller towns, and finally, south to Washington, DC. During those thirty days we had three airline flights, but most of our traveling was, as usual, on Greyhound buses. By the time the tour started, seeing Alan in rehearsals no longer sent me into a tailspin, but I felt stiff and tongue-tied around him in small groups. The only way to avoid him on the tour bus would've been to sit with someone outside our group. Having to give up my lover was hard enough; I couldn't turn away from my friends. We each tried to act as though the affair had never happened, adding another layer of stress to the challenging tour.

As always, Warren was the main source of stress. When we played the Tchaikovsky—every other night of the tour—Warren glared at me right before and after at least one of our solos. For these concerts there were four flutes playing, but even though the assistant principal flute sat between me and Warren for that piece, it made no difference. Would it have been as bad if he hadn't overheard Anne's compliment? I'm sure he still would have tried to undermine me, but his attacks might've been less persistent.

The ASO performed two different programs on the 1971 tour. The program that did not include the Tchaikovsky symphony featured Ravel's *Bolero*, the popular, monotonous piece that repeats one theme over and over, at times played by a solo wind instrument, including bassoon and saxophone. The bassoon statement is in its difficult, extreme high register, including lots of high D-flats, a notoriously challenging note. Night after night, Russ managed to make the solo sound ravishing, even on the high D-flats. Then, one night he cracked one of the D-flats, prompting a scowl from Shaw. From then on, each time we played *Bolero*, Shaw glared at Russ right before the solo. Although note-perfect for the remaining performances, Russ played the solo more carefully, sacrificing some of its sensuality—an example of counterproductive conductor intimidation.

On a very cold night, at the end of a rare day off, I wandered around downtown Chicago. We were staying at the Hilton on Michigan Avenue. Brightly lit and filled with skyscrapers, the neighborhood seemed a safe place to walk alone, though that night I would've been outside anyway; I needed to walk. It had been many months since Alan ended our affair. But in the midst of this difficult tour, I ached for him. I missed him as a lover and, even more, I missed Alan's understanding and reassurances about Warren. Performing concerts alongside Warren, night after night, was eating away at my confidence. After walking for an hour or so, I found myself at the Sears

Tower. The grimy city, with its piles of sooty snow, reflected my mood of despair. For a long time, I stood at the base of the tower, looking up into the starless sky, and wondered if I would make it to the end of the tour, still twelve long days away.

The next night, the accumulated stress finally unnerved me. In the Tchaikovsky symphony, I missed a note in one of the runs, eliciting a glare from Shaw. In five years, I'd never missed a note in a prominent part. The next morning, the personnel manager informed me that Vendla Weber would be playing my part for the rest of the tour. A recent Curtis graduate, Vendla had been hired that fall as the assistant principal flute, a new position. She doubled the first part in loud passages and occasionally played principal on overtures or other short pieces. I was devastated. Not only had I lost my position, but I would now have to take hers: I'd sit next to Warren while Vendla played my solos. Night after night, the rest of the tour.

Warren behaved no differently with Vendla playing second flute. I admit part of me found it satisfying when Warren scowled after Vendla's solos. And I wasn't filled with compassion when she rushed one of the runs, playing it so fast that it was unclear. "That was a mess," Warren muttered. She was so upset by Warren's reaction, she refused to play the second part for the rest of the tour. (Since her contract didn't include playing second flute, she had the right to refuse.)

The next night, I returned to the barrage of scowls and denigrating comments. To my surprise, I enjoyed the remaining concerts. It was oddly liberating to have experienced my worst nightmare—missing a note and being demoted. No doubt Warren thought he had achieved his goal, but it backfired. Missing the note broke the shackles of my constant fear. In the remaining concerts, I was impervious to Warren's badgering, and for the first time in years, I felt free to play my best. The third concert after I returned as second flute, Warren backed off. I think he understood that, at least for the moment, he had lost his power over me.

Shortly after the monthlong tour, we had to sign our contracts for the following year. Despite feeling good about the last few concerts, I was worn out—physically, emotionally, even musically. Over the past five years, I'd often thought about quitting the symphony, more a fantasy than a plan. This year, however, I'd applied and been accepted to the master's program at the New England Conservatory. Before the tour, I had viewed going to Boston as a desperate plan B, a cowardly escape hatch to get away from Warren. But the tour forced me to confront reality: no matter how much confidence I gained from new friendships and reassurances that I was a good player, sitting beside Warren would continue to be destructive. I'd missed a note in a solo; how could I be sure that wouldn't happen again? If it did, Warren could make a strong case for getting me fired. He still wielded a lot of power. The only way to escape him was to take a year's leave of absence. As with all my decisions after I moved out of their house, I never discussed this with my parents. They knew nothing about the problems with Warren.

An added incentive to get away was that Lynette would leave Atlanta at the end of the season to be with her husband in Baltimore. I sent my contract back unsigned, along with the signed form committing both sides to a one-year leave. I would work on my sound by studying with Mr. Pappoutsakis. And maybe, from a safe distance, I could build a stronger defense against Warren's attacks.

A few weeks after our long tour, we played a program that included Dvorak's popular *New World Symphony*. When I saw the piece on the repertoire list, I remembered the bizarre things that had happened the previous year, on another Dvorak symphony. Surely nothing as unnerving would happen this year.

Dvorak is one of the few composers who wrote solos for the second flute; the *New World Symphony* has several, all in the first movement. That movement is the only piece I know with more solos for the second flute than for the first. Warren would be eager to undermine me.

As predicted, during the week of rehearsals Warren stepped up the frequency of his negative comments. After each of my solos, he scowled, shook his head, and muttered, just loud enough for me to hear. "That was terrible," he'd say, or "Christ, that's so out of tune." When the night of the first performance arrived, I was worried but determined: I would not let Warren ruin my chance to play three short but important solos.

My first solo went quite well, as did the next one. When we arrived at the last of my solos, toward the end of the movement, I felt pretty confident — reminiscent of the way I used to feel as a high school student, right before solos in the community orchestra. What a delight, to once again experience pride, and eagerness to play. As I raised the flute to my lips, I took a deep breath. Right before the entrance, my peripheral vision detected sudden movement from Warren, and something shiny popped out very close to my left arm. In the split second before I had to play, thoughts raced through my brain.

Damn, what the heck is that? A switchblade knife? No, even Warren would not risk that during a performance.

He would and he did, aiming it so precisely that the tip of the blade ended up an inch from my upper left arm. After years of his groans and scowls, I'd grown used to his shenanigans, but I was not prepared for this. I have no idea how well I played the solo; the notes were there, but the knife distracted me too much to pay attention to articulation, pitch, and the countless other things that constitute a well-played passage. It was a blur. Many measures passed before I noticed my rapid heartbeat. Warren did it so quickly that no one saw it—he had to because he played soon after my solo. He must've practiced that move so he could snap the blade out, aim it, snap it back in, put the knife down, and come back in on time, all in a matter of seconds, without anyone but me seeing it. If this sounds outrageous, it was. I've heard hundreds of orchestra horror stories, but none that involved a switchblade knife. He wasn't threatening me physically; he was simply trying to make me screw up the solo. Which, I guess, was his highly creative version of a threat.

When I relayed this (now) funny story, a friend made the following comment: "That's one way to cut the ole umbilical cord." True on so many levels. It was time to leave.

Chapter 15: Big City

The week of my departure from Atlanta, I moved out of the house I'd shared with Lynette, deposited much of my stuff in my parents' attic, packed, then flew to Boston on August 28, dragging a huge suitcase through the Atlanta and Boston airports. Though exhausted, I perked up when the cab entered the outskirts of the city. Other than brief trips and the summer at Tanglewood, I'd never been out of the South. (The Whitman reunions of my childhood were all in southern states.) As the cab maneuvered past the Prudential Center at dusk, I marveled at the lights, skyline, and throngs of people. The exhilaration diminished a bit when we arrived at a run-down neighborhood and pulled up to the NEC dormitory, a drab-looking building right across Huntington Avenue from the older, handsome main building of the New England Conservatory.

The Saturday before classes started, the dorm was mostly empty. After retrieving my room key from an envelope left at the deserted front desk, I took the elevator up to the eighth (top) floor, where the heat and mustiness were much worse than in the lobby. Thank goodness the heat was less muggy than Atlanta, but I would need to buy a fan. At the opposite end of the hall from the elevator was a tiny, oblong single room. The distance between the two longer, grayish-white

205

walls was only a few feet wider than the single bed's width. After sharing an entire house with one person, I now lived in a room that resembled a galley kitchen.

I deposited a few clothes in the small built-in chest of drawers, squeezed my suitcase into the closet, and took out my flute. One note was enough. The hard, once-black linoleum floor and the bare walls made the room an echo chamber. Even a junior high flutist would sound good in that room. I'd have to buy a rug and curtains to improve the acoustics. Seeking another place to practice, I crossed the street to the main building. It was locked.

When I returned to my dreary room, the fatigue of traveling and the reality of all I'd given up suddenly overwhelmed me. Alone in the deserted dorm, I collapsed on the bed and sobbed. Eventually, I realized part of my fatigue was hunger. I ate the apple, banana, and nuts I'd packed, but the nuts made me thirsty, and I had neither a drink nor even a glass to use for water from a bathroom faucet. Gazing down the hallway, I saw a water fountain beside the elevator. Such a small thing, and yet, seeing it there rejuvenated me. After all, at long last, I was at a conservatory. And Warren was a thousand miles away.

On Sunday, I explored the neighborhood in search of food: Chinese, McDonald's, local diner—all fast food, all greasy. I settled for a McDonald's chocolate milkshake; if I couldn't eat healthy, I could at least have comfort food. The streets and sidewalks looked like the concrete and asphalt had been there since the 1920s, decorated with trash that funneled into the street gutters. I saw several homeless, apparently drunk men sitting with their backs propped up against dirty buildings. I knew there were such neighborhoods in Atlanta, but not near any place I'd lived.

On Monday, I woke up to rain and cooler temperatures. As soon as the main building was opened, I went in search of a good practice room. Ignoring the handsome Renaissance architecture of the outer facade, I rushed up the wide steps and almost ran into the bust of Beethoven, glaring down at me. Across the modest-sized lobby, the doors to the concert hall were closed but not locked. I opened one and stepped into the most gorgeous concert hall I'd ever seen. The rich, reddish-brown wood of the intricately carved walls and ceiling led to the centerpiece at the back of the stage: a lovely Baroque organ encased in the same color wood. But it wasn't until later that I discovered the best feature of Jordan Hall: the acoustics. All those wooden surfaces made the hall's resonance equal to the best concert spaces, even Carnegie Hall. I spent a few moments admiring Jordan Hall before exploring the rest of the building.

Most of the spacious classrooms were locked, so I descended into the basement, following a sign for the practice rooms. The gloominess of the practice rooms was as striking as the beauty of Jordan Hall. The rooms were small, the acoustical tile of the walls almost the same grayish white as my room, and badly scarred, but at least the rooms were better for practicing than the dorm room. Still, it shocked me that one of the best music schools in the country had such shabby practice spaces, the very rooms where future professional musicians strived to make beautiful sounds.

That afternoon I took the subway to Filene's Department Store and went to the house furnishings section, where I bought the cheapest curtains I could find. Rugs were more expensive, and difficult to carry on the subway, so I settled for four fuzzy bath mats, all black to match the curtains. I thought a black-and-white room might look sharp and contemporary. Alas, after I'd hung the curtains and put down the bath mats, the room was still too reverberant. I would have to figure out something to put on one of the long walls, but I didn't see a

way to attach anything. A few days later, I solved the problem
by buying curtain rods with suction cups that stuck to the wall.
I ended up with six feet of black curtains along one of the walls,
no curtains on the window. That plus a couple more bath mats
turned the space into a decent practice room. Black may sound
gloomy, but everything was new, and the soft materials made
the room seem friendlier.

By the end of the week, I'd learned that half of the residents
on my floor were flutists, including another graduate student.
I couldn't walk from the elevator to my room without hearing
a cacophony of scales, long tones, and flute orchestral excerpts.
With a limited number of practice rooms available, students
often practiced in their rooms. Except for quiet hours from midnight to 8:00 a.m., I felt like I lived in a clamorous flute forest.

A few days after classes started, I witnessed the food
fights that were regular occurrences in the dorm cafeteria. They
would start with one, usually skinny, always male, person who
might toss just a piece of bread across the table. Another too-
old-for-this-behavior kid would respond, and soon the whole
table of seven or eight would be throwing escalating amounts
of food back and forth. Unlike junior high, there was no room
monitor here. Mostly the combatants had the decency (if that
word even applies) to stick to bread, carrots, brownies, and
other non-drippy food. At age twenty-five, I was eating my
meals in a dining hall with eighteen-year-olds who seemed less
mature than seventh graders, and decades younger than some
of my Atlanta Symphony colleagues.

Outside the dorm I discovered broader, cultural differences, in many cases *counter*cultural. In Atlanta, neither
I nor my friends would've given a recital in casual clothing;
at New England, many of the men and several women wore
jeans for their recitals. I hadn't been living in a vacuum—this
was, after all, two years after Woodstock—but my group of

friends in Atlanta restricted our hippie activities to opposing the Vietnam War. We hadn't yet adopted the personal dress codes, experimental drug use, or automatic anti-institutional attitudes already prevalent in the Northeast.

That fall I met a married woman who hadn't changed her last name. It struck me as odd, but within a few months I thought of keeping your name as the norm—the first small step in a deepening commitment to feminist ideas. Before moving to Boston, feminism resided only in my head. Now it was more real. I seemed to be shedding my southern identity rather quickly. Part of it was simply leaving my hometown and finally, at age twenty-five, getting away from the place where my father, then Warren, had defined who I was. The song that frequently ran through my head that year was "I've Gotta Be Me." Cheesy, but the message reflected my mindset. I especially liked the point about choosing a life that was right for me, not for someone else, which included not only Warren and my father but men I might date. No man was going to determine my future.

———

Known throughout the country as a fantastic teacher, Mr. Pappoutsakis had inspired me in the handful of lessons he taught at Tanglewood, but when I studied with him at NEC, he was overworked and suffering from emphysema. Around sixty when I came to New England, he taught students not only at New England but also at Boston University and the Longy School of Music, plus a few at Harvard, Radcliffe, and the Massachusetts Institute of Technology. All this while playing second flute with the Boston Symphony and principal flute with the Boston Pops Orchestra. He was, simply, too busy to put much energy into each lesson. I was glad I had studied with him in the summer when his schedule was much lighter.

Mr. Pappoutsakis, whom students called Mr. P, supported my goal of working on sound but showed little interest in working on other things (breathing, musicality, phrasing, articulation). I learned more about technique from listening to two excellent flutists who lived on my dormitory floor, Ivy Goldfarb and Judy Mendenhall. I began to practice the same technical exercises they practiced, trying to match Ivy's effortless scale patterns and Judy's musical phrasing.

After a few weeks, in one of my lessons I had a breakthrough in the quality of my sound. By concentrating on Mr. P's suggestion to "play on the inside of the lips" (like saying the French word *yeux*), I was able to add depth to the middle register, and warmth to the high register. All of a sudden, Mr. P, a kind but reserved man, practically glowed with enthusiasm.

"You can play whatever you want next week, even 'Twinkle, Twinkle,' as long as you play it with that sound," he said.

Thrilled to have finally excited him, I spent the week making up variations on the "Twinkle, Twinkle" tune, all of them slow to highlight my new sound. (It's harder to gauge sound quality in fast passages.)

"I prepared something different this week," I said at my next lesson. I was eager to show Mr. P that I'd sustained the better sound quality all week. I also thought he'd be amused by my clever variations on "Twinkle."

As I played, Mr. P looked more and more puzzled.

"Well," I said after a few moments of awkward silence, "at my last lesson, you said you'd be happy with anything, even 'Twinkle, Twinkle,' as long as I played it with the sound I got last week."

"Oh, I see. And that's what you were doing just now?"

My cheeks burned with embarrassment. He had forgotten what happened in our last lesson. I thought I'd had a major breakthrough then; now I wasn't so sure. Deflated, I pulled out an étude to play. Mr. P taught me a painful lesson that week: the teacher is far more important to the student than the student is to the teacher. I vowed that, if I ever taught flute students, I would never hurt them in that way.

With his vast orchestral experience, Mr. Pappoutsakis knew the flute orchestral excerpts as well as any teacher, but he was surprisingly negligent in passing along certain basics, perhaps assuming I knew more than I did. That fall I played principal in the NEC Repertory Orchestra on Brahms's Symphony No. 1. After playing most of the part well for the performance, in the fourth movement I got far too excited for the solo that ushers in the allegro—a mere eight bars, but a powerful solo. I poured my soul into the passage, trying to infuse it with the grand passion I thought it deserved. But the first note, high E, tends to be sharp, and by throwing myself into the emotional power of the solo, I played the E quite sharp. I was mortified when I heard the tape of the performance. Later I learned the trick used by most performers: play the E with a slightly altered fingering (the E-flat key closed). Why hadn't Mr. P mentioned that?

In October, Alan wrote asking if he could visit me in two weeks. As he requested, I immediately called him to say yes, keeping the conversation brief. I'd heard from Lynette that Alan was getting a divorce. Hope—unruly, unquenchable—sprang up despite my attempts to extinguish it.

Alan suggested we meet at his hotel, the Marriott near Copley Square. For the first time in months, I applied a little makeup, took time to fluff out my hair, and put on a dress—just your basic little black number but with a flattering, plunging neckline. Grabbing my black raincoat (my only halfway dressy coat), keys, and wallet, I rushed down the stairs, too impatient to wait for the elevator. On the subway I tried to jettison fantasies of getting back together, but why else would Alan fly to Boston?

I walked into the lobby and there he was, looking as suave as ever in black pants and a pale pink silk shirt, open at the collar. Instead of the passionate embrace I'd imagined, he greeted me with a perfunctory hug. My hopes sank a little.

We walked to a nearby Mediterranean restaurant—more casual than upscale, walls of rich, deep red in an otherwise spartan decor. As we sipped our Manhattans, Alan talked about the current symphony season and asked about my life at NEC. By the time our entrées arrived, we hadn't gotten past small talk. I was too nervous to taste the scallops in cream sauce. When a pause in the conversation stretched into an uncomfortable silence, Alan looked at me and, in an oddly (for Alan) hesitant manner, explained the reason for his visit.

As he described his panicked state and the college student who might be pregnant, I felt myself disappear. No shock, no resentment, no hopes dashed. Certainly, no anger. I concentrated on colors: how nice the pink of Alan's shirt looked against the dark red wall, how the black frames of the chairs contrasted with the white tablecloths. Barely glanced at the deep-set eyes that had once conveyed so much love—or so I'd thought.

We talked about options, timelines, resources in Atlanta. I played the role of a good friend, one who listens with sympathy, never inserting her own needs.

Alan had a flight back to Atlanta the next morning. He offered to call me a taxi, but I demurred. The train would be safe this early. Though it wasn't yet 9:00 p.m., I felt like I'd been on a difficult and lengthy journey. I knew I'd never see Alan again.

For weeks after Alan's visit, knowing he'd had other lovers, I thought about our affair. While my head said one thing, my heart remained unchanged. I had loved Alan with an intensity I never experienced with anyone else. Was I as important to him as he was to me? Probably not, but for twelve months I had felt loved. I had no regrets.

———

Like most music schools, NEC required entering graduate students to take tests in music history and music theory. My Emory University degree was essentially a music history major; that exam was fine. Not so with music theory. Although I could analyze scores for themes and large-scale form, I'd either forgotten or never mastered the rudiments of voice leading in four-part harmony. In addition to an advanced course in Beethoven string quartets, I had to take freshman music theory.

It might have been depressing to be in a theory class with eighteen-year-olds, but the teacher, Lyle Davidson, focused on studying scores rather than harmony exercises. We learned part-writing rules by composing and harmonizing our own eight-bar melodies. Like most theory teachers at New England, Lyle Davidson was a composer, and he used the principles of music theory to help students appreciate the craftmanship of great composers. His reverence for the works we studied inspired me. Plus, he was young and good-looking, with gorgeous red hair and matching beard. After a week or so, I began to look forward to each theory class.

Boston is awash in colleges and universities—large and small, excellent and mediocre. It should have been the perfect city for meeting bright, young, single men. The selection at NEC, however, was paltry: lots of self-absorbed, delusional musicians, many of them gay, all with uncertain futures.

Several faculty members were not much older than I, but most of them were married, including Lyle. The dearth of dating prospects contributed to my growing crush on Lyle. Because I was anxious to meet the theory requirements as quickly as possible, Lyle spent extra time with me, addressing the gaps in my background that resulted from attending a liberal arts college rather than a music school or conservatory. In these one-on-one sessions, I struggled to concentrate on score analysis, rather than his sexy hands caressing the piano keys. For a second time, I had fallen for a married man. Unlike Alan in Atlanta, Lyle was a devoted husband; any connection with him beyond teacher/student existed only in my fantasies. I had plenty of those.

Chapter 16: Hard Decisions

The excitement of attending a conservatory and living in a different part of the country was tempered by loneliness. With no friends in Boston, I decided to spend Christmas in Atlanta with my parents and symphony friends. Once there, however, I discovered the orchestra was on vacation, and most of my friends had left town. Only Judy, the one married person in our group, remained.

"Phone for you," Mother called to me, my second day in Atlanta, "someone named Tom." Tom was Judy's husband.

"Hi, Tom," I said as I slid sideways into the chair. The phone sat on a small desk, squeezed into my parents' dining room. If I pulled the chair out too far, it bumped into the large mahogany table that dominated the room. "How have you and Judy been?"

"Hi, Ernestine. We had a good fall, and of course, with all the kids, Christmas is always exciting. How's your visit with your parents going?"

"Okay. I'm glad I'm only here for ten days."

"Yes, based on some things Judy's said about your dad, I can imagine even ten days is long." I was surprised Judy had talked to Tom about my father. Seemed a little odd. "Say," Tom continued, "we'd like to take you out to dinner while you're here, sort of a welcome home. Could you meet us on December 27?"

"Oh, that's so nice of you. I'd love to. It'll be a nice break from my parents. Do you have a restaurant in mind?"

"I thought Benihana's would be good. Have you ever been there?"

"No, and I don't get many chances to have Japanese food. That sounds great," I said. We agreed to meet at the restaurant at 7:00 p.m.

When I first went to one of Tom and Judy's dinner parties, I'd been impressed by their sprawling, interesting house. The contemporary artwork and sleek-looking furniture contrasted sharply with the stodgy decor in my parents' house and my cheaply furnished apartment. Knowing Judy's symphony salary was modest, I figured the luxurious house reflected Tom's success as a life insurance salesman.

At six foot four, Tom towered over his petite wife, although their fourteen-year-old son was catching up. This all-blond, good-looking family of eight never seemed to argue. When the kids joined us for part of a meal, Tom teased them in a friendly, affectionate way, nothing like my distant father. Judy seemed to be the strict parent, Tom the encouraging, supportive one. The last time I went to their house, while we were having appetizers, Tom's five-year-old daughter appeared and climbed into Tom's lap, setting off a wave of longing so sudden and powerful I lost track of the conversation. I kept staring at Tom and his daughter, both so comfortable with this extraordinary display of father-daughter affection. Even as a young girl, I had very little physical contact with my father. I envied Tom's kids for having such a loving father.

At the end of that evening, both Judy and Tom hugged their guests. Was it my imagination, or did Tom pull me into him a little aggressively? I should've paid closer attention.

A gust of late December wind whipped against the door to Benihana's restaurant. After I wrestled it open, the aroma of grilling meats and the sound of chefs' flashing knives greeted me. I spotted Tom right away, seated at the hibachi table between a vacant seat to his left and, to my surprise, only strangers to his right.

"I'm afraid Judy isn't feeling well and won't be joining us tonight," Tom explained as I sat down.

"I'm sorry to hear that," I said. Even seated, I had to look up, Tom's head towering above mine. "Please say hello for me and tell her I hope she feels better soon."

"I will. I hope you don't mind, I ordered some sake for us." Tom filled the tiny cups from a small carafe. "Have you ever tried it?"

"No, but I've been curious."

"Ah," I said after a sip, "it's good. And the warmth is nice on a cold night." I leaned against the back of the high stool and watched the samurai-like motions of the two hibachi chefs. The sounds of conversations around us blended with the scrapes of the flashing knives. After preparing the steak and vegetables perfectly, the chef served us with a flourish, using his knife to flick a piece of daikon off my plate into the top of his tall chef's hat.

"Judy and I have thought about you up North this year," Tom said. "We figured Boston must feel pretty cold to someone from Atlanta."

"It actually hasn't been that bad so far," I said.

"I'm glad. But knowing it will be, Judy and I decided to buy you a winter coat, to ease your transition into northern winters."

"Oh my goodness, that's so sweet of you. But you really shouldn't have. I mean, I'll be fine."

"You say that now," he said, "but it'll be worse in January, and it's a damp cold."

We proceeded to talk about Tom's work, their kids, and the current symphony gossip. I didn't notice when the empty carafe was replaced by a full one, nor did I pay attention to how often Tom refilled my cup.

"So, how about dessert?" Tom asked.

"Oh, I couldn't, I'm completely full. Everything was great. I just wish Judy had been here."

"Me too. Say, the coat we bought is in my office, which is just around the corner. We can stop by there before you drive home, and you can try on the coat to see if it fits."

"Okay, a little walk in cold air sounds good." I hadn't realized how strong sake was, compared to regular wine. I hoped walking would sober me up, but the walk was too short. Before I knew it, we were there.

"So here it is, what do you think?" Tom asked, holding a full-length, tan suede coat, trimmed with white fur down the front as well as on the hood and cuffs. Though the fur was obviously fake, the coat looked expensive.

"It's lovely, but I feel funny about this. It's too much."

"We really wanted to do this for you. You can at least try it on."

"That fits perfectly," he said after I put on the coat. "You look terrific in it."

"Whoa," I said, as I tried to slip my arms out of the sleeves. The room was spinning.

"Maybe you should rest a bit before driving home," Tom suggested as he helped me take off the coat and laid it across one of the plush, white leather chairs.

"Okay, that's probably a good idea." The room had stopped spinning, but I wasn't sure I could drive home safely. Tom led me to the large matching sofa at one end of his spacious office and suggested I lie down for a few minutes. As soon as I lay down, I drifted off.

A pressure across my chest jolted me awake. It took me a few seconds to realize Tom had pinned me down with his massive left arm. My skirt was bunched up around my hips, and I was naked from the waist down. When I tried to move my legs, they wouldn't obey.

"Tom, what are you doing?" My voice sounded far away.

As Tom used his right arm to push my legs apart, I struggled, but I was no match for his large frame.

"No, Tom. Don't!" I pleaded, as he forced himself inside me.

He was violent, hurting me, and wouldn't stop despite my sobbing and saying no, over and over. The longer it went on, the quieter I got, till I gave up. He finally came with a loud grunt.

I have no memory of getting dressed or driving to my parents' house. I was relieved they were both asleep, but my father's angry voice rang inside my head anyway, all through that terrible night. "How could you be so stupid!"

If my parents noticed how withdrawn I was, how little I talked or ate the next two days, they showed no interest in finding out why. Back in Boston I told no one, cut off communication with Tom and Judy, and tried to channel my turmoil into energy for practicing the flute. I ached to listen to the most agonized movements of Mahler and Tchaikovsky, but I had no stereo. Whenever I heard an emotionally wrenching piece on the classical music radio station, I surrendered to it, finding comfort in the profound sorrow I could not put into words.

After two weeks, I could concentrate better. Throwing myself into musical pursuits, I pushed the whole episode to the bottom of my consciousness. But the relief was short-lived. The day before my early February birthday, I bought a pregnancy test kit. Though the odds were against it, I knew I was pregnant. How could such a terrible night not have dire consequences? When the test came back positive, I again felt completely responsible, the guilt all mine.

Politically, logically, even morally, I'd always been pro-choice. An easy belief, in the abstract. But now it was real, now I was the one who had to choose—and soon. The thought of bearing Tom's child was repugnant. How could I love this child? How could I care for someone who might look like him, a constant reminder of a night of violence? Even at twenty-five, I was far from ready to be a parent; I would at best be a resentful mother. I tried to imagine how I could support a baby. The modest scholarship I depended on would disappear if anyone found out about the pregnancy, and other than being a musician, I had no job skills. As if my mother were in the room, her oft-spoken warning came back to me: "If you ever get pregnant, don't come here, because you would not be allowed in this house." Not knowing where to turn, I felt isolated, powerless, and frightened.

Although I had no friends in Boston, I remembered a conversation I'd had with Fran, a fellow graduate student. We'd been commiserating about politics, and the subject of birth control came up. Something she said gave me the impression she'd gone through an abortion. The next day, I found Fran in a practice room and confessed my dilemma. Immediately supportive, she gave me the name of a doctor who performed abortions and offered to come with me for the procedure. Grateful for her offer, I told her she needn't accompany me, but that I'd let her know if I changed my mind.

Four days later, I took the subway to the hospital. I hoped I'd be physically able to take it back to the dorm. After paying two hundred dollars for the abortion, I had no money for a taxi. It was 1973; *Roe v. Wade* had just passed, but abortion was still illegal in Massachusetts. As instructed, I arrived at the hospital after hours and went to an unmarked back entrance.

A nurse unlocked the door, took my cash, and led me into a small room. After giving me a hospital gown to change into, she told me to lie on the table and put my feet in the stirrups. She said I wouldn't have to wait long.

She was right. When he came into the room, the doctor was abrupt—no name, no talking, no eye contact. After the procedure, a sense of desolation swept over me, compounding the physical pain. While I was crying quietly in the deserted waiting room, the doctor walked by and said, with obvious contempt, "Why are you crying now? You got rid of it."

In my shattered state, I felt I deserved that comment. But he did have a point: the ordeal was over. Or so I thought.

In early March, barely three weeks after the abortion, I faced another difficult decision: whether to return to Atlanta. My plan had been to spend one year in Boston, working on sound with Mr. Pappoutsakis, while regaining enough confidence to face Warren. The following year's Atlanta Symphony contract had to be signed and returned by March 15. As the date drew closer, the decision seemed less and less clear.

Studying at New England served as a constant reminder of how difficult it would be to get a job with another orchestra as good as the Atlanta Symphony. Of the nine flutists residing on my dorm floor, eight would be ecstatic to have my job. There were over thirty flutists at NEC, each aspiring to be a professional musician. Thirty at one music school—one of the best, but one of many. For the past six months, each time I walked from the elevator to my room and heard all those flutists practicing, I wondered if I played as well as any of them.

Mr. Pappoutsakis thought I should return to the Atlanta Symphony. He had spent his orchestral career playing second flute to someone with whom he rarely spoke. But a frosty relationship with a colleague is one thing; constant badgering is something else, especially when it comes from a beloved former teacher.

When I thought about *not* returning to Atlanta, inner voices of the two significant men in my life chided me. Initially against my joining the ASO, my father had gradually accepted the fact that I had, somehow, gotten a job earning a living wage. He wished that job were in a field other than music, but at least I wasn't a financial burden to him. His anxiety about my inability to support myself fueled my own self-doubt.

"How can you even consider giving up a lucrative job when you have no guarantee of getting another one? It would be foolish and stupid," I imagined him saying.

The other voice was, of course, Warren's—not just imagined, but remembered:

"What makes you think you're good enough to keep this job? You have no business playing professionally. Why don't you just give up?"

The same comments that had driven me to take a year's leave now taunted me as I considered giving up the job. The money I'd saved would enable me to stay a second year, finishing the master's degree at NEC, but then what? Deplete my savings paying for airfare to heartbreaking auditions? Most painful was the nagging thought that I'd gotten into the Atlanta Symphony not because I played well but because I was Warren's student. How delusional to think I could win another orchestra audition. I should return to my secure job or figure out something else to do with my life. Perhaps, I thought fleetingly, I should use my money to fund one year at a business school instead of a conservatory. But I knew that was my father's voice, not mine. It would be years before I could see that doubts about my musical ability were based on

Warren's negative comments, not on objective assessments of my playing. If only Lynette had been there to insist Warren's comments didn't reflect how well I played. It never occurred to me to call her.

So there I was on March 7, sitting on my narrow bed, staring at the ASO contract. One piece of paper containing one paragraph—so few words, so much riding on them. How likely was it that Warren had mellowed during the past year? Frustrated by endlessly circling thoughts, I left the room and went downstairs to check my mailbox, where I found an envelope addressed in an unfamiliar hand. In the elevator going back to my room, I tried to place the location of the return address in Atlanta. From Jill somebody, a name that sounded vaguely familiar.

Inside were two handwritten pages. Wasting no space on pleasantries, Jill described her difficult situation, beginning with two paragraphs about Warren's behavior, paragraphs I might have written. Jill was my replacement in the ASO. Less than a year ago, when she had won the audition, she'd been thrilled. Although it was only a one-year contract, she'd hoped the experience with a professional orchestra would be the cachet she needed to be invited to audition for other jobs. (With so many applicants for flute positions, professional orchestras often eliminated dozens of flutists based solely on their résumés.) Warren's constant abuse had destroyed her dreams of playing professionally. With three months left in her contract, she wondered whether she would make it to the end of the year. Disillusioned and struggling through each rehearsal, she was considering other careers. It was a bitter, heartbreaking letter, ending with the sentence I'll never forget: "You would have to be crazy to come back to this job."

After reading the letter, two things were finally clear: I would *not* subject myself to another year of Warren's attacks;

second, no matter how grim the odds, I would keep pursuing a career in music. Getting another job would be difficult, but I was determined to chase the dream as far as I could. After writing *I resign* across the contract, I sealed it in an envelope, walked down the street with renewed energy, and dropped it in the corner mailbox.

Would I have made the same decision had I not received Jill's letter? I'd like to think so. Even in the tough world of professional orchestras, Warren's behavior was egregious and especially hurtful to me. Still, giving up that secure job felt like letting go of a trapeze bar without knowing whether I could catch another one. Flying through the air, with no net underneath.

Development, Part II

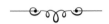

The arc of the story might end here, with the pivotal decisions to quit the symphony and leave Atlanta for good. The shape of the memoir would then reflect the proportions of a typical eighteenth-century sonata form, where the development is the same length as the exposition: the hundred or so pages of the exposition would be balanced by a hundred pages in the development. The section would conclude with me breaking free from the shackles of both my father and Warren and escaping the town where I'd been raped.

Life, however, is messier, and leaving one's hometown does not erase the past. The release I felt after returning the unsigned ASO contract lasted through most of the second year at New England, but the damage from years of Warren's harassment—his gaslighting—as well as the rape and its aftermath, eventually resurfaced. Underneath the guilt and self-doubt caused by those things lay the nagging thought that my father was right: I could never make a living in music. Getting into the ASO was a fluke, an unrepeatable anomaly.

The story of escaping my father and Warren was far from over. Consequently, the development continues, similar to Beethoven's 1804 *Eroica Symphony*, and many nineteenth-century pieces, where the development section is much longer than the exposition.

Chapter 17: Conservatory

My second year at NEC, I escaped the dorm and joined a small coed co-op in a two-story, slightly run-down rental house in Malden, a short bus ride from the northern end of the MBTA Orange Line. Among the six of us, all in our late twenties, the only other student was Hiroshi, a Japanese doctoral student in neurobiology at Tufts University. The other four had various jobs, but we coordinated our schedules to eat dinner together most nights, each person cooking one night a week.

Hiroshi taught us the right way to serve rice: with a little soy sauce and a generous amount of freshly grated ginger. Hiroshi was the glue that made our motley group gel into a sort of family, as we gathered around the dinner table and talked about how our day had gone. Much less companionable than my Atlanta dinner group, but far better than eating alone. And no food fights.

In the five-bedroom house, my room had been a sewing room, no bigger than my dorm room at NEC, but with a large bay window that took up all of one wall. Just outside the window, on the right as I looked out, was a scrawny, tulip poplar tree. Though its leaves were sparse, they added a splash of rich golden color that fall. The bed was a single mattress on the floor, the rent forty dollars a month, less than half what the others paid. Three men, three women, friends only.

One of the best improvements was my practice space. Because my housemates left early in the morning, I could practice in the large, acoustically appealing living room. Most classes at NEC were in the late morning or afternoon. Even with the forty-five-minute commute, I could practice from 8:00 to 9:30 a.m. and still get to NEC on time. In the evenings, I practiced in my small room—not ideal, but easier to concentrate without the distraction of others practicing.

My second year at NEC was extraordinary: a year without male harassment of any kind. I couldn't remember the last time I'd escaped pressure from men for such an extended period. If flute lessons were somewhat disappointing, other courses provided unexpected joys. The faculty at NEC were not only experts in their fields but also gifted and devoted instructors. As teachers, composers, and conductors, they were in positions of power, but unlike Warren, they taught effectively without taking advantage of their positions. No suggestive flattery, no belittling insults or other manipulative behavior. My interactions with the faculty at NEC were blessedly uncomplicated.

Both years in Boston I had the privilege of working with John Heiss—flutist, composer, and towering intellect. As kind as he was brilliant, Mr. Heiss taught music theory and composition, coached chamber music, gave occasional flute lessons, and organized concerts of new music. I'll never forget his meticulous dissection of Varèse's *Density 21.5*, his insistence on constant mental subdivision of each beat, which is the only way to accurately perform Varèse's intricate rhythmic subtleties.

Mr. Heiss balanced his obsessive focus on detail with equal attention to musical shape and expressive phrasing.

Unfailingly enthusiastic and energetic, Mr. Heiss shared his wealth of knowledge to enlighten, but never intimidate, students. He was encouraging, personable, and interested in all his students, even those who, like me, had only a few lessons with him.

Early in my second year, I played principal flute under Gunther Schuller for a performance of Beethoven's Symphony No. 6, *Pastoral.* When I found out I'd be principal, I was pleased but worried. Schuller sometimes lacerated students in the orchestra if he was unhappy with their playing. In the early 1970s, verbal abuse from conductors was still common. I also knew, from playing under his baton in Atlanta, how tricky it could be to figure out who he was looking at when he made comments in rehearsals. With one good eye and one made of glass, the focus of his gaze was never where it appeared to be. His intimidating presence and reputation for impatience made players hesitant to ask, "Are you talking to me? Do you want *me* to play louder?" In Atlanta, I merely observed it; as principal flute, I would be in his crosshairs.

But the first few rehearsals went smoothly. Then I received a note to go to Mr. Schuller's office. He must have been unhappy with my playing, I thought, and had decided to put someone else on the principal part. Nice of him to tell me in person. Or maybe it wouldn't be so nice. More like being summoned to the principal's office.

The main building of NEC, though imposing on the outside, had only a few offices, many of them small and dilapidated. Schuller's was by far the biggest and best maintained, though it was crammed with books, scores, records, and file cabinets. Schuller sat behind a large, handsome desk made of dark wood.

"Have a seat," he said, looking at the person to my right. I figured he meant me.

"So," he said, leaning back in his large chair, "you played with the Atlanta Symphony."

"I did."

"I conducted there a few years ago."

"I remember it well. We played your *Seven Studies on Themes of Paul Klee*."

"Yes, the performances went very well," he said. "You've already been here a year. Why didn't you stop by to say hello?"

Because you scare the hell out of me.

"I don't know. I guess I didn't think you'd remember me."

"Of course I remember you," he said. "You were second flute, sitting beside a large man with black hair."

What a memory.

"That's right," I said, "and in fact, your piece is the reason I'm here."

"What do you mean?"

"When I listened to the *Seven Studies* recording, I thought the flutist had the most beautiful sound I'd ever heard. I wanted to study with him, just to be next to that sound. So I came here to study with Mr. Pappoutsakis."

"That's quite a story." He smiled, looking—much to my surprise—friendly. "Thank you for coming in. I hope you enjoy the rest of your time here."

"I will," I said, resisting the impulse to bow as I left the office.

Even with such esteemed faculty, I learned at least as much from the other flutists, especially Ivy and Judy, the two mentioned earlier. In addition to noting what they practiced, I made a point of playing duets with them and with other flutists whose sounds I admired, trying to imitate whatever aspect of their sound I liked. One of the best things about being at NEC was hearing so many different, excellent flute sounds.

As for a social life, my first year in Boston I made very

few friends. Although the second year was better, the friendships with my co-op housemates were casual. After the rape,
I had no interest in dating, but I missed the support of musician friends, especially the easy camaraderie of our woodwind
quintet. Shared meals, lots of laughter, challenging chamber
music performances—it all seemed like a lifetime ago.

Now that I'd made the difficult decision not to go back
to Atlanta, I had to figure out what to do next. (In Atlanta
at that time, the ASO was the only professional outlet for
classical musicians.) To make a living as a flutist, I could either
take auditions for other orchestra jobs or apply for teaching
positions in colleges and universities. Most schools preferred
hiring someone with a doctorate, but earning a doctor of
musical arts (DMA) degree would take years. The odds of
getting another orchestra job, however, were slim: over a
hundred applicants for each job and only three or four flute
positions open in a typical year. My modest savings would run
out quickly if I paid travel expenses to audition sites. Because
of the tight job market, when flutists got orchestra jobs, they
usually stayed there. No wonder both Mr. Pappoutsakis
and the other flutists at NEC thought I should return to the
Atlanta Symphony.

Midway through my second year at NEC, Lynette called.

"Hey, Ernestine." Lynette made my name sound like a
burst of joy. "Do you know about the second flute opening
in Baltimore?"

"Yes, I just saw it posted in the *International Musician*."
The *IM* is the official journal of the musicians' union.

"You're going to audition, aren't you?" Lynette's husband,
Frank Cohen, played principal clarinet with the Baltimore
Symphony. She played with a chamber music group in Bethesda,
Maryland.

"Actually, I'm kind of on the fence about it," I said.

"Gosh, I hope you take it. You can stay here, so you wouldn't have to pay for meals or lodging. You really should audition. Not many flutists have your experience of playing second flute with a major orchestra."

"That may be true, but I get really nervous for auditions," I said.

"But think about why you're auditioning, how different this job would be from Atlanta. I can guarantee no one in the flute section, or anywhere else, would treat you like Warren did. Remember, you're free of him! Besides, I'd really like to see you."

"Yes, seeing you would be great, but what you said about being free of Warren? Unfortunately, when I get nervous, he's still in my head."

We argued for several minutes. Always my biggest fan, Lynette persuaded me I had a good chance of getting the job. It had been a year and a half since we'd lived together, but I still missed Lynette's warm support. She could always banish my self-doubt, whether about flute or anything else.

"Okay, I'll do it."

"Great! Just let me know when your flight gets in, and I'll pick you up."

"Actually, I thought I'd take the Greyhound bus." Lynette had forgotten what it's like to be a student with no money.

"Are you sure? It's such a long trip."

"True, but much cheaper than flying. I'll let you know which bus I take."

A few days after I sent my résumé to the Baltimore Symphony personnel manager, I received an audition time and a list of the twelve orchestral excerpts that would be on the audition. (For professional orchestras, audition excerpts are selected from the particular instrument's group of twenty or so well-known orchestral pieces.) Like most flutists, I knew the standard excerpts; the challenge was to play them all note-perfect, with a beautiful sound, flawless intonation, and dazzling technique. For the next three weeks, I practiced nothing but the excerpts. When Mr. P seemed impressed after I played a few of them in a lesson, I allowed a little hope to creep in.

Lynette was right about the long trip. The bus left Boston at 12:30 a.m. and arrived in Baltimore at noon. The audition was on Thursday, so I took the bus Tuesday to give myself a day to recover from the trip.

"I'm so glad you're here!" Lynette said, embracing me at the bus station. "That ride was so long. How are you?"

"A little stiff and definitely sleep-deprived, but it's worth it to spend time with you," I replied, happy to see her wide, always-slightly-mischievous grin again.

"Yes, this is great." Then her grin faded a bit. "Just to warn you, we had a surprise visit from Frank's brother Aaron, who's a little strange, but don't worry, we have plenty of room."

From my visit the previous summer, I knew the Cohens had a lovely three-bedroom Tudor house in a leafy neighborhood of fine homes, all about sixty years old.

I liked Frank a lot and loved his exquisite clarinet playing. His brother had Frank's dark eyes, strong chin, and short-but-fit build. Otherwise, alas, he was nothing like Frank. A nerdy, awkward man, Aaron spoke with a nasal voice and stood a little too close when he talked to me. But the pleasure of Lynette's company far outweighed that minor annoyance.

During a tasty dinner of clam spaghetti, Aaron, a non-musician, said very little while the three of us talked about mutual musician friends and about Sergiu Comissiona, the conductor of the Baltimore Symphony. Frank both liked and complained about Comissiona, as orchestra members tend to do. I went to bed early and woke up refreshed, but whenever I thought about the audition, my stomach clenched.

From 9:00 to 11:30 that morning, Lynette's house filled with the intertwining voices of flute, clarinet, and bassoon. Lynette insisted I use the music room in their basement, where I barely heard the sounds coming from the upstairs rooms. There was also intermittent squawking, as Lynette and Frank whittled away and tested reeds by blowing through them (called "crowing the reed").

"You sound really great," Lynette said at the end of my morning practice session. "Your double tonguing is fantastic."

She'd heard me practicing the excerpt from Mendelssohn's *A Midsummer Night's Dream*. The infamous flute solo in the Scherzo consists of fast tonguing, nonstop for several minutes at high speed. Breath control is also a challenge. There are only two places for fast breaths, and the last phrase is very long. Mr. Pappoutsakis suggested a trick: leave out one note and sneak in an extra breath, which ensures that the player won't run out of air at the end of the solo.

All afternoon, at least one of us was practicing, usually me. When I wasn't practicing, Lynette and I reminisced about Atlanta Symphony days; when Frank wasn't practicing, he and Aaron talked. I overheard Aaron describing his stringent health food diet, featuring massive amounts of herbs. After another good dinner, I went to bed around 10:00 p.m. Anxious about the audition, I didn't get to sleep until well after 2:00 a.m.

On Thursday, Lynette and Frank left early to go to their respective rehearsals. After a quick breakfast of granola, I started to go through the excerpts for the last time. Aaron kept barging in, wanting to talk. I kept shooing him out.

My audition time was 1:30 p.m. After a light lunch, I called a taxi at 12:15 p.m. to get me to the hall around 12:45 p.m. A few minutes before the taxi appeared, Aaron offered me a cup of greenish-yellow tea.

"I just made this with some herbs and stuff I found in

the backyard. Try it. If you're nervous about the audition, I bet this will settle your stomach."

I didn't want to waste time arguing with him, so I drank the earthy, slightly bitter tea. To avoid Aaron's distracting presence, I decided to wait outside. I'd just shut the front door when Aaron opened it again and stuck his head out. As the taxi turned the corner onto Lynette's street, Aaron said, "I now think some of those weeds are poisonous, so I made myself throw up. You should probably do the same."

"Poisonous?" my voice croaked. He nodded. I reminded myself he was my good friend's brother-in-law and choked down the swear words. As the cab pulled into the long drive-way, I just glared at him.

Arriving at the hall at 12:50 p.m., I decided not take Aaron's advice, though I certainly felt queasy. The usual gray-haired lady (they always seem to manage auditions) led me backstage to a large warm-up room, which sounded like an audio track from *The Birds*, with swarming flute sounds. There were probably only eight flutists, but all were playing fortissimo. Every time the cacophony subsided enough for me to hear one flutist, that person sounded terrific. What the hell was I doing there?

At 1:30 p.m. the personnel manager, after warning me not to utter a word during the audition, led me down a narrow hall and onto the large stage of Orchestra Hall, a stately old building that smelled a little like a musty cellar. I walked to the two music stands, placed side by side in the middle of the otherwise bare stage. The excerpts had been cut and pasted onto several large sheets of paper, all sitting on the stand to the right.

Before I started, I looked out into the dimly lit, mostly empty hall—a sea of pale blue seats, with a wide partition set up about halfway to the back of the hall. Behind it, I knew, sat the conductor, the principal flutist, Frank, and a couple of other woodwind players. Surely they could all hear my heart pounding. A disembodied voice in the hall said, "Please start with the first excerpt and play down each page." I tried to block out the negative Warren comments going through my head.

The main solo from Ravel's *Daphnis et Chloé* was the first excerpt, followed by several passages from Beethoven's *Leonore* Overture No. 3. My sound was a little tight on *Daphnis*, but I was pleased with *Leonore*. I slid the first page to the stand on the left and looked at the next page: Scherzo from *A Midsummer Night's Dream*. I breathed a little easier. Lynette was right; rapid tonguing was one of my strengths.

"Now play it again without the extra breath," the voice said as soon as I'd played the excerpt.

In a concert, no one would notice the omitted note because it was in the low register and went by so fast. On auditions, I learned that day, they noticed. I took as big a breath as I could going into the final long passage, but I ran out of breath and the last few notes were weak.

"Thank you. Please go to the next excerpt."

Rattled by the breath issue, I played the remaining excerpts without the focused concentration I needed and missed a note in Strauss's *Till Eulenspiegel*. Later Lynette tried to console me. "The fact that they asked you to play the scherzo again, and then had you play the rest of the excerpts is a good sign. Darn that scherzo. I know once you practice it, you'll be able to play it without the extra breath."

Sworn to secrecy, Frank could say nothing, but his look of discomfort confirmed what I already knew—the extra breath had destroyed whatever chance I might've had. From that day on, I always practiced the scherzo without the extra breath and got pretty good at it. But I couldn't do it on the spot. I was annoyed Mr. Pappoutsakis hadn't told me I should play the note on auditions.

It could have been worse. They could've said, "That's all we need to hear," after only one or two excerpts. After paying for airfare and hotel, applicants often play for two minutes. Two very expensive minutes. I wondered if giving up the Atlanta Symphony job had been a mistake.

My conclusion from the Baltimore experience might've been that I needed more time to recover from Warren's abuse, but in the all-or-nothing thinking my father had drummed into me, I took it to mean I'd never be successful competing in auditions for professional orchestras. Which left only the teaching path.

The auditions I took later that year—with confidence—were for admission into the DMA programs in flute performance at the University of Wisconsin (UW) and Indiana University (IU). The teaching assistantship at the UW paid pretty well, but IU had a slightly better reputation. I decided Wisconsin would be a better fit for me. My sister and her family lived in Madison, and it seemed a more interesting town (in the 1970s) than Bloomington.

While I was considering which school to attend, Capital University in Columbus, Ohio, invited me to an on-site audition and interview for their flute professor position. The visit went well, and I liked the faculty, especially the terrific Hungarian pianist who played for the recital portion of my interview. At the end of the two-day interview, the department chair offered me the position. My final meeting was with the president, who asked about my plans if I didn't accept the position. When I said I would pursue a DMA degree, he revealed that all faculty at Capital must have doctorates to get tenure. I appreciated his candor.

Teaching full-time would leave little time for practicing or playing in an orchestra, the two things I most enjoyed.

The large graduate music program at UW meant their student orchestra was probably very good. The salary Capital offered was, of course, much greater than the teaching assistantship stipend. As I considered my dwindling savings, my father's anxiety—still a palpable presence in financial decisions—argued in favor of accepting the position at Capital.

In the end, I did what I had done exactly a year previously: I took the riskier alternative. A year and a half away from both my father and Warren made this decision easier. I still felt like I was letting go of one trapeze bar with no guarantee of catching another, but this time there was a net underneath.

Chapter 18: Isthmus

The summer before moving to Madison, I played second flute at the Grand Teton Music Festival. That year the festival was a two-month season of orchestra concerts performed in Jackson Hole, Wyoming. Despite a ho-hum conductor, the orchestra was terrific, the setting, spectacular. We stayed in a ski lodge at the base of Rendezvous Mountain, highest point 10,927 feet. Instead of going to the usual gloomy practice room, each day I took a music stand several yards up the mountain, where I gazed on a profusion of blue, purple, and yellow wildflowers, set against the snowcapped peaks.

In addition to performing inspiring music in beautiful surroundings, I enjoyed a summer romance with a cute cellist. Single, horny, and exhilarated by musical and scenic highs, we had a brief affair with no expectations and no baggage.

When I got to Madison, I looked for a house like the Malden co-op—a place to share good food and fellowship. The co-op I found on the near east side was identical in size—six people sharing a two-story house—but with two disappointing differences. There was no attempt to eat meals communally, and two of the six inhabitants were a couple who constantly quarreled and had sex, both at high volume. After one semester, I moved to another shared house, this one on Madison Street, a nicer house on the near west side. There were six women, no couples, and no attempts to interact with each other. Housemates who remained strangers.

At first, I thought the people in Madison were boring. About a week later, I realized my mistake. Far from boring, they were simply less neurotic than the people I knew in Boston. Good, solid Midwestern values — like southern hospitality but more genuine.

Opened in 1969, the humanities building that housed the UW School of Music was a brutalist style, concrete monstrosity with windowless classrooms, low ceilings (except my office, tucked into an awkward corner), and confusing passageways. Faculty offices on the top floor had attractive, tall but narrow windows that iced over in the winter. Within a few months of construction, the windows began to leak. The practice rooms in the basement formed a large square around an open courtyard, the only place on the bottom floor with any natural light. Funding must have dried up, because instead of a lovely garden, the courtyard was a functionless gravel pit, its doors permanently locked. Students called it the Inhumanities Building.

The main concert venue, Mills Concert Hall, was aesthetically similar to the rest of the bunker-like building, with the added drawback of mediocre acoustics, a striking contrast to the elegant, acoustically perfect Jordan Hall at NEC. Morphy Recital Hall wasn't so much ugly as strange. The attractive wood of the stage and surprisingly comfortable seats were offset by the shape of the hall: tall and narrow, with seats so steeply banked that performers faced a tower of people who seemed about to topple onto the stage. The audience felt that, too, with vertigo adding to the weirdness. Acoustically, Morphy was so reverberant that crisp staccatos were impossible.

My office, in a corner of the humanities building basement, was in a cul-de-sac of five practice rooms used as small offices for graduate music students. Because of the setup, I ran into the other graduate students frequently and became especially close to pianist Mary Hunt, another DMA student. Mary and I were both twenty-seven and the same short height. We both had dark eyes and hair, though her hair was short, mine waist-length. In other ways, we were very different. A devoted Catholic who'd been married several years, Mary lived with her husband in their house on Few Street, close to Tenney Park, and seemed very settled. I was single, agnostic, had grave doubts about my future, and moved three times during my four years there. But she was a supportive, steadying friend whose calm manner belied a ferocious dedication to ever-higher standards for her own playing. She performed with me on several recitals, including pieces with wicked-hard piano parts, such as Schubert's *Variations on "Trockne Blumen"* and the Sonata by Prokofiev.

From my parents' basement to the remodeled room at NEC, I'd sought dead practice rooms. My little office in Madison was peculiar. Due to a quirk in construction, the corner room had a ceiling that rose as high as a second story. Although I'd added a rug, the bare cement walls made the room too live. For some reason, acoustical tiles hung only in the tallest part, starting about six feet up. To get closer to those tiles, I tried standing on my desk. Voilà, perfect acoustics.

One night, after most people had left the building, I turned out the lights, stood on the desk, and played through beautiful melodies. Alone with my sound, I poured my heart into flute solo melodies, operatic arias, and cheesy love songs, remembering the freedom and joy I felt, years ago, singing on our swing set. I was in my own lovely sound world . . . until the sound of a key in the lock and sudden, blinding light. The janitor had come in to empty the trash can. There I was, standing on my desk, with the lights out. And I'd been practicing on one leg, in a yoga tree pose. How to explain? I mumbled something about the lights not working but couldn't explain why I was standing on my desk. The guy looked at me doubtfully and flicked the light switch off and on a few times.

"Seems to be working fine," he said.

———

Earning the doctor of musical arts degree served the long-range goal of getting a teaching position; I also thought studying with another flute teacher would fill the pedagogical holes in my background. Warren Little's demanding regimen taught me how to develop facile technique, and Mr. Pappoutsakis had shown me ways to work on sound, but neither teacher worked on vibrato, breathing, or even holding the flute in the most relaxed way possible. I thought by studying with another master teacher, one less overworked, I would learn how to explain things to students, assuming I'd eventually get a teaching position. Unfortunately, although Mr. Cole was a great teacher for undergrads, he never said much in my lessons other than "very good." Perhaps Cole, like Mr. Pappoutsakis, thought I knew more than I did simply because I'd played in the Atlanta Symphony.

I gradually learned what most teachers know: the best way to understand something is to teach it to others. For my assistantship, I taught several very good freshmen music majors as well as a graduate student working on her master's in music education. I also had two adult students who studied flute just for fun, and we had plenty of that.

With its large graduate program, I'd assumed UW would have a fine student orchestra, which had factored into my decision to choose UW. My hunger for orchestral playing, diminished by years of sitting beside Warren Little, had rebounded at NEC. The first year at UW, however, the orchestra was weak, due to a terrible conductor. I decided not to audition for it. The following year, they hired Phillip Lehrman, a talented young man, fresh from his post with the New York Philharmonic as assistant conductor to Leonard Bernstein. I auditioned for the orchestra and was delighted to get the principal position.

"Wow, Mr. Lehrman is amazing," I said to Martha, the graduate student playing second flute in the UW orchestra.

"Yes, I guess he didn't make up the part about conducting the New York Philharmonic last year," Martha said with her slow, sardonic smile. "He seems a little cocky, though."

"Well, he's a conductor."

"Hah, true, at least for successful conductors."

From the first rehearsal, Lehrman began to transform the UW orchestra, and as he demanded more and more, we rose to his standards. Maestro Lehrman chose difficult music that challenged and excited us. He kept rehearsals moving, often using his East Coast humor to soften a critical remark. Some of my polite, Midwestern peers thought him abrasive, but I found his humor witty and his musicianship inspiring.

As principal flute, I was under constant scrutiny from the conductor. At first, I was too nervous to think much about Phil Lehrman, other than to hope he liked my playing. Gradually, my admiration for his intellect, musicality, and conducting skills metamorphosed into the familiar hero worship of a male authority figure. I began to crave his approval. That he was short, balding, and slightly heavy mattered not at all.

That semester I enrolled in Lehrman's music theory course, "Advanced Analysis of Symphonic Literature," one of the best courses I took at UW. I loved digging into a score, trying to pinpoint exactly what made each work a masterpiece. Unlike the autocratic maestro on the podium, in class Lehrman encouraged us to voice our own insights, even to contradict him—more of a seminar than a lecture class. When he laughed after some comment I made (an appreciative laugh), I noticed his cute dimples and the way his eyes sparkled when he thought something was funny. Although he was clearly the one with greater knowledge, Lehrman treated the students as equals.

I looked forward to writing my first paper for the class, until Mr. Lehrman announced all papers must be typed. I balked. Lehrman wasn't swayed by the fact that I'd made it through two degrees writing papers by hand, or that I'd had only one semester of typing, back in high school. He did, however, offer to let me use the typewriter in his office, but only at night when he wasn't around, which suited me fine.

The first paper was due on a Friday morning. Thursday night I arrived at Lehrman's office at 9:00 p.m. After the custodian let me in, I got to work. At 2:30 a.m., barely halfway through the movement of the Mozart symphony, I decided to cut part of the analysis and simply get the thing done. At 5:45 a.m., I typed the last word and added, handwritten, "I could say more, but it's 5:45 and I'm exhausted."

A week later, Lehrman returned our papers. Right below my handwritten comment, Lehrman had written, "*Schlaf gut mein Freund. Deine Arbeit ist erledigt.*" ("Sleep well, my friend. Your work is done," in German because Mozart was an Austrian composer.) By this point—three weeks and six rehearsals into the term—I'd noticed that when our eyes met in rehearsals, Lehrman's gaze lingered just a bit longer than necessary. He also smiled after some of my solos, which he didn't do for anyone else, no matter how well they played.

The comments on the paper confirmed what I suspected: my feelings weren't one-sided.

Why are conductors so sexy? Conductor infatuation may seem juvenile, but even jaded, middle-aged lifers in professional orchestras, on the rare occasions when a conductor inspires them, feel an intense connection with the conductor, especially during performances. When that connection is one-on-one—such as an encouraging smile right before a solo—the bond is personal. Partners creating fleeting, magical moments. Like the best lovemaking.

In my case, the pattern was admiration, then infatuation, then desire. These crushes always involved a man who shared my passion for orchestral music and filled my need for approval from a male authority figure.

After resisting the pull toward each other for a couple of months, midway through the semester we began dating. Off the podium, Phil was affectionate and very funny. Plus, he really liked my playing, always a turn-on. Faculty-student dating was frowned upon, and Phil was untenured, so although we were the same age, we kept the relationship secret.

Debussy's *Prelude to the Afternoon of a Faun* is one of those pieces flutists long to play. Named after a poem by Stéphane Mallarmé, Debussy's 1894 work ushered in the Impressionist period of Western classical music. (As usual, music came later than the comparable style in art.) The faun is a man-goat. The piece loosely describes the faun's dreams of pursuing woodland nymphs, the faun represented by the flute, in its sultry low register. Like Impressionist painters exploring color for color's sake, Debussy explored different sonorities through his brilliant orchestrations.

My delight in seeing *Afternoon of a Faun* scheduled for the December concert turned to anxiety when I saw that Phil (no more Maestro Lehrman) had put the piece at the beginning of the program. *Afternoon of a Faun* begins with one of the longest single-breath solos in the flute repertoire, right up there with the scherzo from *A Midsummer Night's Dream*. Long phrases are especially challenging for petite females. With smaller lungs, we have to find ways of conserving air without sacrificing the quality or projection of the sound. Flute requires more air than any other instrument except tuba.

Opening the program with *Faun* meant that the first notes of the concert would be mine and mine alone, with no time to settle down. Breathing problems are worse if you're nervous, so I prepared for the concert by running up and down a flight of stairs several times, then grabbing my flute and playing the solo with a pounding heart and compromised air supply. There are many flute solos in the piece, but the very first one, when the flute is all alone, is the one flutists worry about the most. Once the orchestra comes in, you're not so naked.

Even at the first rehearsal of *Faun*, I was nervous. It didn't help that the graduate student playing second flute resented me because she'd been principal flute the previous year. However, the first time I played the opening solo, Martha said, "You know, I've never really liked this solo. The way you play it, I get it, I see why it's such a big deal." That generous compliment from an unlikely source calmed me down.

Because *Faun* was such a revered solo, I wanted to play it for Professor Cole. Having played in the Philadelphia Orchestra many years, he knew the excerpt well. I'd worked hard to find just the right tone color for the opening—sensuous yet sweet. I hoped Cole would also notice the way I used vibrato on the long first note to keep it alive and moving. But when I played the solo at one of my lessons, he said nothing. Anxious moments stretched into an awkward pause, as Mr. Cole gazed thoughtfully at his feet. I steeled myself for severe criticism.

"Know anyone who wants to buy a pair of slightly used Earth Shoes?" he asked.

I didn't know what to say. As I swallowed my disappointment, he explained that he'd bought the expensive shoes two days ago and was very dissatisfied with them.

"What did you think about the Debussy?" I asked, trying to mask my irritation.

"Oh, that was fine," he said, smiling.

The other two pieces on the program, Strauss's *Till Eulenspiegel* and Shostakovich's Symphony No. 5, also had lots of flute solos. On any other program, those pieces might've made me nervous, but once the Debussy was over, I relaxed and enjoyed the rest of the concert. The orchestra performed each concert twice; the first night, *Faun* went pretty well, the next night, even better. I felt lucky to be playing principal on pieces with such fabulous flute parts. That orchestra program, I realized with delight, contained more flute solos than any single program Warren got to play while I was in Atlanta.

Like many relationships based on infatuation, the first few months of dating Phil were the best. In addition to his prowess as a conductor, Phil's sophisticated wit delighted me. Having grown up in California, then living in New York, he exuded the same intensity I'd admired in many of the NEC faculty and in Alan Balter. Phil took me to the most expensive restaurants and ordered the best wine, my first experience with such an extravagant lifestyle. Keeping the relationship secret also added to its allure, for a while.

Successful conductors usually have big egos; Phil was no exception. I've often wondered if egotistical men—and less often women—are drawn to conducting because of the glory, or whether they become egomaniacs after basking in all the applause. As a lover, Phil's pedestal—or podium—made him just sexy enough to fuel my desire.

After we'd dated a few months, cracks in the pedestal began to appear, right before my March 22 solo performance of the Nielsen Flute Concerto. In the fall, I'd won the concerto competition, along with Mary, who would play the last movement of the Bartók Piano Concerto on the same program. Behind most concerto performances is a tug-of-war between two big egos—the conductor and a renowned, highly paid soloist who expects the conductor to follow her. Not so when the soloist is a student, even a doctoral student. Being the conductor's secret lover only added to the tension.

The orchestra part for the Nielsen is quite difficult, with tricky interplay between flutist and orchestra, and lengthy soloistic parts for both clarinet and trombone. In our one rehearsal, the clarinet and trombone parts were fine; the tough string parts in the opening of the piece were not. I wanted a fast tempo to create an edgy opening, but instead of intense and energetic, the violins sounded scratchy and out of tune. When Phil stopped the orchestra, I thought he was going to work on that passage with the violin section. Instead, he turned to me.

"Your tempo is much too fast. Let's start again at a reasonable tempo," he said, in an abrupt manner.

Would I have stood up to him had we not been lovers? Doubtful, given my assumption of Phil's superior musicianship. Even as I meekly agreed to take his tempo, something nagged at me. Later that evening, I identified what it was. Working with almost anyone else, Phil would've been more diplomatic. He might have insisted on a slower tempo, but he wouldn't have criticized the soloist—certainly not a male soloist.

Despite these tensions, the night of the concert I played well—clean technique, intense sound, well-shaped phrases, and dramatic cadenza. After the performance, Phil's comments to me about the Nielsen mirrored the feedback he would've given any soloist, positive but perfunctory. He went on to compliment himself on how well he'd followed me. (He had not; I followed him.) After other concerts, since Phil was the conductor and I merely an orchestra member, focusing on him made sense, or so I had rationalized. But I'd just played a solo concerto. Even I recognized Phil's self-absorption that night.

After the March concert, our relationship unraveled. I noticed how often Phil's clever sense of humor was at someone else's expense—similar to my father in that respect. During April and May, I had no rehearsals with him, which lessened the tension a bit, but even in casual conversations, he often belittled me.

Playing in the orchestra that spring, however, was awe-inspiring. The last concert of the year, with the UW Choral Union, was a performance of Verdi's *Requiem*, conducted by Wisconsin's choral director, Robert Fountain. Recognized as one of the country's top collegiate choral directors, Fountain inspired student choirs to reach beyond their abilities. Rehearsals with him were intense but not stressful. After the friction between Phil and me, playing under Fountain was exhilarating—no mixed messages from the podium, no fear of disappointing the conductor, no complicated extra-musical relationship. Once again, I experienced the deep satisfaction of playing my best, contributing my part to a stirring performance of a powerful piece.

"Why can't you go out to dinner tonight?" Phil asked, one day in late April.

"Phil, I already told you, I have to finish a paper for Les Thimmig's course."

"Oh yeah, Les is your new idol, right? Because he's tall and sexy." An undertone of mockery belied his teasing smile.

"Of course not. I'm just glad I'm taking this course. I never liked atonal or twelve-tone music before, maybe because I'd never heard Berg's Violin Concerto."

"Sure, everyone loves the Berg concerto, but what else?"

"Webern's *Five Pieces for Orchestra.*"

"Aha, you like the flutter tonguing."

"No, it's not that." I wanted to stand up for myself, to insist I'm more discerning than to judge pieces merely by the flute parts. But as so often happened with Phil, I couldn't find the right words quickly.

"What's your paper on?" he asked.

"Berg's *Lyric Suite.* It's also a terrific piece."

"Yes, I studied it years ago at USC." (The University of Southern California, known for its excellent music program.) "Which recording did you listen to?" Phil asked.

"The Juilliard Quartet, I think."

"You don't actually know, do you?"

"I'm pretty sure it was Juilliard." My certainty was waning.

"You should've listened to the Alban Berg Quartett. You know the love story behind that piece, don't you?"

I did, but only because I'd recently read the LP jacket notes. Phil's photographic memory made him a quick study. Was there any piece he didn't know? I was excited about the contemporary masterpieces we studied in Thimmig's course, but whenever I tried to share my enthusiasm with Phil, his vast musical knowledge reminded me how little I knew.

There it was again, the comparison trap. Phil's boundless musical expertise triggered the old feelings of inferiority, the legacy of growing up with a brilliant sister. I slowly realized that Phil encouraged this, relished being the authority. He didn't need to put me down; the more he expounded on his musical knowledge, the more keenly I felt my inferiority.

Phil's intellectual gifts meant he spent little time perusing scores and preparing for his classes. I, on the other hand, took full course loads, taught students as part of my assistantship, and practiced several hours a day. He wanted to spend more time together; I wanted to practice more. With Phil demanding what little time I had, there was no time for friends.

As I became more isolated, Phil's egocentric worldview enveloped me. My own accomplishments seemed meager. What was playing in the Atlanta Symphony compared to *conducting* the New York Philharmonic? I'd worked under Robert Shaw; he'd worked with Leonard Bernstein. I felt myself disappearing, much as I'd felt during the worst days in the Atlanta Symphony. I needed help.

Chapter 19: Therapist

When the psychiatric resident assigned to me opened the door to the waiting room and called my name, I looked up and met the gaze of Ichabod Crane. Tall, thin, and slightly stooped, Mark had a ruddy, pockmarked face and scruffy beard, framed by dirty black hair that fell below his shoulders. Concave chest. Melancholy expression. This character from Sleepy Hollow was supposed to help me work through issues of low self-esteem? What kind of self-image did *he* have?

Despite my misgivings at the first appointment, I saw Mark twice a week for almost ten months, starting in mid-April. The first sessions covered the usual family and childhood background. Because I now lived in the same town as Melinda, I talked a lot about the lesser-sister-comparison baggage. Mostly, I talked; Mark listened. I wondered if Mark would be as passive a therapist as Dr. Norton, the Atlanta analyst, had been.

In the third week, however, Mark began to interact more. He asked me to expand on a couple of issues, starting with why I was in therapy. I explained that my first eighteen months in Madison had gone well. I described what I enjoyed about my classes and what I liked about teaching. Over the past year and a half, I'd gained a great deal of confidence in my strengths as a flute teacher. I knew how important it was to establish a personal connection with each student, and to maintain a sense of humor, especially about myself.

"But," I explained, "my real passion is for playing in an orchestra. It's the one time I feel part of something essential and profound. For a while, playing principal flute in the orchestra was exciting. I loved it."

"What changed?" Mark asked.

I tried to explain the growing problems with Phil, and how being romantically involved with the conductor complicated things.

"What first drew you to Phil?" Mark asked.

"His musicianship, his musical knowledge. He's an excellent conductor, and a good classroom teacher. I took one of his courses last fall," I said.

"It sounds like you're drawn to men in positions of authority over you," Mark suggested.

"No, I wouldn't say that," I said. "I just like men who are smart, articulate, and funny."

"Funny?"

"Yes, I love Phil's wry sense of humor. He's clever and has lots of zany stories about people he's worked with, including some pretty famous musicians."

"Like who?" Mark asked.

"Well, Leonard Bernstein."

"He worked with Bernstein?"

"Yes, Phil was an assistant conductor with the New York Philharmonic, right before he came to Wisconsin."

"I can see why Phil impressed you."

"But it wasn't his credentials that impressed me; it was the way he transformed the orchestra," I said. "It's now as good as the top orchestra at the New England Conservatory, and that's a high standard because—"

"Let's get back to Phil." Mark seemed impatient with musical details. "You do agree that part of Phil's appeal is his position of power, don't you?" he asked.

"I don't think so. I've never thought of it that way."

"Isn't the conductor the one who controls the orchestra?"

"Sort of, but it's more leading than controlling."

"Doesn't the conductor determine the tempo? Doesn't he choose the music?" Mark persisted.

"True, but—"

"And if you're in his orchestra, you're under his control."

"You make it sound so perverse, but it's just the way large musical groups operate."

"Yes, with one person at the top, calling the shots," Mark went on, "and that's the person who attracts you."

"Okay, I'm attracted to men who are accomplished musicians, but it's because I value that, and I don't meet many single men who have those traits." My words were true, but I knew Mark was partially right. After all, hadn't I fallen for Michael, the conductor in Atlanta? And maybe Schuller would've appealed to me had he been younger.

Mark was silent, staring at me with unnerving intensity. I thought about his stare for days afterward. At the next session, wanting to refute Mark's theory, I charged right in.

"I don't think you're right about Phil's appeal being his authority over me," I said. "That makes it sound like I want someone to take charge of my life."

"I would put it a different way." Mark was using a hushed voice that disconcerted me. "You want someone to take care of you."

"No. I want my own life. In fact, that's why we're having problems. Phil's too self-centered to acknowledge my goals and accomplishments." I went on to describe how conversations with Phil had changed from equal exchanges of mutual support to conversations focused exclusively on his conducting.

"Besides," I continued, "if I were after a conductor who was a father figure, then the rehearsals I'm in now with Robert

Fountain would set off the longing. Fountain is older, white-haired, and quite fatherly, but I'm very comfortable with him on the podium. I don't have the slightest desire for more attention from him."

"I'm not saying you fall for every man who's in a position of authority, just that there is a strong connection here between authority and desire."

I left frustrated. At the first therapy session, I'd worried Mark would be too taciturn. Now I had the uneasy feeling he might be too directive.

I went straight from the session to a rehearsal—from frustration to inspiration. I loved playing under Mr. Fountain, especially for a terrific piece like Verdi's *Requiem*. I've often wished I could play the bass drum for the intense "Dies Irae" (Day of Wrath) movement, pounding the drum with offbeats. It must feel good to beat the hell out of a big, resonant instrument. Flute solos are often beautiful, but never have the raw, menacing power of that bass drum part.

For the next week or so, Mark dropped the subject of Phil. I spent the next sessions talking about my anxiety about making it in the competitive world of music. Then, toward the end of a session, Mark again brought up Phil.

"You've said you admire Phil's command of the orchestra," he said.

"Yes, I think he's a really good conductor."

"You like being with someone assertive."

"Wait, no, it was Phil's musicianship, not his assertiveness, that attracted me."

"In either case, it's the same person," Mark said. "An assertive conductor is likely to be sure of himself in other areas."

"Okay, I guess confidence does appeal to me." I had the vague feeling I'd lost an argument; before I could figure out what it was about, time was up. A week later, we again discussed Phil.

"Does Phil ask your opinion of his interpretations of pieces?" Mark asked.

"No, conductors don't really do that, but Phil does tell me his ideas about the music he's rehearsing. I'm in his orchestra, so I experience firsthand how he shapes a piece. Since I played a lot of the same works when I was in the Atlanta Symphony, I know the repertoire."

"Sounds like he's using you to boost his ego."

"N-no—"

"And perhaps being around someone who's so successful boosts *your* ego."

"You're twisting things. And I hate the idea that a woman's self-worth depends on a man. It's unfair and outdated."

"I didn't say your self-worth was based entirely on Phil. But I am suggesting, since his success as a conductor is very visible, that it's part of his appeal." I recognized some truth in Mark's statement, but why did Phil's impressive musicianship mean my needs and interests didn't matter? Somehow, I couldn't articulate those thoughts in sessions with Mark.

Though problems with Phil were what first brought me to therapy, I was beginning to think we were focusing too much on him. Perhaps Mark read my mind, because for the next few weeks, he didn't ask about Phil.

Slowly, despite his unkempt appearance, I began to trust Mark. His kind and gentle manner reassured me. I thought he was perceptive in pinpointing the factors that made me subject to male infatuations. But it was mostly his eyes—black, intense, boring-into-you eyes.

Mark prescribed Elavil to help with depression; unfortunately, it made my mouth too dry to practice. With each day the side effect got worse, so on the fourth day I stopped.

When I told him why I'd quit taking it, Mark reprimanded me for trying to undermine his authority. I felt like a bad patient, but I couldn't give up practicing.

In all the hours of therapy with Mark, I never mentioned my experience in the Atlanta Symphony. Warren's denigration of my playing lay at the heart of the doubt about my musical abilities, yet I avoided talking about him. Perhaps, even though I hadn't seen him in three years, I still feared Warren was right, I was an incompetent flutist. Or I may have avoided talking about Warren because I thought that part of my life was over. And yet, here I was again, questioning my musical abilities after the withdrawal of support from a male authority figure. This situation differed in that Phil was my lover as well as conductor and, unlike Warren, Phil hadn't overtly insulted me; he simply stopped being interested in my life.

That spring I gave the fifth of seven recitals required for the doctoral degree. When the last piece was over, the audience applauded warmly. Next came the three-part, post-recital ritual. First, accepting compliments backstage, both genuine ("You sounded great!") and obligatory ("I love your dress," which means "There was nothing good about your playing"). Phil's comments fell somewhere in between, as did Mr. Cole's, but everyone else, including several music faculty, seemed impressed.

The other two parts of the ritual were the small, post-recital party at my apartment and, finally, the unraveling. After the party, as I picked up the empty wine glasses and cheese trays, the familiar cloak of despondency wrapped around me. Practicing hard had kept the emptiness at bay, but now the recital was over. I took off the floor-length, graceful dress I'd bought. I'd thought the empire-waist dress, with its subtle peach floral pattern, was lovely, but now it taunted me. No matter what I wore, the outcome was the same.

"You seem out of sorts today," Mark said at my appointment the following Monday.

"Did the recital not go well?"

"It was okay," I replied dully. "It's always this way."

"What do you mean?" he asked.

"I work so hard for a performance, and when it's over I feel depressed."

"And that happens every time?"

"Pretty much," I said. "The more important the concert, the worse I feel. I thought it would be better after I left NEC."

"Why is that?"

"NEC had lots of good flutists. In Madison, I thought I'd feel less . . . I don't know . . ." I couldn't find the right word.

"Discouraged?" Mark suggested.

"No, it's more than that. Less of a failure, maybe."

"Do most performers experience a letdown after a big concert?"

"Some do, but not this extreme." I thought about performers I knew well. "No, that's not true. Most performers I know feel pleased, maybe even proud, after their concerts." I kept circling through players I'd known over the years. "And those who do feel a letdown bounce back after a day or two."

"How long does your reaction usually last?"

"Weeks, sometimes longer. It only goes away when I have another performance to work toward."

"Have you ever been proud of a performance?" he asked.

"I don't think . . . wait, yes. Several times. In high school."

"That's a long time ago. Any more recent performance come to mind? Maybe at NEC?"

"Gosh no. At NEC I felt so inferior. For months I didn't tell anyone I'd played in the Atlanta Symphony."

"Why not? Wouldn't that have impressed people?"

"No, no, I'd be embarrassed." I glanced at my watch. Good, the hour was almost up. My palms were sweating. I wanted to get out of there.

"Why would you be embarrassed?"

"I don't know," I said.

"It's okay," he said gently. "We don't have to talk about this if you don't want to."

———

"I'd like to go back to something you said last week," Mark said the following Monday. "Can you describe a performance you were happy with?"

"Let's see. I played a solo with the Atlanta Community Orchestra when I was a senior in high school, Griffes's *Poem for Flute and Orchestra*."

"And you were happy with how it went?"

"Yes, I think I was."

"Was Mr. Little there?"

"No. He never came to my performances. I don't think he went to any of his students' concerts. But it didn't matter. Mr. Sieber, the community orchestra conductor, was there; he had to be, since he was conducting. And he seemed really pleased with my performance. But I just remembered something. I had a memory slip toward the end, where there's a short cadenza."

"Did you stop?" Mark asked.

"Gosh no, that would've been a disaster."

"What happened?"

"I made up stuff, I just let my fingers fly, trying to make it sound like Griffes, and because it was a cadenza, it didn't matter. I got back on track before the orchestra came in."

"So, you missed a lot of notes—"

"No, only a few, really."

"—and yet you still felt happy about the performance," he said.

"Yes, that's odd, now that I think about it. I didn't berate myself, and because it was a modern piece, most people in the audience didn't notice the wrong notes. I'm sure I would've felt terrible if I'd screwed up so badly that the orchestra had to stop."

"If that same thing happened now, how do you think you would feel?" he asked.

"Okay, I see your point. I would feel ashamed."

"Even if no one knew you'd made a mistake?"

"Yes, if it's not perfect, or close to it, I feel like a failure." I sensed we were, finally, getting at something important. But we didn't return to that topic.

"Are you having more problems with Phil?" Mark asked at a session in June. I'd been in a bad mood since the session started.

"Yes, we argue a lot. When we're not arguing, we're talking about him. Only him. My goals don't matter anymore."

"Maybe what first attracted you is incompatible with what you want," Mark said gently.

"I'm not following you."

"His assertiveness makes it hard for you to voice your own needs, so you become more and more passive."

I wanted to yell at Mark that he was wrong. I hated being called passive, like my mother, but I recognized that the intensity of my reaction meant there was some truth in his words.

A few weeks later, when I went back to the subject of Phil, Mark interrupted me.

"Why don't we talk about what's really on your mind," Mark suggested, leaning forward.

"What do you mean?"

"Let's start with this. Why do you wash your hair before each of our appointments?" Mark asked.

"But I don't do that."

"What about this morning? Did you wash your hair?"

`"Yes, but that's just a coincidence," I said, annoyed. I almost asked if he *ever* washed his hair.

"If you do, that's okay, you know," Mark said gently. "You can say anything in here," he added, lowering his voice to almost a whisper.

Later I thought about Mark's comment. My sessions were on Mondays and Fridays. Since I washed my hair about twice a week, Mark may have been right, but had I planned my schedule around sessions? I didn't think so. The exchange made me uneasy.

At the next session, Mark didn't encourage me to talk about my feelings for him. He was shrewd. He implanted his theory carefully, unveiling it slowly. Several sessions later, I came in discouraged about the steep competition in flute. That morning I'd checked the musicians' union paper; in the entire country, only two orchestra jobs were listed for flute.

"Maybe my father was right, maybe it's stupid to try to be a professional musician," I said.

"You've said this before, but let's talk about what's really bothering you," Mark said.

"I am. Flute positions are hard to get."

"But you don't have to solve that problem today."

"Maybe not," I responded, "but it's hard to keep working toward something if you think it will never happen."

"In here, you can talk to me about anything, but you won't get much out of therapy if you focus on the distant future. Think about what you want today."

"Okay," I said, determined not to take the bait, "today I want to be reassured that I'll be able to make a living in music."

"Look more deeply into what you want now, in this moment," he said quietly. "Getting a job in music isn't all that's on your mind. You're using that to avoid talking about more personal issues."

"You don't understand." I was getting angry and wanted to argue my case, but time was up.

"We'll come back to this," Mark said as I left.

Over the next few weeks, Mark revealed his theory. My low self-esteem and depression were caused by not being brave enough to go after what I wanted. Because of the patient-therapist bond, or transference, I had become attached to Mark—simply a natural part of the process.

"You can avoid talking about this, but until you admit your feelings, you'll remain stuck."

At first I was suspicious, but Mark had my undivided attention for an hour, twice a week, brainwashing me session by session. Much later I recognized the parallel with Warren who, day by day, brainwashed me into thinking I was a terrible flutist.

By the third month, Mark had lured me into his transference den. He'd convinced me to set aside concerns about Phil and anxiety about my music career in order to focus on the therapist-patient relationship. I was engaged in the sessions and began to find Mark's strange appearance attractive. I'd seen him riding a distinctive lime-green racing bike, which was often parked outside the student union. I began stalking him, trying to run into him in the student union. It wasn't hard. He spent hours there playing Go.

One day after a therapy session, I waited outside the hospital till Mark left, and stealthily biked after him to find out where he lived. The Inez Apartments, at the eastern edge of campus, weren't on the route from the humanities building to my house, but I often went by there. I knew the Inez units were all studio apartments, and I soon figured out which apartment window was his.

In Atlanta, with the passive analyst Dr. Norton, I had also formed a strong bond with the therapist, but Norton used that bond to build trust. Transference was merely the backdrop, a means for getting me to open up about issues that troubled me. Mark seemed to consider the therapist-patient relationship the crux of therapy, the end rather than the means.

For a while, talking to Mark twice a week and stalking him occasionally on weekends fed my fantasy that Mark cared about me. But after a few weeks, I realized it was only that, a fantasy. Disenchanted with Mark's focus on transference, I began to resent his impatience when I brought up anything else. My interests were unimportant. Similar to what had happened with Phil—and with my father.

The next fall, as usual, auditions for placement in the ensembles were held right before classes started. At that time, I hadn't seen Phil for two months. The auditions, behind a screen with multiple faculty listening, consisted of the usual combination of a solo chosen by the candidate, orchestral excerpts, and sight-reading. Despite being nervous, I played well enough to again get the principal flute position in the orchestra. Although reluctant to resume the relationship with Phil, I was eager to see him on the podium. My infatuation may have disappeared, but my admiration for Phil's conducting remained undiminished, and I was excited about the repertoire for the fall season of the UW orchestra.

Of all the repertoire we performed during my three years with the UW orchestra, the piece with the best flute part was Stravinsky's *Le chant du rossignol*, the orchestral suite based on Stravinsky's opera of the same name. In the suite, the flute takes the role of the nightingale. Not surprisingly, the score is laden with flute solos, many of them lovely and expressive. The piece was on the first concert of the 1975–76 orchestra season. Because *Le chant du rossignol* is not one of the standard orchestral excerpts, I had no idea the flute part was so extensive.

At the time of the first rehearsal, Phil and I had seen each other only once, the weekend after the auditions. Summer's imposed absence may have made our hearts grow fonder, but a residue of strain remained, each of us pretending it wasn't there. I wondered if rehearsals would be awkward. When I opened the music folder and saw the *Rossignol* flute part, I was both delighted and dismayed—delighted to see a long cadenza plus many other passages marked solo, dismayed because Phil hadn't warned me, hadn't suggested I practice the part before the first rehearsal. Sight-reading cadenzas written by contemporary composers is often challenging, as it was for me the day we first read through *Rossignol*.

"Well, well, you seem to take the term *cadenza* to mean improvise freely," Phil said. "That would make sense if Stravinsky were an eighteenth-century composer. Perhaps you can go over that part before our next rehearsal."

Phil's sarcasm stung. Yes, I had played some wrong notes in the cadenza, but he wouldn't have spoken that way to any other orchestra member. Was it a careless remark, or did he enjoy embarrassing me in front of the orchestra?

By the next rehearsal, I'd learned the part well. After I played the cadenza, orchestra members shuffled their feet (musician's version of applause), but not a word from the podium. At our Friday night date the next night, Phil talked about his excitement over conducting *Rossignol*, a piece new to him too. As he continued his monologue, pointing out ways his conducting would highlight Stravinsky's genius, I lapsed into my usual role of supportive listener. As he droned on,

I felt myself disappearing. So what if I played the flute part well? Such a small thing compared to Phil's command of the entire orchestra.

The mid-October performances of *Le chant du rossignol* were excellent. Ignoring the tension with Phil, I savored each solo and gave that *Rossignol* a beautiful voice. Outside of rehearsals, however, I dreaded spending time with Phil. His assertiveness ate away at my confidence. Listening to him talk about conducting made me question whether I had any talent of my own.

Mark played a part in this disintegration of confidence, showing no interest in talking about my goals as a musician, much less about problems with Phil. If it wasn't about transference, Mark wouldn't listen. He was right about my avoiding issues in therapy, wrong about what those issues were. In all the sessions with him, I never mentioned rape. Or abortion.

Chapter 20: Darkness

Fall wore on, the days getting shorter, the darkness last-ing longer as we approached the months that brought me face-to-face with my past. One thing, however, kept pulling me back from the descent: in early December, the orchestra was scheduled to play Ravel's *Daphnis et Chloé*. We would be joined by the UW Chorale in performing both Suite No. 1 and Suite No. 2. Although I'd played the second flute part in Atlanta, this time I would get the principal part.

Ask flutists which orchestral solo is their favorite and most will say the *Daphnis* solo from the second suite, not because it's easy—far from it—but because the main solo is one of the longest and most ravishing flute excerpts in the entire orchestral repertoire. The solo calls for a rich, alluring tone, and provides numerous opportunities for artistic shap-ing. Flutists get to show off their dynamic range, imaginative use of vibrato, and different tone colors. One could argue the most expressive orchestral writing for the flute was by impres-sionist composers Debussy and Ravel; the two quintessential examples are, respectively, *Afternoon of a Faun* and *Daphnis et Chloé*. There are several fairly short solos in *Faun*; in *Daphnis* the flutist has one big moment, lasting a full two minutes.

So many things make the *Daphnis* solo difficult, begin-ning with the opening run, which should sound clear, supple, and floating. It is just an A major scale, but it's hard to play smoothly; the version with E-sharp (Ravel liked both versions) is only slightly easier. Like the solos in *Afternoon of a Faun*, there are many long notes requiring a sensuous sound, but unlike *Faun*, the first long note is not on the flute's most flexible note but on a high G-sharp, which can sound thin. I tried to make the note sound open, like "ah" or "oh" and not the vowel sound of a long E, where the throat is less relaxed. Each measure begins with a long note and ends with faster notes, but even the fast notes should be languorous. For the solo to sound spontaneous, the flutist can stretch those faster notes, but only if the conductor allows the flutist that rhythmic flexibility. In auditions, flutists must play the solo so it sounds free while conforming to a rigid tempo.

In Atlanta, we'd performed only Suite No. 2. At the first UW orchestra rehearsal, I discovered Suite No. 1 begins with a flute solo—shorter than the well-known one in Suite No. 2, but just as lovely.

My excitement about playing *Daphnis* shoved depression aside for a few glorious weeks. Even though my relationship with Phil was strained, he allowed me the freedom to play the solo the way I wanted. Once again, I experienced the exhilaration of adding my voice, my artistry, to the presentation of a magnificent piece. Even without the flute solo, Ravel's music dazzled me—from the shimmering opening of *Daphnis* through its bacchanalian ending—I found the piece as captivating as when I'd first performed it in Atlanta.

Because performing *Daphnis* was such a rare opportunity, I wanted everything to be perfect. At the first of the two concerts, my sound was a bit tight. Phil gave me a solo bow when the piece ended, but he didn't look especially pleased. Too upset to accept praise from friends in the orchestra, I rushed to my office after the final note and cried. In my mind, it had been a disaster. The second performance went quite well. I found exactly the sound I wanted; in the runs following the solo, Sue (second flutist that year) and I dovetailed perfectly, and the long run that goes from piccolo to alto flute was seamless. The four of us in that flute section were pleased with the performance and proud of our section.

And then I went out with Phil.

Phil was ecstatic about how well the concert had gone—for him. I fell into my role of agreeing with his self-congratulations. Eventually, he did compliment me, but because it was tepid, I began to question whether I'd played well. The *Capital Times* review praising the flute solo and compliments from other musicians were tainted by Phil's lack of enthusiasm.

Already depressed, I reluctantly returned to Atlanta to spend Christmas with my parents. By then, all of my good friends from the Atlanta Symphony had moved away. Two long weeks with my parents—maintaining the cheerful facade, reassuring them that yes, things were going well at UW and yes, I'd chosen the topic for my dissertation. In the Whitman house, where any talk about feelings was forbidden, I dared not admit to being sad, much less depressed. As always, Daddy dominated dinner conversations with stories about someone's stupidity, either students or his dean. Mother and I laughed dutifully. At least in Atlanta the days were slightly longer, the temperatures much warmer. If only I could block out the memories.

Unlike most victims of trauma, I never experienced flashbacks in the sense of losing track of where I was, but the memories were bad enough. Although I was in the city where the rape happened, it was the abortion scene in Boston that haunted me during that visit to Atlanta. Not reliving it so much as being defined by it. By the guilt and shame. My belief in a woman's right to choose did not apply to me. Getting past the day of the rape provided no relief. I still had to get through

January, my most difficult month. But I knew exactly where I'd put that bottle of antidepressants.

Back in Madison, I went through the motions of being a student—classes, rehearsals, teaching, practicing, ignoring Phil, who had agreed to take a break from our relationship. Like every January since the rape, I found no joy in practicing—no pleasure in striving for a more beautiful sound, no satisfaction in conquering a difficult passage. Teaching even my favorite students was arduous. I struggled just to get out of bed.

Dragging myself to my appointments with Mark, I showed up without being present. The less I reflected the infatuation of transference, the more Mark insisted my depression would get worse unless I expressed and acted on my feelings for him. He reminded me transference was the driving force that made therapy effective. I got a reprieve the third week of January when he was out of town at a conference. I dreaded going back.

"You look nice today," Mark said on Monday, January 26.

Didn't he notice the bags under my eyes, my dirty hair?

"Were you okay, not seeing me last week?" Mark asked.

"Fine."

"You don't sound very sure about that."

"I am sure. I'm just very, very tired."

"Suppressing desires is draining," he said.

"It's not that." I glanced at his intense stare, then looked away.

"If not that, what is it?"

"I just . . ."

"You just what?"

"I've lost interest in things," I said, staring at the dingy, beige linoleum floor.

"What things?"

"Practicing, teaching . . ."

"Anything else?"

I finally looked directly at him. "Yes, playing in the orchestra, and that's usually what pulls me out of depression," I said with a brief burst of energy, fueled by irritation at Mark's lack of understanding.

"Why isn't that working now?"

"I don't know. I hate January." I wanted to get up and leave, but I knew he'd claim I was running away from therapy.

"What makes January significant?" he asked.

It's the month I carried my rapist's child. But I couldn't say that. Mark would blame me, and maybe he should.

"You're upset because I was gone for a week."

"No, I told you." The brief burst of energy was gone. Forming each word was like slogging through a snowdrift.

"You're deceiving yourself about the reason you're depressed."

Silence. Too much effort to respond.

"Did you think about what I suggested last time?" he asked.

I struggled to remember. Finally, it came to me.

"You said I wanted to put my head in your lap."

"Ah, so you *do* remember." I heard the triumphant smile in his voice.

More silence.

"If you take this one small step, you might begin to recover. You won't know till you try. Here, I'll make it easier."

Mark moved to the chair beside me. At least his face wasn't right in front of me.

"Okay, Ernestine, relax. Put your head in my lap, stop fighting it."

So, so tired. Contradicting him exhausted me. To silence his badgering, I leaned over and put my head in his lap.

"Just rest for a bit and you'll start to feel better."

The huge clock on the wall ticked off the seconds.

"You're thinking about what else you want to do," Mark said.

"What do you mean?"

"I'm sure you want more than this."

"No, you're wrong," I mumbled.

"Go after what you want," he said softly.

I remained in the awkward position, staring at long, skinny thighs encased in black jeans. Slowly, I became aware of his arousal.

With a sudden wave of revulsion, I sat up quickly and stared straight ahead.

"It's okay if you want to stop there. I know you're resisting, but you've made good progress today." He sounded pleased.

I rushed out of the room. Too upset to go to class, I went to my office and tried to practice, but I kept hearing Mark's voice and seeing his beady eyes. I sat slumped in my office chair, staring at blank walls. I felt filthy, repulsive. Mark had stirred up the self-disgust I'd carried around for four years.

After the appointment I'd been too exhausted to act, but a few hours later a wave of shame and self-loathing energized me. Walking to my house, I stopped by a small liquor store. Ignoring my usual beer and wine coolers, I looked at the bottles of Scotch. I hadn't bought any since the worst days of dealing with Warren, years ago. It seemed like the right choice tonight. I bought the cheapest bottle and put it in my backpack.

When I got to the house, I grabbed a glass from the kitchen and trudged up two flights of stairs to my room in the attic. After dropping my coat, mittens, and backpack on the floor, I opened the drawer in the small nightstand and retrieved the almost-full bottle of Elavil. On the nightstand I lined up the Scotch, pill bottle, and glass. Sitting on the edge of the bed, I poured some Scotch into the glass and drank quickly, ignoring the bitter taste. After opening the pill bottle, I couldn't make myself drink more of the Scotch. I went down the stairs and filled the glass with tap water from the second-floor bathroom. Back in the bedroom, emotionally numb, I systematically swallowed pill after pill. When only two pills remained, weariness gave way to euphoria. I again went down the stairs and called the UW Hospital to ask if the amount of Scotch and Elavil my friend had taken were enough to kill her. When they said yes and urged me to call 911 or bring her to the ER, I hung up and laughed.

Maybe the survival instinct took over. Whatever it was, in my crazed state I decided to leave my fate to chance. I would walk the two miles to the hospital. If I made it, fine; if not, I would at least spare my housemates the shock of finding me in my room. Since no one went up to the attic, my body might remain undiscovered for days.

Despite the minus-ten temperature, my bare face didn't feel the cold. The euphoria left as quickly as it had arrived. I didn't care if I made it; I simply kept walking, oblivious to my surroundings. Shortly after I arrived at the hospital, I became unresponsive and remained unconscious for the next forty-eight hours.

My throat felt blocked and raw, as if someone had scraped it with something sharp and left part of it lodged in there. I sensed people coming and going around me but had no idea who they were or what they were doing. After more cycles of waking up and slipping back, things began to make sense. I was in a hospital bed, but I still didn't know why. Visually nothing but blurry shapes. It may have been minutes or hours before I understood the reason I couldn't see: I had neither glasses nor contact lenses. I wanted to ask someone for my glasses, but it was too much effort. Easier to slip back into the welcoming darkness.

At some point when I awoke, I began to remember things: the creepy scene with Mark, the utter despair, the desperate need to escape the pain and self-hate, and finally, giving in to my monthlong plan to swallow the pills. But what had happened to the depression? I felt light, peaceful.

A nurse came into the room and asked me if they should call my parents. I shook my head from side to side to indicate no. I wanted to emphasize how much I did *not* want them called, but I couldn't do that with a tube in my throat. I looked around for a pen and some paper but saw only tubes and monitors. I gave up, hoping they got the message.

Later two nurses stood by the bed, fiddling with something beside my head. One of them told me they were going to remove the tube. After a brief but very unpleasant sensation of choking, it was out.

"Could, could you . . ." I croaked, unable to finish the question. One of the nurses held up my glasses case. I nodded and she put them on. Better. I couldn't talk very well, but at least I could see. In a hoarse whisper, I asked her what day it was. When she said Thursday, I must have looked confused.

"Yes, you had us quite worried there for a couple of days. We moved you out of ICU just this morning."

Later that day, I woke up to find my sister leaning over the bed. Though she wore a big smile, she seemed embarrassed. She asked if I was feeling better, her voice high-pitched, as if she were talking to a child. I couldn't talk very well, so I just nodded. She left shortly after that.

Friday I woke up with an uneasy feeling. On Fridays I usually saw Mark at 2:00 p.m. I had arrived at the hospital Monday night, the day of our last appointment, which seemed like a lifetime ago, and in some ways, it was. Thank goodness I wouldn't see him today, or would I? No. The hospital had probably contacted him. If Mark showed up, I didn't know what I would say to him.

I didn't have to say anything. He walked in at 2:15 p.m. and wasted no time.

"What the hell were you trying to do?" Mark was livid.

The answer seemed obvious. I said nothing.

"Did you think about consequences? Do you know how this looks on my record?"

I turned my head away, couldn't look at him.

"If you wanted my attention, there are better ways."

I remained silent.

"We won't have any appointments until you get out of here," he said, making no effort to disguise his disgust.

Realizing I wasn't going to respond, Mark turned abruptly, zipped up his dark blue parka, and stomped out of the room. I was glad he was gone, but his visit brought back the horrible thoughts I'd had the day of our last appointment.

Mark's visit deflated me; after he left, however, I recovered quickly. Why didn't I feel depressed and ashamed, as I had just four days ago? Perhaps surviving the attempt had given me a new respect for life—*my* life. I remembered there were things I wanted to do, but it had been months since I'd believed I could do them. Mark's harsh words prompted a hard question: Was therapy helping me? I'd have to figure that out, and soon.

In the late afternoon, I had another visitor.

"How are you feeling?" Phil asked. He seemed genuinely concerned.

"Okay, better today."

"Melinda told me what happened. I'm sorry."

I was touched but couldn't think of anything to say.

"How are rehearsals going?" I asked, hoping to steer the conversation away from why I was in the hospital.

"Pretty well. Sue sounds good, but we miss you." (Sue was playing my part in the orchestra.) "She asked about you, by the way." He smiled. It had been a long time since I'd seen this gentle side of Phil.

"I'll be back soon," I said with more confidence than I felt.

"Hope so. Hey, you know that Melinda called your parents, right?"

"Shoot, I distinctly said no to calling them, or at least I indicated it. Why would she do that?"

"She told me why."

"Well?"

He looked uncomfortable.

"I hope you don't tell her I told you this, but she said, 'She's been suicidal before. Someday she'll succeed, and what will I tell my parents then?'"

I must have looked shocked.

"I'm sorry. I probably shouldn't have told you."

"No, *she* shouldn't have told *them*," I said.

"Have they called?"

"No." His question clarified one of the reasons I didn't want my parents notified. I knew I'd be disappointed by their response.

"Have you talked to Melinda?" Phil asked.

"Just briefly. She came by yesterday. I don't imagine she'll come again." It was years before I considered how disturbing this might've been for her, at a time when she was under constant stress from a demanding job and caring for two young children.

Before he left, Phil came over to the bed and squeezed my hand.

"I care, you know."

After Phil left, I thought about how affectionate and funny he could be. His visit left me missing those days, but I knew we couldn't go back. Trying to recapture the good times would also bring back the bad.

The rest of the weekend was uneventful, other than the arrival of a beautiful azalea plant, full of deep pink blossoms. A typed card from the florist said it was from Dr. and Mrs. Whitman. The flowers were lovely, but the absence of a personal card hurt.

By Sunday I was walking around, feeling bored and restless. I wanted to get back to practicing. Late in the afternoon, a couple of nurses came in and did some quick, easy tests: stand up, touch your toes, close your eyes and touch your finger to your nose. Plus, the reflex tests with knees and the bottoms of my feet that had been so worrisome when I was admitted. They told me I'd done well and would be discharged within a day or two.

On Monday a physician examined me and approved my release for the next day.

Tuesday, February 2. My thirtieth birthday. Though I didn't want to, I called my parents to tell them I was okay and thank them for the flowers. After wishing me a happy birthday, they rang off—a brief, awkward call. No interest in talking about what happened. On my way out, I left the azalea plant at the nurses' station.

As I waited for the elevator, I turned around and took one last look at the brightly lit, generic hospital corridor where I'd almost lost my life. I thought about those who weren't as lucky as I, people with guns, or those who arrived at the hospital too late. And what about those who jump—in midair did they wish they could take it back, could *un*jump? Filled with gratitude for my survival, I promised my future self that even if the black shroud of depression returned and enveloped me, I would never again attempt suicide. Ever.

A short cab ride from the hospital took me back to the house on Madison Street. When I walked in the door around 11:00 a.m., it hit me: I needed to move. Even though I spent little time there, living with strangers contributed to my sense of isolation. The tiny bedroom, with its two hooks to hang things and no space for a chest of drawers, felt like a prison. I was tired of pulling clothes out of a trunk and ducking my head to avoid hitting the ceiling. Somewhat relieved to have pinpointed something I could change, I picked up a section of the *Isthmus* that was lying around and looked at the apartment ads.

Having no special plans for my birthday didn't bother me. The brush with death had clarified my priorities. In a few hours, I'd be in a rehearsal; playing principal flute in an orchestra was much better than any birthday party.

Several players greeted me warmly when I sat down for the first rehearsal after a week's absence. Sue was especially welcoming. I could tell she knew my explanation was incomplete. I said I'd unwisely combined prescription drugs with alcohol, causing me to lose consciousness, all true. I left out only the intentional part. At the end of the rehearsal, Sue gave me a sweet card that described her own struggles with depression and doubts about her playing. It surprised me, as she was both an excellent flutist and a terrific person. But I understood self-denigration.

The next day, I was fully back—practicing, rehearsing, teaching, attending classes, all with a renewed sense of purpose, and ready to make some important decisions, beginning with Phil. Although we had agreed not to see each other for a few weeks, things between us were far from settled. Because he'd been so sweet at the hospital, I was tempted to renege on my vow to stay away from him. But with my sharpened perception of things, I saw that the pull toward Phil was fueled more by guilt than by desire to continue the relationship. Did

I feel guilty simply because he was nice to me in the hospital? Or was it the old assumption that I didn't have the right to say no to a man? As I thought more about how we related to each other, I realized how much Phil's need to feel superior contributed to my feelings of worthlessness. A brilliant and talented musician, Phil was too caught up in his rising career as a conductor to be supportive of me. I would break things off completely. As long as we related to each other simply as fellow musicians, Phil and I got along just fine.

With that settled, I faced the more difficult question. Why was I continuing the therapy with Mark? I shuddered when I remembered the last session. Why did I follow his suggestion that I put my head in his lap when I didn't want to? Because I'd been too tired and depressed to care, so I'd simply acquiesced. But I felt stronger now, more clearheaded. Although I didn't understand how or why Mark had been able to manipulate me, I knew I had to get away from him. Right after a suicide attempt would be an odd time to quit therapy. Did I have the guts to do that?

Yes! I made the uncharacteristic, audacious decision to stop seeing Mark and gave myself permission to explain the decision to him on paper. Although Mark's power over me had waned, I wasn't ready to test it by confronting him face-to-face. Late Thursday afternoon, I biked to University Hospital. When I got to the therapy wing, strong and conflicting feelings made me hesitate. Then I thought of the last appointment— only ten days ago. I handed my letter to the secretary who scheduled sessions. After canceling the next day's appointment, I told her I wouldn't be coming back, and asked her to give the letter to Mark. The letter was brief. I didn't have sufficient distance from the events to understand my reasons for quitting, but I trusted my gut instinct.

Despite the seriousness of the suicide attempt, I later recognized that I was much stronger when depression hit the second time. But there were simply too many issues that collided at once: buried feelings about the rape and abortion, plus the immediate problems of an unsupportive boyfriend and a manipulative therapist who, like Phil, used me to feed his ego.

Did the momentous decisions to end the relationship with Phil and quit therapy make me feel empowered? No. I simply eliminated things that had contributed to my depression. Far from feeling liberated, I concentrated on surviving. After handing in the letter, I biked to my office with a smile on my face. Music would be my path back to sanity.

Chapter 21: Endings and Beginnings

I'd looked at only a few apartments when Richard Knowles, a Shakespeare scholar on the English faculty, told me about an undergraduate who needed a roommate to share her apartment on the top floor of a house. (Richard sang in the University Chorus and had admired my playing in *Daphnis.* After the program, he'd introduced himself to me.) He assured me Carmen, the aptly named voice major, was an exceptionally mature undergrad. He was right about that. As soon as I met her and saw the apartment, I knew 423 West Doty Street would be my next living space.

The top floor of the old, run-down house consisted of a modest-sized central space flanked by two bedrooms, plus a narrow, oblong kitchen and tiny bathroom. A small table, two chairs, and a worn brown sofa filled the central room. My bedroom contained a double mattress on the floor, and a scarred, secondhand wardrobe. Opposite the door into the living room was a door that opened onto a balcony. Although it was unsafe to go out there, the door let in light and fresh air. The house was smaller, cheaper, and not as well maintained as the house on Madison Street, but I found it charming. I could finally hang up my clothes, and no matter where I stood, I was in no danger of bonking my head on the sloped ceiling.

Carmen Pelton had grown up on a farm in Reedsburg, Wisconsin, about an hour's drive from Madison. She and I quickly became friends, sharing many late-night talks, eating popcorn while we voiced our self-doubts about being good enough to make it in the competitive music world. Flute and soprano were—and continue to be—two of the most over-populated fields in classical music. (Carmen became a terrific singer, active as a soloist on the national stage, and professor at the renowned University of Michigan School of Music.)

Sharing the apartment with Carmen made me realize how toxic my previous situation had been, living with strangers who had no interest in getting to know me. I noticed a revealing parallel: seven years ago, moving in with Lynette had hastened my recovery from the first depression, and the same thing happened this time, more quickly. In early March, less than five weeks after my release from the hospital, I applied for a competitive, international, summer master class given by world-famous flutist James Galway. If I had remained in therapy with Mark, and continued living with strangers, I'm sure I wouldn't have had the confidence to apply.

Years ago, I'd heard Pappoutsakis's flute sound on a recording, which had prompted me to find a way to study with him. Likewise, hearing Galway's sound on a recording rekindled my desire to find a richer sound. I was determined to hear Galway's sound up close. Once I got in, there were several barriers. The two-week class was in England. I'd never been abroad and had very little money, but I found a cheap flight from Chicago to London, and I could take a bus to Chicago. So I emptied my little savings account and scraped together enough money for the trip.

The class was awe-inspiring, including its location—the Stowe School in Buckinghamshire, an eighteenth-century estate consisting of several run-down but magnificent buildings, on extensive grounds that were dotted with old, impressive marble sculptures.

The first note Galway played, the morning of the first full day, was the middle D at the beginning of Chaminade's Concertino, a piece we all knew very well. Galway's D was the richest, most gorgeous D I'd ever heard. Sitting ten feet from his sound was like entering aural paradise. As soon as we had some free time, I rushed to the ugly basement of the main building. The acoustics in the dorm rooms of this eighteenth-century manor were terrible echo chambers, but I'd discovered a place where the acoustics were like a heavily carpeted living room: the boiler room in the basement, with lots of exposed pipes and irregular surfaces to break up the sound. And lots of cobwebs. Not so different from the basement in my parents' house that had been my first practice room.

Over the next few days, I spent considerable time practicing middle D, trying to imitate Galway's luscious sound. One day, there was a tap on the door, which was too warped to close completely. I looked up and saw Galway, grinning broadly, flute in hand. Even though I'd known this for days, it continued to surprise me that he was so short—maybe five foot six.

"You found yourself a great practice room," he said, with his charming Irish lilt.

Awestruck, I just stared at him.

"Here," he said, holding his flute out, "would you like to try my flute?"

"Uh, sure, I'll be very careful."

I played a few notes on his beautiful gold flute, trying to summon my best sound.

"You're about the only one around here who's figured out you can't work on sound in a bathtub."

Out of a large black bag he pulled out another flute case. After he put the silver flute together, he again invited me to try it. Not quite as special as the gold flute but still several cuts above my Powell.

"You can play on that for a few days if you want to."

"Oh, wow, are you sure?"

"Well," he said, looking around the dismal room, the characteristic twinkle in his eye, "I don't really see how you can flee the country from here."

After hearing Galway's sound up close and having him show up at my practice room, my performance in class was somewhat anticlimactic. Each participant got a twenty-minute lesson with Galway, in front of an audience of thirty or so accomplished flutists from all over the world. After I played Varèse's *Density 21.5*, Galway praised my rhythmic accuracy and dynamic range, but the best comment came when I returned his flute the next day. "You know, I think you're going to be one of those flute players who really gets the sound thing."

With Galway's flute I'd discovered a new dimension in my sound. Now that I had that sound in my ear, I could work toward duplicating it on my own flute. He was right: I was really into the sound thing.

After the class, I took a ferry across the Channel, then a train to Cologne for a short visit with a pianist friend, Jodi Gandolfi, who was studying that summer at the Hochschule für Musik in Cologne. More exhilarating experiences, starting with the Cologne Cathedral in the center of town. Having visited Westminster Abbey and St. Paul's in London, I'd now seen three magnificent cathedrals in as many weeks. I wished I could spend hours simply sitting in one of them, but the summer crowds of tourists made reflective contemplation impossible.

Jodi packed a lot into my four-day visit, including a boat trip down the beautiful Rhine to Koblenz, where the Rhine and Mosel rivers meet. We sampled lots of great wine, all white, from both regions. I preferred the less sweet Mosel wines.

Jodi also helped me sort through my conflicting feelings about Phil. Despite having ended our relationship, I worried that Phil believed the breakup was temporary. Before the spring semester ended, Phil had asked my exact travel plans. His summer plans included a few days in London. Knowing I'd be in London the day before my flight back to the US, he sent a postcard to Jodi's address, in which he said, "If our relationship has meant anything at all to you, meet me in front of Big Ben at 2:00 p.m. on Tuesday, August 10." Phil must have thought ours was *An Affair to Remember*.

Jodi pointed out Phil's manipulative behavior in appealing to my overdeveloped sense of guilt. She asked if anything had changed in my view of how Phil and I related to one another. She knew that I knew the answer as well as she did, but it's always easier to be clear-eyed about someone else's relationship.

In London, on August 10, I watched the two o'clock hour come and go. Staying not far from Big Ben, I looked out my grimy hotel room window and pictured Phil, under the iconic clock. How long would he wait for me? An hour? More? It took all my self-control to resist leaving the hotel room and running toward the clock. Did I have the right to refuse such a reasonable request? After all, I wouldn't be agreeing to restart our affair; I'd be merely affirming that yes, our affair *had* meant something to me. I stared out the window for over an hour, arguing with myself. Eventually, I acknowledged the obvious: acquiescing to Phil's request would undo the progress I'd made over the summer in distancing myself from him. I would continue to pursue my dreams without depending on male approval.

⸻

Auditions for ensembles that September were not behind a screen, but at least the director of bands joined Phil to hear auditions. Phil addressed me quite formally, less friendly than he would've been with any other student. I'm sure he was angry about my not meeting him in London, and I wondered if that would influence his decision about who played principal. I played well, and the assignments showed Phil was not vindictive; again, I was principal flute.

In contrast to the previous year, the repertoire for the UW orchestra 1976–77 season didn't feature outstanding flute parts. Did our breakup have anything to do with that? The October concert featured Beethoven's *Eroica Symphony*, not a big flute part but one hell of a good piece. When Robert Shaw conducted *Eroica* in Atlanta, the first movement was viscerally powerful. Second chair flutists rarely get direct cues from the conductor, but at each performance of the piece, Shaw gestured to me to bring out the dissonant high E-natural that clashed with Warren's high F in the fortissimo chords that precede the new theme in the development section. The two flutes stick out because they are the highest voices and because they're playing a minor second, the harshest interval in tonal music. Highlighting screaming minor seconds that precede a calm, lyrical theme is but one example of Shaw's attention to details.

By contrast, Phil's first movement projected a more noble, less passionate vision of heroism. He wanted those chords loud but didn't draw attention to them as Shaw had. One could argue Phil's steadier tempo sustained the movement's momentum better. Both interpretations worked well; the true hero was Beethoven.

The other musical highlight of the semester was Poulenc's lovely choral work *Gloria*, performed in December with my roommate Carmen as the soprano soloist. She sounded fabulous, an early sign of the many superb performances in her future.

If the 1976–77 orchestral repertoire was disappointing, the pieces on my doctoral recitals made up for it. The gutsiest choice was Elliott Carter's Sonata for Flute, Oboe, Cello and Harpsichord, perhaps the most challenging and rewarding piece I ever performed. No one at UW—students or faculty— had performed the work. Mr. Cole thought I was nuts to choose it and warned me he'd have nothing to say about it. That was fine with me. I relished the challenge.

Written in 1952, the sonata uses metrical modulation (a complicated way to change time signatures), which took us a while to figure out. I loved the unique sounds Carter created from this eighteenth-century combination of instruments. (The harpsichord and organ were the main keyboard instruments of the Baroque period in music; composers in the nineteenth and twentieth centuries rarely wrote for harpsichord.) To fit the pieces together in this complicated puzzle, we rehearsed a lot, but no matter how much time we spent, the piece always sounded fresh. The recital went well and ended with a party at Melinda's house.

Melinda and I hadn't seen much of each other the previous year, when I'd been so depressed. But after I quit therapy and stopped dating Phil, I spent more time with her and her brilliant husband, also named Phil. In addition to being an outstanding chemistry professor and administrator (eventually dean of the college), Phil excelled at telling stories. You had to be careful, though, because he could appear deadly serious while spinning a yarn. If you missed the twinkle in his eye, you'd believe his every word.

With no babysitting experience, I wasn't a particularly good aunt, but I enjoyed getting to know their lively son Andrew and his cute, sassy sister Heather. Melinda and Phil were excellent cooks, so having dinner at their house was a treat, even though the two rambunctious children sometimes created a Fellini-like atmosphere. During my four years at UW, Melinda and Phil attended all my recitals and most of the orchestra concerts—a lot of nights out for a busy couple with young kids.

In addition to coursework and recitals, the DMA degree at the University of Wisconsin required a thesis. I chose to write about the flute works by Claude Debussy, much beloved by flutists not only for *Afternoon of a Faun* but for his popular solo piece, *Syrinx.* Rather than opting for the flute's dazzling facility (like the rapid runs in the bird part for Prokofiev's *Peter and the Wolf*), Debussy was the first composer to bring out the sensual, sultry side of the flute. My thesis covered the two non-orchestral works Debussy wrote for flute: *Syrinx* and the Sonata for Flute, Viola and Harp. The difference between my analyses and those of music theorists was that I linked the analysis to performance, pointing out places where a deeper understanding of the pieces would influence how flutists performed the works.

In *Syrinx* I described in detail how the opening motive, with its sensual chromaticism and embellishments, is gradually transformed into the relatively shapeless whole-tone scale at the end of the piece. I drew a parallel with the mythical transformation of Syrinx from a curvy wood nymph into a perfectly cylindrical reed. In the 1970s, *Syrinx* was a particularly good candidate for this type of analysis. Due to its popularity and the fact that it was unaccompanied, flutists often performed it very freely, ignoring Debussy's meticulous markings. I wanted to draw attention to details in the score that indicated the exact opposite of the way many flutists chose to perform the piece.

Despite its being one of the flute's most beautiful chamber music pieces, the Sonata for Flute, Viola and Harp had received far less attention than *Syrinx*, from theorists as well as performers. Excellent harpists were—and still are—hard to find; the few able to play the piece's difficult part were usually too busy to spend the required practice and rehearsal time on a chamber work. During the spring of that year, I was lucky to find wonderful colleagues who played for my lecture recital, where I discussed and performed both pieces.

Because of the Sonata's relative obscurity, I felt more confident that my analysis would offer a unique perspective on the piece. I wrote about the important role dynamic markings (loud and soft) played in creating the shape—a graceful arc—of each movement. To illustrate this, I made charts showing the dynamic levels throughout each movement, a ridiculously tedious job before the days of word processors and graphic design software. My only tools were a ruler and a drafting compass.

As the end of my doctoral studies approached, I wondered what I would do next. During the six years since I'd quit the Atlanta Symphony, anxiety about getting another job was my constant companion. That year, only a few universities had openings for flute positions. I applied for two of the jobs but got nowhere. Perhaps my chances of getting a college teaching position would improve once I had the degree in hand.

In late spring, the Saint Paul Chamber Orchestra (SPCO) advertised an audition for principal flute. Because there was a direct, inexpensive flight from Madison to Twin Cities, I could get there relatively cheaply; as a world-class orchestra, however, the SPCO would attract top flutists from all over the country. My chances of winning were slim. I decided to go for it despite the odds, and I enjoyed having the goal of perfecting fifteen orchestral excerpts in three weeks. Far from discouraging, those weeks were among my happiest at UW. Mr. Cole was out of town and had invited me to use his office to practice. In addition to being eight times the size of my cramped office, it had four windows — narrow but tall, and on the south side. Natural light, lots of space, and four floors above the cacophony of the practice rooms, I could be alone with my flute.

Practicing for the audition was the fun part. Once I boarded the flight to Twin Cities, nervousness set in, triggering the familiar self-doubt. What was I doing? Why spend money to take an audition that was such a long shot? The next day, after taking a cab to St. Catherine University, I walked into audition-circuit hell: a warm-up room with a dozen flutists trying to hear themselves amid other flutists playing the same excerpts. I didn't win the audition, but I was proud of myself for trying. My eagerness to go after something so ambitious revealed a level of confidence I hadn't felt in a long time.

Now that I had completed the required coursework, recitals, and comprehensive written and oral exams, I was officially ABD — all but dissertation. Doctoral students writing theses could claim one of several tiny offices in the Memorial Library. Furnished with one uncomfortable wooden chair and a built-in shelf which served as a desk, it was far removed from the sounds of practicing and human conversation. Richard (the Shakespeare professor who had connected me with Carmen) lent me an old typewriter, which gave the text a whimsical look when the sticky keys jumped above the line.

Devoting the summer to writing the thesis, I finished in late July. Except for the tedious chore of making the graphs, I enjoyed the three-stage process: doing background research, coming up with my own analyses, and writing a well-articulated argument. The thesis defense would be August 15, the earliest date all committee members were back from summer travels. Having nothing lined up for the fall, I had decided to move back to Boston. Two years ago, my friends at the Malden house decided not to rent my tiny room, which they now offered me. They were confident I could find a job of some sort. Like New York City, Boston had a surplus of excellent flutists, but at least I knew the area and had friends there.

All summer I fed chapters of the thesis to my doctoral committee, which included music theorist Les Thimmig and musicologist Walter Gray, but I received feedback only from pianist Howard Karp—all laudatory, nothing critical. Mr. Cole, as expected, had nothing to say; his Curtis background did not include writing papers. Assuming no news was good news, I approached the thesis defense with confidence.

Assembled in Mr. Cole's office, the committee asked the usual questions: why I'd chosen the topic, what had surprised me about the research, specific details about my analyses. Things seemed to be going well. Then Walter Gray asked, given my extensive background as an orchestral flutist, why I hadn't included a chapter about Debussy's use of the flute in the orchestra. I stated the obvious: I had decided to focus only on the solo and chamber works of Debussy. He queried me on various orchestral pieces and seemed impressed with my answers. Mr. Cole then asked me to step out in the hall while they discussed my defense. About ten minutes later, Howard Karp came out and told me Professor Gray had recommended I add a chapter about Debussy's use of the flute in the orchestra. Seeing my dismay, he hastily assured me that the committee had approved the document and were confident I could write the chapter quickly.

All I heard was that I had failed my thesis defense. *Failure.* The power of that word eclipsed everything else. I managed to restrain my emotions until I reached my office. When I told

Mary, she was appalled the committee hadn't asked for that chapter before the defense. We were pretty sure it was because Professor Gray hadn't bothered to read the thesis until very recently, maybe even the night before.

I was scheduled to leave town in three weeks. Although part of me wanted to just get the damn thing done, I knew I'd be unhappy with a hurriedly written chapter. Sadly, I canceled my plans for moving to Boston. Carmen hadn't found a new roommate, so I had housing, but I'd received the last check from my fellowship, so I'd have to find a job. I estimated it would take me at least six weeks to complete the chapter, plus time for a professional typist to produce the final draft.

Finding a job, when I could commit to only three months, proved difficult. I didn't have any nonmusical work experience, and restaurants had already hired students returning for the fall. I settled for a boring but easy job close to the library: working at the key desk in the basement of the humanities building, a job usually done by freshmen. All day I sat at a tiny desk in the windowless basement, giving out practice room keys, surrounded by the din of practicing undergrads. No classes to go to, no orchestra to play in, no teaching, and— worst of all—no office. Barely a week into the job, I had four impacted wisdom teeth pulled. In addition to being stuck at the desk, I was unable to practice and looked like a chipmunk.

Each day I left the key desk at 4:00 p.m. and went straight to my library cubbyhole. Because I already knew which pieces to include, and what to say about them, the writing went quickly, but with no other activities, the monotonous weeks dragged by.

In early October, I received an intriguing job offer. Famed solo flutist Paula Robison was about to have a baby and offered me a free studio apartment in Manhattan if I would be her full-time babysitter. I would also receive free lessons with Paula and fifty dollars a month. I'd fallen in love with Paula's playing when I heard the first phrase of the Hummel flute sonata on her recording *The Romantic Flute*. I'd taken a few memorable lessons with her during one of the summers I spent in Boston. With her imaginative, expressive approach to flute playing, she was easily the most musical flutist I'd ever heard—the Isaac Stern of the flute. Of course I said yes. I'd never done any babysitting, but how hard could it be? Perhaps I could break into the New York freelance music scene.

Energized by my new plans, I finished writing the additional chapter in late October. Professor Gray was impressed with the chapter and did not feel a second defense hearing was needed. As soon as all the members of the committee had approved the manuscript, I took it to a professional typist. I'd heard stories about doctorates being withheld due to some problem with the dissertation formatting. I asked the typist how many doctoral theses she'd done. Over a hundred, she replied. Reassured, I turned to the task of packing.

The schedule was tight. Paula wanted me in New York by late November, so I booked a relatively cheap flight to New York on the twenty-fourth, Thanksgiving Day. The typist had other projects ahead of mine but said she'd have it done in three weeks. I called her every few days. She started my thesis November 17, promising to have it ready before she left town on the twenty-second. I picked up the thesis on the twenty-first. Since all I had to do was climb Bascom Hill to the Administration Building and deposit it in the archives, I brought the thesis to the Doty Street apartment and continued packing—boxing up half my stuff to ship to Atlanta, the other half to New York. Neither Carmen nor I had a car, but Richard lent us his car to take the boxes to the post office.

After sending the boxes mid-afternoon on the twenty-third, I made my fateful trip up Bascom Hill. Descending into the basement of the Bascom Hall Administration Building, where dissertations go to die, I found the gatekeeper and handed over my thesis. I was done! But not so fast. She asked me to stay while she measured the margins. To my dismay, she found over thirty pages with lines that strayed into the forbidden territory of the right margin. It was unacceptable.

I went to Richard's office in a panic. When he saw my face, thesis in hand, he knew exactly what had happened. Since my flight was the next day, I couldn't just take the thing back to the typist, who was out of town anyway. Richard calmed me down and came up with a brilliant solution. He purchased three X-Acto knives and rolls of thin adhesive tape the width of a typed line. He proposed we invite Carmen to an all-night pizza party at the apartment. For hours we three meticulously cut out and moved words ever so slightly to the left, sometimes moving four words per line, then laid the words on the adhesive backing. After finishing at about 3:00 a.m., I deposited the thesis on the way to the airport, ending the journey to a doctorate with a cut-and-paste job.

I moved to New York to study with Paula Robison; living in Manhattan on the posh Upper East Side (225 East Seventy-Ninth Street) was a side benefit. I hoped it might be a good place to meet well-educated, single young men—successful businessmen and lawyers, instead of lofty-minded, out-of-work musicians.

Two days after I arrived, I went down the block to a small grocery store. I loved the convenience of having a store so close, until I discovered that the price of one potato was equal to the price of a five-pound bag in Madison. I would have to plan carefully to live on fifty dollars a month. The only culinary indulgence I allowed myself was a teaspoon of Häagen-Dazs vanilla bean ice cream, which I stole from Paula's freezer every few weeks, usually on days when baby Elizabeth was exceptionally fussy. Sort of like hazard pay.

I hadn't given much thought to the babysitting part of the arrangement. Reality hit about ten days into the job, when I realized caring for a baby was exhausting. I looked after Elizabeth all day and was on call for evenings and weekends, with one day off most weeks, though the day varied according to their complicated concert schedules.

Paula thought it important that Elizabeth get fresh air each day, so I took her to Central Park at midday. And yes, over the lunch hour some very attractive young men hurried down the street, but they didn't look twice at the young woman with the baby carriage. And those freelance jobs I'd hoped to get? The few times one of the flutists I knew (from NEC) asked me to sub, I was babysitting.

In New York City, even highly successful artists live with spatial limitations. Paula and her husband, violist and entrepreneur Scott Nickrenz, had the penthouse apartment in an impressive old building on East Seventy-Ninth, but it was essentially two rooms—a modest-sized living room and a bedroom, with a galley-sized kitchen and a bathroom tucked between the two, no bigger than the Madison apartment I'd shared with Carmen. After Elizabeth's arrival, the bedroom became the nursery, and Paula and Scott slept on a foldout couch in their living room. Years later they bought the apartment directly below, connecting the two with a spiral staircase, but that year they lived in very close quarters. Their office consisted of a small desk in a corner of the nursery.

Ten floors below their penthouse, my furnished studio apartment consisted of one small room dominated by a double bed, with a tiny kitchen area at the opposite end, against the same wall as the one narrow window. The view out the window was standard NYC: the back sides of other high-rise apartment buildings. If I stuck my head out the window at noon, I might catch the sun briefly, at its pinnacle. In addition to the bed, there was a kitchen table with two chairs, plus a small desk with a third chair, tucked into the one interesting feature of the apartment, a little alcove a step higher than the main floor.

On the same floor lived a writer who couldn't concentrate when I practiced, so I ended up back in the basement. I should have known: every town I'd lived in, I had practiced in either a basement or, at NEC and UW, a basement practice room. This basement housed the laundry facilities. Despite being in an elegant old building, it looked like a typical unfinished basement: exposed, dusty pipes, concrete floor, lots of unimpressive washers and dryers, and, of course, cobwebs.

On New Year's Eve, I was in the basement practicing when a very assertive middle-aged man with a huge black mustache got off the elevator, strode right up to me, and said in a booming voice, "Hi, I'm Gene Shalit."

"Hi, I'm Ernestine Whitman," I answered, trying to match his volume.

He was very gregarious and asked lots of questions: Why do you practice down here? What are you doing in New York? Aren't you going to a New Year's Eve party later? He finally left for his party. I didn't own a TV; I had no idea Gene Shalit was a well-known TV personality.

Living in a studio apartment on a tight budget with no social life, I was lonely. Most weeks, the only people I interacted with were Elizabeth, who didn't uphold her end of the conversation, and Paula or Scott, when I picked up or brought Elizabeth back. I had no money for concerts, theater, or dance programs. It was even hard to find time to visit the Metropolitan Museum, only a few blocks away. The lessons with Paula weren't as riveting as my previous lessons with her. Under-standable, since she was a new mom with a very demanding career. Occasionally she taught lessons with a fussy Elizabeth in her lap, distracting both of us.

In late January, when it was too cold to take Elizabeth out, my little apartment seemed to shrink further. I thought getting lost in a great novel would help, so I purchased *The Brothers Karamazov* at a used bookstore. After reading a few chapters, I needed exercise to cheer me up. In Madison, I'd discovered the quickest way to get my heart rate up was to run up and down stairs. I lived in a high-rise building; I had no excuses.

One day, as I ran up the ten flights to the top floor, I heard a flute echoing in the stairwell. I stopped and listened; it was the first two bars of the Mozart Concerto in G Major, over and over. Paula was trying to get just the right inflection for the appoggiatura (an expressive note that isn't part of the underlying chord) at the beginning of the second measure. Such dedication to perfection. Eavesdropping turned out to be my most inspiring lesson.

Caring for a two-month-old baby is an intense intro-duction to babysitting. Under Paula's detailed but patient guidance, I learned quickly. Elizabeth was, of course, adorable, with a feathery version of Scott's curly, reddish-blond hair, his blue eyes, and Paula's intense gaze. On her fussy days, only one thing from my limited repertoire of baby entertainment helped: singing, "Hush, Little Baby, Don't Say a Word" while I paced the apartment with her over my shoulder, jostling her gently.

Elizabeth's mealtimes were challenging. Paula had strict orders about the number of spoonfuls she had to consume at each feeding. When I did the evening feeding, I was in Paula's apartment. One night, Elizabeth seemed determined to spit out every mouthful of mashed bananas. Over and over, we repeated the sequence: I put a spoonful in; she spat it out. An endless loop. After twenty minutes, I got so frustrated that I said loudly and—I admit—angrily, "Goddamn it, Elizabeth, for once can't you just swallow one fucking spoonful?"

And then it happened. She laughed. A real, loud, belly laugh. I can still see her in the pale green onesie, strapped into the carrier seat on Paula's kitchen counter. Impossible not to fall in love with a baby who laughs at your frustrations. I'd already grown fond of her; from that moment on, I was attached. I can't remember whether she ate, but I'll never forget that first, delightful laugh.

In April, a most unlikely visitor stayed in that tiny apartment for several days. I was surprised and pleased when Mother accepted my invitation to come to New York. She'd never traveled without Daddy, and even their trips were only to Whitman family reunions or to visit Melinda in Wisconsin. Without Daddy's domineering presence, I decided to make the most of our shared love of the arts. We took the A train to see the Cloisters, raced up to the peanut gallery in Carnegie Hall to hear Janet Baker (Mother surprisingly spry at sixty-eight), walked around the corner to watch *The Turning Point* starring Mikhail Baryshnikov, and splurged on great tickets for the Dutch Royal Ballet, with featured soloist Rudolf Nureyev. What fantastic luck to see two of the greatest male dancers of the century in one weekend! No one would've appreciated their incredible leaps more than the two of us. We'd never attended anything together before (or since), and we hadn't slept in the same bed except in Missouri, twenty years earlier. Fortunately, she was a still, quiet sleeper.

Mother obviously enjoyed this vacation from my father, and, because I'd not lived at home for over ten years, I felt no need to get away from her, no automatic recoil from her hugs. It reminded me there was much more to Mother than the passive wife role I detested. We shared a love not only of ballet and classical music but also of birds, kittens, and desserts. The trait of Mother's I'm still trying to emulate was her ability to pause and really savor things—a prom dress she helped select, an exceptionally rich chocolate mousse, a tableau of fall colors in the Great Smoky Mountains.

For years, Paula and Scott had been featured artists at both Spoleto Festivals—one in Spoleto, Italy, the other in Charleston, South Carolina. My babysitting days ended in May with two weeks in Charleston, where we shared a handsome old house. (I was born in Charleston but don't remember much, having left when I was eighteen months.) My bedroom was small, but I had access to a real kitchen. For two months Elizabeth had been in that delightful stage between four months and a year, an abundance of smiles, even while eating mashed banana. At the end of the two weeks, I flew to Madison, where I would spend the summer. I had cared for Elizabeth for only seven months, but as soon as the plane took off, I choked up. I already missed her terribly.

Right before I moved back to Madison, the journal of the College Music Society listed the flute professor position at Lawrence University in Appleton, Wisconsin, one hundred miles north of Madison. I knew Lawrence's reputation for excellence in both academics and music, and that it was one of only a few schools with a conservatory attached to a small liberal arts college. Unlike its bigger rival Oberlin, Lawrence was solely an undergraduate institution. One month after I sent in my application materials, Colin Murdoch, dean of the Lawrence Conservatory of Music, called to invite me to campus for an audition and interview. Finally, a chance to realize the goal that had seemed so distant when I began the doctoral program. It was late May; if I didn't get the Lawrence job, I had no idea where I'd go or what I'd do, yet I was surprisingly calm about the interview.

After months of doing very little other than babysitting, I enjoyed the packed schedule: an audition, individual and group interviews with faculty, a master class and private lessons for current flute students, sight-reading with a faculty chamber group, and a short lecture on an aspect of music theory. (Music theory would constitute half my teaching load.)

Shortly after my flight landed, I had dinner with the dean. The schedule listed a half hour after dinner to warm up before the audition, but we were running late, so I walked right into a classroom (the recital hall was booked) and started playing my program for the search committee and the flute majors. Because there was no pianist, I played several unaccompanied pieces and the Kuhlau Grand Solo No. 3, which has such a minimal piano part, it sounded fine without it. I ended with a short lecture and performance of Debussy's *Syrinx*.

The job description had included a salary range. Two days after the audition, Colin called and offered me the job, but instead of offering a salary, he asked me what salary I would accept. I hadn't thought about it, so I picked the absolute middle of the range mentioned in the job posting. With a doctorate, years in a professional orchestra, a minor in music theory, and a degree from a liberal arts college, I might have asked for the high end, as I realized after I'd been at Lawrence for a while. It didn't matter. Salary was far less important than job fit, which turned out to be just right.

Recapitulation

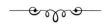

In a typical sonata form, the recapitulation is about the same length as the exposition, because it contains all the material from the exposition, with the crucial difference that the second theme is presented in the same (home) key as the first theme, reconciling the tension created by contrasting keys. Such repetition makes no sense in a literary work. On a deeper level, however, these last two chapters function like the recapitulation in sonata form: they resolve the tensions inherent in the themes, in part by separating them—musical achievement is no longer intertwined with male approval. In some sonata forms, the second theme precedes the first in the recapitulation, as it does here.

Chapter 22: Resolution, Second Theme

Although a university position hadn't been my original goal, teaching flute quickly became a second calling. To journey alongside a student and witness their development, both as a musician and as an emerging adult, was as rewarding as playing in an orchestra. Aware of the irony, I used Mr. Little as a role model for much of my teaching. Remembering how special he made me feel during lessons, I tried to bring my full attention to every lesson, seeking for each student the best balance between encouragement and challenge. In addition to developing my own materials, I used Mr. Little's technical patterns of scales, intervals, and chord outlines, which proved challenging, even for the best players. To ensure students kept practicing these fundamentals, I instigated regular technique juries—tests each term where students performed technical exercises for a faculty panel. Seeing my students struggle with the patterns, I marveled at the rigor of Mr. Little's regimen, which I had not appreciated as a teenager.

When I left Atlanta, I went to Boston because I wanted to sound like James Pappoutsakis, whom I'd heard on a recording. Years later, after hearing a James Galway recording, I flew to England for his master class so I could hear his sound up close.

That constant search for a richer flute tone guided my teaching, and nothing thrilled me more than hearing a student's gorgeous sound soar above other instruments in the student orchestra. Even the less ambitious students—those who wouldn't get into the orchestra—had breakthrough lessons when, after months of painstaking work that seemed to yield no results, their sound would burst forth with color, beauty, and depth. I got just as excited for them as I did for the gifted performance majors. The student and I, through working together, had created something lovely, something that had not previously existed for that student. It wouldn't have been nearly as moving if I hadn't been at a school where I could really connect with students, personally as well as musically. Their joy was my joy. For decades, teaching flute remained fulfilling because every lesson held the possibility that a student might produce a more beautiful sound, that day.

Large music schools, such as NEC, tout their artist faculty, but frequently those artists spend many weeks touring, and/or take too many students (Mr. Pappoutsakis) to become involved in their students' lives. I loved being at a small school where the student-teacher ratio was low, allowing faculty to become true mentors. In addition to attending our students' band and orchestra concerts, conservatory faculty (college faculty also) often attended students' athletic games and presentations of their academic research projects.

Like most teachers, I found the first year of teaching the hardest. I knew I could teach flute effectively; my doubts were about music theory. The doctoral courses I'd taken for the music theory minor covered subjects far removed from the rules of four-voice part writing, the bedrock of freshman theory curricula. Thank goodness for Marge Irvin, a formidable Lawrence grande dame who taught piano and music theory. An articulate, intense middle-aged woman, Marge could be intimidating. Had she been male, the relationship between us might have been complicated; instead, I accepted her generous guidance freely, with no subtexts on her part or mine. In addition to helping with music theory, Marge supported me in other ways, hosting parties after my recitals and inviting me and other young faculty to dinner at her home.

Even with Marge's help, classroom teaching was challenging and time-consuming. The theory course met five days a week, seventy minutes per class, two or three assignments per week. A music theory section and fifteen flute students hadn't sounded like a heavy load, but I'd underestimated the time required for class preparation, piano practice (for theory class), and paper grading. Even when I'd set aside an hour or two for practicing, class prep expanded to fill any available time. I practiced mostly after 9:00 p.m., at the end of a tiring day.

Did having a job rid me of self-doubt? Of course not, but for a year or so the focus switched from playing the flute to teaching music theory. Every few weeks, I said something misleading or downright wrong in class. I'd realize my mistake right after class, feel stupid, and wait impatiently for the next day, eager to own up to and correct my mistake. Students were generous in giving me second and third chances to get it right. They seemed to respect me in spite of my mistakes—or maybe because I admitted them.

My father was wrong about my inability to make a living in music, right about the odds: unless a student planned to teach in public schools, the chances of making a living in music were slim. I tried to be encouraging but honest with flutists who aspired to careers as performers. College teaching jobs are hard to get; orchestra jobs, even more difficult. The painful part of teaching flute was guiding students who, with no understanding of the competition, thought they could waltz into the flute section of the Chicago Symphony. My goal was to guide them gently toward reality without crushing their dreams.

One of Lawrence's best features was—and still is—a five-year program in which a student earns both a bachelor of music degree in the conservatory and a bachelor of arts degree in the college, in whatever major they choose. This gives students a plan B for their career if music doesn't work out. Unlike many of the top music schools, music majors at Lawrence take a third of their courses in the college, thus getting a liberal arts background as well as music training.

As often happens in teaching, I learned as much from my students as they did from me, though more about life than about flute. Their quick recovery from setbacks astonished me. The way they reacted to discouraging auditions helped me see how harshly I'd judged my own failures, beginning with that one-chance-in-a-hundred audition for the Curtis Institute at age eighteen. My father instilled in me the belief that if you were not the best at something—as indicated by one unsuccessful audition—you had no right to pursue it.

My goal was to develop students who no longer needed me, and I was thrilled and humbled when they played something better than I could. I never envied students' playing abilities, but I did envy the encouragement they received from parents who showed genuine interest in their musical studies and traveled great distances to attend their recitals. Meeting so many supportive parents underscored how little encouragement I'd gotten from my parents. I began to understand the importance of Mr. Little's support and why the withdrawal of that support had been so devastating.

The yearly evaluations were very positive from both flute and music theory students. Confidence about the quality of my teaching was reaffirmed when, six years after my arrival at Lawrence, I received tenure and the Outstanding Young Teacher Award, a university-wide honor.

Chapter 23: Resolution,
First Theme

The position of flute professor at a good conservatory validated my identity as a musician, resolving the question of whether I was good enough to succeed in the music world. With regard to yearning for support from father figures, part of that theme's resolution was pure luck: there were no older men at Lawrence in positions of power over me. The conservatory dean was about my age, the university president only seven years older. President Warch might have been a real danger, as he was an outstanding public speaker and quite handsome, but my interactions with him were minimal. Warch treated me with great respect, attending many of my recitals and supporting me when I faced a crisis later in my career.

Neither Lawrence nor Appleton was teeming with unattached males in their thirties, and even though a serious relationship wasn't a high priority, I needed a social life. I winced each time someone touted the best virtue of Appleton: a great place to raise kids. Though dating options were limited, at least rehearsing and performing provided social interactions with conservatory faculty. Through our weekly music theory meetings, and because his office was across the hall from mine,

I got to know Carl Rath, the bassoon teacher, quite well. We commiserated about the challenges of teaching theory and often met for a quick dinner at Damrow's, three blocks from the conservatory and the cheapest place in town. I was older than Carl, and he was interested in younger women, which alleviated any dating subtexts between us.

After we formed the faculty woodwind quintet, I became good friends with oboist George Riordan and his wife, Karen Clarke, the violin professor. Rehearsals with the convivial quintet included moments of hilarity, usually prompted by a funny comment from George or Carl. And we got well acquainted with each other's idiosyncrasies.

One time, at a dress rehearsal for the next day's concert, we were rehearsing the difficult quintet by Jean Francaix. George kept screwing up one of his runs—rare for him—and got so frustrated he took the reed out of his oboe.

"I hate you!" he yelled, smashing it into the music stand with great force. He'd spent hours making that reed.

"That should fix that!" he said triumphantly. "Destroying that reed sure felt good. Too bad it was my only good reed for the concert," he continued, grinning the whole time.

Oboists are often a bit crazy, maybe because they are at the mercy of fragile, unpredictable reeds. The next day, George sounded great on one of his bad reeds.

Most of the Lawrence faculty were older, with kids, and not eager to socialize with a single woman. Thanks to Carl, George, and Karen, it didn't matter. Toward the end of my third year, Karen was offered a job at a much larger university, with a lighter teaching load. By then Carl had left, and I was crushed to see my remaining two friends move away.

In late April, as soon as George announced he was leaving, I was appointed to the search committee to find another oboist. As an oboist, George would be hard to replace; as a friend, impossible. I tried not to resent the people who applied for his position.

At 8:00 a.m. in late May, groggy from being up late the previous night, I met Howard Niblock. Out of an applicant pool of seventy-two, we'd invited three oboists to campus for an interview and audition; Howard was the final candidate. The first thing I noticed was his shirt, a most unattractive shade of green. Although he seemed nice enough, I couldn't help comparing him with George, an exceptionally gregarious person who was always grinning. Because the recital hall was booked, Howard had to audition in a second-floor classroom, on a record-breaking hot day. The un-air-conditioned room was about ninety degrees.

Though small, this classroom had tiered seats. With the audience almost on top of him in the hot room, Howard began to sweat as he made his way through the six pieces he'd selected for the audition—a taxing program, with no breaks as you'd have in a regular concert. Between pieces he paused just long enough to mop his face with a handkerchief. Considering the heat, the unflattering room, and the importance of the occasion, he was remarkably composed during that sweaty performance. He played well and, most important to me, had a lovely sound with a fluent, expressive vibrato. I might not particularly like him—especially his taste in shirts—but I'd be delighted to have him in our woodwind quintet. His other qualifications were equally impressive: he had taught both music theory and music history, and in addition to obtaining a master's degree in oboe performance, he had majored in philosophy and English as an undergraduate, perfect for a liberal arts college. The day after Howard left, the committee met briefly; hiring Howard was an easy decision. I still resented him a bit. He wasn't George.

In order to spend time with friends and my sister's family, that summer I sublet an apartment in Madison. In July, I received an interesting phone call.

"Hello," I said.

"Hi, Ernestine? This is Howard Niblock."

"Oh yes, Howard, how are you?"

"I'm fine. Say, I'm in Madison for the summer, and Marc told me you're here too." Marc was the oboe teacher at UW. "I was wondering if you'd like to meet for dinner and maybe go to a movie."

We agreed on a date—though not really a date, merely a chance to get to know a new colleague. When Howard came to pick me up, he seemed anxious. I didn't remember him being the least bit nervous, either at his interview or on the phone. After we sat down to dinner at a nice restaurant on Lake Mendota, he apologized for his agitation.

"Just as I was about to leave to pick you up, I got a call from my best friend Gary," Howard said. "He's the clarinet teacher at Luther." I knew Howard had taught at Luther College for five years.

"Is he ill?" I asked.

"It's more complicated than that."

He proceeded to tell me that Gary struggled with alcoholism, that he was gay, and that when Howard taught at Luther, he and Gary had lived together for years.

"See," he explained, "as soon as I got the call offering me the job at Lawrence, I called Gary and told him. He'd known about the interview and was excited for me. But when he called just now, he asked whether I'd ever heard about the Lawrence job."

"It's odd that such a close friend would forget something like that."

"No, you don't understand," Howard said. "Gary was in a rehab program last year, and I thought he'd managed to quit drinking. In fact, I know he didn't drink for a long time after he got out."

"So if he forgot about your getting the job . . ."

"He wouldn't forget something so important to me. He must have been drinking so heavily the night I called him that he had no memory of our conversation."

Howard's dismay over Gary's drinking was palpable. He clearly cared deeply for this man.

"I'm sorry, that must be disappointing—"

"It's not just disappointing. He may lose his job over this. Luther granted him a leave of absence and paid for his rehab program."

After that weighty conversation, we saw the movie *History of the World*, not one of Mel Brooks's best. Despite having just watched a comedy, the evening ended somberly. At least I'd gotten to know my new colleague a bit. Well, perhaps more than a bit. I added up the facts: Howard cared deeply about Gary. They had shared a house for years. Gary was gay. And Howard had some mannerisms that might be considered gay. Ergo.

In early fall, before classes started, Howard and I talked about the challenge of cooking for one and eating alone every night. We decided to form a dinner group, similar to the one I'd enjoyed with three friends in Atlanta. We invited two other musicians to an audition potluck to see how it would be to cook for one another and, more importantly, to spend time together.

The evening provided all the things we'd hoped for: great food, good wine, interesting conversation, lots of laughter. From then on, we each cooked one night a week, Monday through Thursday. Given our busy schedules and frequent evening rehearsals, we arrived promptly at 6:00 p.m. and left at 7:00 p.m. Life was much better with the comfortable companionship of two recent divorcées—Dan, our clarinet teacher, and Sharon, a violinist who taught in the public schools—and, I thought, a gay man who might become a good friend. To the surprise of all of us, we were so compatible that the dinner group continued to meet for eight years.

The Lawrence faculty woodwind quintet often performed concerts around the state, at high schools with good music programs. When we scheduled a four-day tour for early November, I knew it would cut into practice time for my solo recital at the Elvehjem Art Museum scheduled for November 15. The concerts at the Elvehjem were broadcast live on public radio stations throughout the state. I'd planned to be so well prepared that I wouldn't need those days for practicing, but the extra rehearsals of the quintet plus the demands of teaching theory left me hoping for an early November blizzard (not unheard of in Wisconsin), severe enough to cancel the tour.

One night at dinner, a week before the tour, Sharon mentioned her plans for Thanksgiving break, prompting Howard to reveal his plan to meet his girlfriend, who lived in Nebraska. They were meeting halfway, in Iowa. *What?* I barely kept the food from falling out of my open mouth. I already admired his expressive oboe playing and enjoyed his zany sense of humor. Even though I thought he was gay, I'd certainly noticed his long, slender legs, right next to mine in all our quintet rehearsals. But now I viewed his clear blue eyes, slightly lopsided grin, and tall, slim frame differently.

I wasted no time. So what if he had a girlfriend. Since we had to take two cars, I contrived to be in his car—the *only* one in his car. By the end of the second day, enough sparks were flying that we met for drinks and conversation about things other than music. On November 5, in a Days Inn room on Madison's west side, we shared our first kiss. Howard claims I asked, before the kiss, "Do you kiss non-girlfriends?"

The next day, I made a request that could have ended our budding romance. I asked if I could practice in the back seat of his orange VW Rabbit, while he drove from town to town. With the flute stretched out to my right in order to avoid banging into the window, the head joint of the flute, where most of the sound comes out, ended up a few inches from Howard's right ear. His only restriction: nothing above high G.

The week before an important concert like a recital at the Elvejhem Art Museum would normally have been a frantic week, with me grabbing every spare moment to practice, but the memory of a first kiss, with the hope of many more, made that final week more joyful than harried. With a big grin on his face, Ted Rehl, my mischievous pianist, asked me if there was anything new in my life. Oh no, just the excitement of the recital. He knew I was lying.

The recital featured two of my favorite flute pieces: Luciano Berio's *Sequenza*, an avant-garde, unaccompanied piece written in 1958, and Henri Dutilleux's lovely *Sonatine*, written only fifteen years earlier but in a lush, neo-romantic style. I ended the program with the *Sonatine* because, when performed well, it's a guaranteed crowd pleaser. It opens with a beautiful, floating theme in 7/8 time played first by the piano, then the flute, a waltz but in an irregular meter. The piece's three movements flow together, the third movement ending with a frenzied accelerando of fast triplets, which is as exciting for the performers as for the audience. The previous weekend's romantic development added a little extra verve and expressiveness to my performance. Driving back to Appleton, alone in the car, I relished the double high of a successful recital and a new love interest, crooning cheesy love songs like "Just in Time."

Despite my enthusiasm, Howard did not break up with his girlfriend immediately. He had already planned to visit her in Nebraska that December, which he did, but by then it was to end rather than continue the relationship. On the drive back to Appleton, he stopped by Melinda's house, where I'd spent Christmas. Howard immediately fit into that family of five (a second daughter had arrived), which reassured me; I'd grown very attached to Melinda's children. The clincher was when four-year-old Laura climbed into Howard's lap. *Okay, this man is special.* It had nothing to do with my wanting kids (never a priority for me), but rather with Howard's immediate connection to each member of Melinda's family.

Melinda and Phil would have welcomed anyone I cared about. In the four years since I'd moved to Appleton, their support for me extended way beyond making the hundred-mile trek to attend recitals at Lawrence. I spent every Thanksgiving at their home and always saw them during the Christmas holidays. My first few years at Lawrence would have been far more lonely had it not been for the Certain family. It was both wonderful and a bit odd that we two Georgia girls ended up in Wisconsin.

The winter of 1982 was brutal. On January 17, Milwaukee recorded its lowest temperature ever: minus twenty-six, much lower with the windchill. One hundred miles north of Milwaukee, Appleton was even colder, with the windchill approaching minus sixty. The streets turned into pathways between six-foot-high walls of packed, icy snow, and even avid skiers and skaters stayed inside. But a blossoming romance made the harshness of winter easy to bear, and by March we were considering wedding dates. Because the conservatory at Lawrence, like most small schools, was a goldfish bowl, we'd tried to keep our relationship secret. We decided to reveal our plans on April 5, five months after our first kiss.

One of the first people I told was my student Terri Sundberg, a phenomenally talented junior. At her first lesson, Terri and I bonded instantly, a rare and wonderful thing. I had an exceptionally good class that year and the next three.

In my early years of teaching, I found it hard to maintain the student-teacher boundary with my first group of good flute students. Jan, Kathy, Terri, Ellen, Ruth, and Katie were bright, talented, and interesting, and I was barely fifteen years older than they were. Terri later earned a master's degree at Yale and became a tenured professor at the University of North Texas, her students winning an exceptional number of national competitions and auditions. The other five had equally impressive but different careers, four in music, one in college administration.

That spring, when I stepped over the boundary and told Terri about Howard and me, I asked her not to tell anyone because Howard and I hadn't yet told the students. She replied, "Oh, everybody knows about you two. We call you Nibbles and Wits."

At 5:30 p.m. on August 24, the deluge started. Good timing: a few minutes before, I'd rushed from the car to the church with my dress in a bag, folded over one arm. As I looked down from a window in the small, second-story changing room, I saw Terri emerge from a taxi. Hugging her flute to her chest, she rushed across the street to the shelter of the church awning, where she wrung out the skirt of her bright blue dress before coming inside.

The musicians, who were as important to us as the bridal party, were tied up doing numerous summer festivals at Aspen, Banff, and Tanglewood, with a narrow window before their fall commitments, so the wedding took place on a Tuesday night. We chose to have the wedding in Madison, because our Lawrence/Appleton friends scattered in the summer, and we both had friends, plus my sister's family, in Madison.

Melinda and my nieces, four-year-old Laura and seven-year-old Heather, wore floor-length, empire-waist dresses of pale green with a pattern of small peach-colored flowers. I spent more time picking out the fabric for those dresses than I did shopping for the bridal gown, which was a gently flowing dress of satin with a voile overlay, and sheer voile sleeves. The bodice had lace on the flattering scalloped neckline and at the ends of the sleeves. The tuxedoed half of the wedding party included my brother-in-law Phil and his eleven-year-old son Andrew as ushers, and Gary, Howard's dear friend from Luther College, as the best man.

Every wedding has its surprises. The day before the wedding, Laura fell off her bike and cut her upper lip. The pain didn't bother her as much as the thought of losing her spot as a bridesmaid, but all three bridesmaids, processing in at three very different heights, looked so lovely that no one noticed a busted lip. The day of the wedding, Howard lost the key to his car and had to call a locksmith. Right before the ceremony, Gary realized he'd lost the tie for his tux, so he used Andrew's. A cute eleven-year-old boy in a tux doesn't need a bow tie.

As the musicians began playing a Mozart sextet, I was surprisingly calm up there in the bridal room. I thought how meaningful it was to have Howard's and my friends joining together to play Mozart chamber music for the prelude and postlude: bassoonist Lynette from my Atlanta Symphony days; oboist Marc, who'd taught Howard and performed in my recitals at UW; the other oboist John, a student of Howard's at Luther; the French hornists from Howard's graduate school time at Michigan State—all from different parts of our lives.

When I kissed Mother before she went downstairs, I savored the moment of seeing her so happy. But then, everyone was happy, as they should be at weddings. Even my father, who looked slim and regal as he walked me down the aisle in the black suit that matched his hair, still dark at age seventy-two.

During the service, my UW friends flutist Sue Klick and pianist Mary Hunt played one of my favorite flute pieces, the lento from Bach's Sonata in B Minor. Later in the service, Terri joined Sue and Mary for Bach's aria, "Blast die wohlgegriffnen Flöten" (Blow the well-played flutes), with my UW roommate Carmen singing the joyful soprano part.

After the ceremony, when Howard and I were greeting friends in the entryway, my brother-in-law gently pried us away and led us outside to the church steps, where we saw that the storm had passed. The most stunning wedding picture shows Howard and me in profile on the church steps, holding hands and gazing into each other's eyes. The background is the Madison skyline with a perfect rainbow, which ends on the bald top of Howard's head.

The reception was in the front yard of Melinda's house. It would've been a muddy mess if my father, pessimistic about everything, including weather, hadn't insisted we rent a tent. My favorite picture from the reception is of me, again in profile, talking to Daddy, who is facing the camera. His right hand holds a glass of champagne and he's grinning—in fact, he's obviously *laughing*—at something I said. A precious moment. Despite my successes in music, the moment Daddy truly relaxed about my future was when I got married. My feminist hackles rise at that, but it didn't matter; on my wedding day, Daddy and I were, in that moment, at peace.

Because Howard and I got to know each other first as friends, there was never any awkwardness between us. Howard hadn't considered dating me because he already had a girlfriend. I'd been focused on my career, plus I thought he was gay. My interest in him had nothing to do with male authority. I was, in fact, slightly higher on the academic ladder—closer to getting tenure at Lawrence and somewhat better paid. From the start we were equals, and it has remained that way to this day, through four decades of marriage. I'm glad I didn't meet Howard earlier, when I was too involved in my career and father-longing to recognize the man who was right for me.

Like all long marriages, ours has endured many challenges. In our first two decades together, Howard's controlling mother generated much of the tension by being hypercritical of me. But Howard has also put up with a lot, especially my insecurity about flute performances, plus a few odd quirks. I'm still a bit prickly about being independent, so I sometimes flinch when he tries to help me put on a coat, which amuses us both. When I'm defensive, Howard reminds me he is not my father; when Howard's defensive, I remind him I am not his mother.

I've often thought of the ways our marriage refutes my mother's comment about men—they want only sex and a cook. Howard and I have multiple roles in each other's lives; if I had to pick the most important one, it would be supporter. Howard encourages me to keep developing as a person, pursuing my goals, not his. As for being his cook, after fifteen years of sharing cooking duty, we finally figured out we were both happier when Howard cooked and I cleaned up. For years Howard has been the cook; I'm glad Mother was right about the other part.

To this day, years after his death and decades after I last saw him, I still have extreme, contradictory feelings about Warren Little. I shall always be grateful for his excellent and inspiring teaching. Because of him, I fell in love with the flute and developed a passion for orchestral music. Without his care and guidance, I would not have become a musician. That doesn't erase the psychological damage from years of his mistreatment. When I consider the men who left scars—father, flute teacher, rapist, therapist—Warren Little is the one who struck closest to my identity and left the deepest scars. I rarely had doubts about myself as a woman; after Warren turned against me, I always had doubts about myself as a flutist.

The discord with Warren forced me to choose between a stressful but secure job and a risky but more hopeful future. I made the right choice. If I'd stayed, Warren's abuse might have sent me into another depression, one too deep for recovery. Even if I'd survived, most of the things I treasure wouldn't be part of my life: I wouldn't have developed a passion for teaching, nor would I have met the wonderful students I've taught, many of whom remain good friends. Most significantly, I would never have met Howard, and my amazing son would not exist. The very thing that excited me about music—love of orchestral repertoire—would also have suffered: after playing the same symphonies for decades, I'd be tired of them.

My longing for male approval, the first theme in this sonata form, was not resolved by a transformation of the relationship with my father, which remained distant and strained. Instead, the first theme became intertwined with the second— the search for a loving father commingled with the quest to become a musician, and the more success I achieved as a flutist, the less I needed a father figure's encouragement. Thus, both themes resolved when the second theme became independent of the first, no longer in need of a countermelody.

Afterword

I have lived long enough that most of the men who made my life difficult are deceased, which greatly reduces concern about upsetting people. I do, however, regret that this story paints an incomplete picture of my father. To hundreds of students and dozens of colleagues at Emory University, Tate Whitman was unfailingly kind and supportive. At his memorial service, I was grateful to read and hear many eulogies to a person who rarely appears in these pages.

Acknowledgments

It takes a lot of help to make a nonfiction writer from scratch, especially one who begins writing in her late sixties. My deepest thanks to:

Howard Niblock, first, last, and always—best friend, constant ballast, life partner alongside me every agonizing step of the way—and our son, Elliott, who said offhandedly one day, "Hey, Mom, you should write down some of those stories."

Jill Swensen, whose memoir classes started me on this journey and who later reviewed each chapter with patience and insight.

David McGlynn for encouraging me after reading only a first, extremely rough draft of the book's opening pages, which were all scrapped.

Peter Murphy, who developed my writing skills in six excellent classes, and who insisted, despite my resistance, that I was a writer.

My exceptionally supportive Monday Night Zoom Group—Rachel Bunting, Maureen Cawley, Roberta Francis, Isabel Lewis, David Milley, and Christine Waldeyer, all Peter Murphy alumnae. I've been in only one writing group; what fantastic luck to have stumbled upon your collective wisdom and encouragement!

Eleanor Henderson for believing in me based solely on one unforgettable class, and for her perceptive analysis of the early manuscript's weaknesses.

About the Author

Ernestine Whitman began her career as a professional flutist at age twenty, the youngest and one of few women in the Atlanta Symphony. Her passion for teaching brought her to Lawrence University in Appleton, Wisconsin, where she was professor of flute for thirty-three years. At the end of her performing career, she began practicing martial arts and earned two black belts in her sixties. A passionate advocate for restorative justice, she volunteers frequently in programs at several Wisconsin prisons. Ernestine and her husband, oboist Howard Niblock, divide their time between their longtime residence in Appleton and their condo in midtown Atlanta.

Author photo © Rachel Crowl

Looking for your next great read?

We can help!

Visit www.shewritespress.com/next-read
or scan the QR code below for a list
of our recommended titles.

She Writes Press is an award-winning
independent publishing company founded to
serve women writers everywhere.